ANTHROPOLOGY
AND
CONTEMPORARY
HUMAN PROBLEMS

ANTHROPOLOGY AND CONTEMPORARY HUMAN PROBLEMS

SECOND EDITION

John H. Bodley
WASHINGTON STATE UNIVERSITY

 Mayfield Publishing Company

Library of Congress Catalog Card Number: 84-061381
International Standard Book Number: 0-87484-671-4

Manufactured in the United States of America
10   9   8   7

Mayfield Publishing Company
1240 Villa Street
Mountain View, CA 94041

Sponsoring editor: Janet M. Beatty
Manuscript editor: Mary Anne Stewart
Managing editor: Pat Herbst
Production editor: Jan deProsse
Art director and designer: Nancy Sears
Cover designer: Jim M'Guinness
Production manager: Cathy Willkie
Compositor: Columbia Phototype
Printer and binder: Thomson-Shore

CONTENTS

2

ADAPTATION, TRIBAL CULTURE, AND THE ENVIRONMENTAL CRISIS 23

3

NATURAL RESOURCES AND THE CULTURE OF CONSUMPTION 59

CONTENTS

2

ADAPTATION, TRIBAL CULTURE, AND THE ENVIRONMENTAL CRISIS   23

3

NATURAL RESOURCES AND THE CULTURE OF CONSUMPTION   59

4

WORLD HUNGER AND THE
EVOLUTION OF FOOD SYSTEMS   *85*

5

INDUSTRIAL FOOD SYSTEMS   **117**

6

THE POPULATION PROBLEM   **145**

7

INTERNAL ORDER 171

8

WAR AND INTERNATIONAL ORDER 191

PREFACE
TO THE SECOND EDITION

This book is intended to supplement introductory courses in anthropology. Its purpose is to bring into focus the value of the cross-cultural, evolutionary, and cross-disciplinary perspectives that are unique to anthropology and to explain how these perspectives are applicable to a more profound understanding of large-scale, complex problems of contemporary industrialized societies.

The book is a treatment of and a call for more anthropological research into the problems of overconsumption, adaptation to environment, resource depletion, hunger and starvation, overpopulation, violence, and war. Anthropologists have dealt with these issues in many ways, in many times, and in many cultures. This book attempts to relate these anthropological insights to the contemporary world.

To evaluate one's own culture objectively is a most difficult task, yet it is necessary if long-range and effective measures are to be developed to ensure human survival. Anthropology, of all the disciplines, should be centrally involved with this concern, and has been to a large degree, as is evidenced by current research and the numerous case studies used in this book to advance the general thesis.

This edition retains the chapter structure and overall viewpoint of the first edition. The most conspicuous change in the present edition is the replacement of the term *primitive* with the term *tribal*. I recognize that the term *primitive* has now been almost entirely abandoned by anthropologists because to many people it suggests inferiority. From my perspective, it makes little difference what labels are used, as long as the importance of small-scale, relatively self-sufficient, politically autonomous peoples is recognized. These peoples constitute a cultural type that affords a significant contrast to peoples living in large-scale political states. I apply the label *tribal* to these peoples and their cultures, with the recognition that even this term has disadvantages. In this edition I have also included a discussion of the problem of "noble savage romanticism" and a review of those who view tribals in negative terms.

Important new material on the environment has been added to Chapter 2. The status of areas of special concern, such as tropical rain forests, has been updated, and new findings from the "Global 2000" presidential commission on the environment are included. I also discuss the problem of Pleistocene extinctions and stress that tribal cultures do modify environments and manage natural resources, as the example of traditional burning practices clearly demonstrates.

The treatment of world hunger in Chapter 4 is slanted somewhat differently than in the first edition. I now emphasize more directly the importance of social inequality and stress that hunger is less a problem of overpopulation and technological underdevelopment than it is a sociopolitical problem. A new case study based on Bangladesh is included to illustrate this perspective. Diverse new viewpoints are presented on the relationships among population, technology, and resources. The concepts of carrying capacity, subsistence intensification, optimization, and risk minimizing are all examined. New interpretations of infanticide, pastoral adaptations, and Rappaport's famous New Guinea equilibrium model are also included. Chapter 8 on war is updated with a discussion of the "nuclear winter" that could result from even limited use of nuclear weapons.

The final chapter concludes with a review of proposals by economist Leopold Kohr and anthropologist Sol Tax for solving global problems by drastically reducing the size of nation-states.

PREFACE
TO THE FIRST EDITION

In many respects the present work is a continuation of my earlier work, *Victims of Progress*, which dealt with the destruction of primitive cultures by our expanding industrial civilization. *Anthropology and Contemporary Human Problems* argues that many of our most serious difficulties are inherent in the basic cultural patterns of our civilization, and indeed in civilization itself. Tribal cultures are designed along fundamentally different lines and therefore managed to avoid most of the problems that now seem about to overwhelm us. The contrasts between these two major types of culture—tribal and civilized—are so great that they must be virtually incompatible, and with the appearance of civilization the eventual disappearance of tribal cultures became inevitable. What we are now seeing is perhaps the final irony of cultural evolution—the latecomer, industrial civilization, has suddenly arisen as a clear dominant and a brilliant short-run success. We have eliminated the earlier tribal cultures, which were proven long-run successes, and there are now clear indications that civilization has accumulated enough internal problems to be self-terminating. There is a real possibility that we could become victims of our own evolutionary progress. To avoid such an outcome, it is imperative that we view our contemporary problems in as wide a context as possible. We must go back and re-examine tribal cultures and compare their solutions to basic human problems with our own solutions. Perhaps this is anthropology's most critical task.

This book is not an exhaustive treatment of all modern problems. Instead, we have surveyed some of our most serious problem areas and have attempted to place them in an anthropological perspective. The reader must be cautioned that much of the data drawn from the archaeological and ethnological record is fragmentary and open to more than one interpretation. I have tried to be objective and have indicated several places where serious doubts are present. My own bias, that tribal cultures were generally well adapted to their environments and were in many other ways "superior," has undoubtedly colored my interpretation of the facts, but such a bias has proven a useful heuristic device.

This work could be subtitled *A Critique of Civilization,* like Stanley Diamond's *In Search of the Primitive,* from which I have drawn great inspiration. To criticize one's own culture is a difficult task and opens one to charges of hypocrisy and misunderstanding. If it is hypocritical to enjoy the benefits of civilization while still recognizing its shortcomings and working toward their solution, then I am guilty of hypocrisy. It must be clear that I am calling into question some of the most basic features of our culture. For convenience many of my examples are drawn from the United States, but I do not wish to single out any particular nation for special criticism. I also disavow any political-economic ideology and am emphatically not calling for a capitalist, socialist, Marxist, or communist solution. Perhaps my greatest frustration in writing this book is that—although it emphasizes how profound the cultural changes must be if real solutions are to be found—how the necessary changes can be implemented and precisely what form they should take are open questions.

Acknowledgments

My students and colleagues at Washington State University contributed many useful ideas and criticisms to this book, and much of the material in the first six chapters was critically reviewed by my Anthropology and World Problems class during the fall semester of 1974. Linda Jovanivich provided material on the Green Revolution. I also drew freely on data supplied by Barry Hicks on the future; the typology of futurists in Chapter 9 is modified from a scheme he developed. Portions of the original manuscript were read by Barry Hicks, Bob Kiste, John Nelson, Dan Stark, and my wife, Kathleen Bodley.

In addition to these individuals, a number of people generously provided materials that I have drawn upon in the preparation of the second edition. Others have given me valuable ideas and critical comments. The following list is certainly incomplete: Diane Bell, Gerald Berreman, Michael J. Cisimir, Mark Fleisher, Richard A. Gould, Franklin C. Graham, Fekri Hassan, Brian Hayden, Howard M. Hecker, Arthur E. Hippler, Allen Johnson, Richard G. Klein, P. A. Lancaster, Henry T. Lewis, R. A. Littlewood, Thomas J. Maloney, Paul S. Martin, Robert K. McKnight, James G. Peoples, Rudy Reyser, Linda Stone, Sol Tax, B. H. Walker, and Thomas Weaver.

ANTHROPOLOGY AND CONTEMPORARY HUMAN PROBLEMS

1

ANTHROPOLOGICAL PERSPECTIVES ON CONTEMPORARY HUMAN PROBLEMS

A knowledge of anthropology enables us to look with greater freedom at the problems confronting our civilization.

Franz Boas, *Anthropology and Modern Life*

Cultural evolution, through processes that many would label *progress*, has brought humanity to major turning points many times: the adoption of upright posture, the first use of tools, the development of language, culture as an adaptive strategy, food sharing, food production, social stratification, urbanization, state organization, and now industrialization. All of these changes have been decisive ones—crucial developments with critical implications for the future. However, at this point the outlook is suddenly different, because industrialization has dramatically intensified all the potential problems created by earlier developments. It is difficult to imagine a continuation of present trends without civilization destroying itself in any of several ways. In that sense, civilization is at a crisis point—drastic changes must take place or it might not survive.

In many respects the present work is a continuation of my earlier work, *Victims of Progress*, which dealt with the destruction of tribal cultures by our expanding industrial civilization. It now seems clear that many of our most serious contemporary problems are inherent in the basic cultural patterns of our civilization, and indeed in civilization itself. Tribal cultures are designed along fundamentally different lines and therefore managed to solve most of the problems which now seem about to overwhelm us. The contrasts between these two major types of culture—tribal and civilized—are so great that they must be virtually incompatible, and with the appearance of civilization the eventual disappearance of tribal cultures became almost inevitable. What we are now seeing is perhaps the final irony of cultural evolution—the latecomer, industrial civilization, has suddenly arisen as a clear dominant and brilliant short-run success. We have eliminated the earlier tribal cultures, which were proven long-run successes, and there are now clear indications that civilization has accumulated enough internal problems to be self-terminating. We seem about to become victims of our own evolutionary progress. To avoid such an outcome, it is imperative that we view our contemporary problems in as wide a context as possible. We must go back and re-examine tribal cultures and compare their solutions to basic human problems with our own solutions. This is perhaps anthropology's most critical purpose.

Nature and Scope of the Problems

What we face is a *global* crisis. The entire species is in jeopardy; more is at stake now than merely the existence of isolated tribes or nations. A further complication is that we face not one, but *multiple* crises in many areas; and as they multiply, we may be suddenly confronted with an overwhelming "crisis of crises" (Platt 1969). The pace of cultural change is now so rapid that new, unforeseen problems, each of crisis proportions, appear even before the earlier problems have been adequately identified. In effect, crises are now bigger (i.e., they bring greater potential for disaster), there are more of them, and they are arising more rapidly than ever before.

We are undergoing an accelerating rate of cultural change that strains our ability to adapt, and threatens to leave us in the vulnerable condition that Alvin Toffler (1971) aptly labeled "future shock." This pace of cultural change is apparent when the ages of the major archaeological periods are compared. The Paleolithic period lasted perhaps 3 million years, possibly much longer, during which time we can assume that early humans and their immediate hominid ancestors remained hunter-gatherers in small, thinly scattered bands. The transition through the Mesolithic period into food production and to the brink of urbanism in the Neolithic required perhaps 8,000 years; nearly 5,000 years more were required to reach the beginnings of industrialization. The industrial era is now barely 200 years old, and futurists are already proclaiming the arrival of the "postindustrial" era. As Toffler (1971:14) and others point out, much of our material culture has only been with us over the past 60 years or so—the space of one lifetime. Many of the most significant technological innovations, including antibiotics, TV, computers, nuclear energy, mass-produced organic compounds, and jet propulsion, have arrived within the past 25 years. The present generation is experiencing the most profound changes humanity has ever seen. Whereas earlier crises were certainly "revolutionary" in their long-run impact, they occurred so slowly that they were imperceptible to the individuals involved, and their outcomes would not have been obvious for hundreds or even thousands of years. Cultural institutions were able gradually to adjust, but today we are often totally unprepared to deal with the unexpected impact of such rapid change.

Not only has the *pace* of change increased, but its *scope* has dramatically widened. The early evolution of human beings was not a global crisis. Humans have occupied all of both hemispheres for only perhaps 15,000 years, barely 0.005 percent of their existence. The Neolithic "crisis" was passed independently in several areas, and was an event of basically local significance but with long-run implications. Even as recently as 200 years ago, perhaps 50 million politically autonomous tribal people still occupied vast areas of the world and were only marginally affected by either nation-states or the Industrial Revolution. Now, however, industrialization has become a global process that has destroyed or transformed all previous cultural adaptations and has given humanity the power not only to bring about its own extinction as a species, but also to speed the extinction of many other species and to alter basic biological and geological processes as well. If industrial society were to disappear overnight, it would leave an impoverished planet; in contrast, the extinction of humans during the Paleolithic era would have been of no more global significance than the passing of the woolly mammoth. Even "local" crises now occur simultaneously throughout the world. The *human* impact of the present crisis is also far greater in scope than that of any previous crisis, because far more people are alive now than at any time in the past (the average population during the Paleolithic was approximately 0.001 percent of its present level) (Deevey 1960; Coale 1974).

Crisis Levels

We are presently confronted with crises on at least three levels: global, national, and personal. At the global level the biosphere's capacity to absorb human insults is being seriously strained, world resources are rapidly shrinking, and devastating armed conflicts threaten. Individual nation-states must meet these crises while at the same time they confront a multitude of domestic threats in the form of political instabilities and social and economic distress. Many nations are now hard pressed in their efforts merely to continue satisfying minimal human needs for food, shelter, health, and education, and seem totally incapable of meeting rising demands for increased levels of material consumption. Individuals may temporarily ignore certain global and even national-level crises; but at the personal level, we are now being confronted with health, family, and value crises of unprecedented frequency, scope, and complexity.

Whatever level we consider, our cultural means of individual and collective survival seem to be falling behind in their ability to cope with crisis.

Crisis Intensity

> Whether we have 10 years or more like 20 to 30, unless we
> systematically find new large-scale solutions, we are in the gravest
> danger of destroying our society, our world, and ourselves in any of a
> number of different ways well before the end of this century.
> (Platt 1969)

More than a decade ago, an attempt to evaluate the intensities of current crises was published in *Science* by John Platt (1969), in an effort to establish priorities for a massive mobilization of scientists to deal effectively with the most critical world and national problems. In Platt's analysis, crises were cataloged by probable time of arrival into three categories spread over the next 50 years and into eight grades by probable intensity or degree of effect (see Table 1-1). The most dangerous crisis in terms of both imminence and intensity is, of course, the potential for total annihilation due to nuclear or radiological-chemical-biological warfare. Second-order crises, with the potential for massive destruction if not the immediate end of modern civilization, are famines, ecological catastrophes, failure of economic development, local wars, and the gap between rich and poor. Since this analysis was published in 1969, several of these second-order crises have actually already arrived. Third-order crises will mean widespread, nearly intolerable tensions and may well contribute to first- and second-order crises. Lower intensity crises could bring distress to millions of people, but do not threaten civilization immediately, or else they are likely to be distant enough in time that we can prepare for them at our leisure, as it were. The ice caps might indeed begin to melt (or expand) at a rapid rate within 30 to 50 years, but if we don't make it through the next 20 years for other reasons, we will never face such a "remote" crisis.

TABLE 1·1 Classification of global problems and crises by estimated time and intensity

Grade	Estimated crisis intensity (number affected × degree of effect)	Estimated time to crisis*		
		1 to 5 years	*5 to 20 years*	*20 to 50 years*
1.	10^{10} Total annihilation	Nuclear or RCBW escalation	Nuclear or RCBW** escalation	(Solved or dead)
2.	10^9 Great destruction or change (physical, biological, or political)	(Too soon)	Famines Ecological balance Development failures Local wars Rich-poor gap	Economic structure and political theory Population and ecological balance Patterns of living Universal education Communications-integration Management of world Integrative philosophy
3.	10^8 Widespread, almost unbearable tension	Administrative management Need for participation Group and racial conflict Poverty—rising expectations Environmental degradation	Poverty Pollution Racial wars Political rigidity Strong dictatorships	?

4.	10^7	Large-scale distress	Transportation Diseases Loss of old cultures	Housing Education Independence of big powers Communications gap	?

5.	10^6	Tension producing
		  responsive
		  change
			Regional organization
			Water supplies
				?	?

6.		Other problems—
		  important, but
		  adequately
		  researched
			Technical development
			  design
			Intelligent monetary
			  design		

7.		Exaggerated
		  dangers and
		  hopes
					Eugenics
					Melting of ice caps

8.		Noncrisis problems
		  being
		  "overstudied"
			Man in Space
			Most basic science		

*If no major effort is made at anticipatory solution

**Radiological-chemical-biological warfare

Source: John Platt, "What We Must Do," *Science* 166(1969): 1119, Table 2.

Crisis Awareness and Response

> There is a question in the air, more sensed than seen, like the
> invisible approach of a distant storm. . . . "Is there hope for man?"
> [The] question asks . . . whether we do not foresee in the human
> prospect a deterioration of things, even an impending catastrophe
> of fearful dimensions. (Heilbroner 1974:13)

Industrialization has intensified many preexisting problems and has
touched off a variety of new crises. Qualitatively unique social problems,
international political problems, and now an environmental crisis have
all suddenly materialized in rapid succession over the past 150 years and
have widened to include the entire globe. Cultures perceive and respond
to crisis in many different ways; but in view of the pace and scope of the
present "multiple crisis," our capacity to adjust is clearly in doubt. As
industrial civilization has progressed into its crisis, many individuals and
institutions have sounded the alarm, the initial negative feedback mechanisms have been activated, but corrective response has been painfully
inadequate.

Certainly the earliest and most bitter resisters of progress have been
the tribal peoples who have become forced participants, but they have
not been alone or unsupported in their resistance. During the height of
colonial expansion in the late 19th and early 20th centuries, a very active
group of British anti-imperialists (Porter 1968) condemned the entire
colonial adventure that was then feeding progress, and called for reduced
industrial output. These scattered protests, however, were easily swept
aside.

The first major industrialization crises to be widely perceived were
the enormous social upheavals touched off by drastic economic transformation—the factory system in particular. These changes proved profoundly disruptive of the social order and spawned an almost instant
outpouring of social criticism, dire predictions, and outright resistance.
On the eve of the Industrial Revolution in England, the Luddites attempted to halt the entire process by attacking the new machines directly;
and by the mid-19th century, Karl Marx and others predicted the collapse
of at least one form of industrial civilization, because of its "inherent
contradictions." Many of these more obvious difficulties were partially

met with belated laws setting minimum wages, providing social welfare, prescribing work conditions, allowing workers to organize, and attempting to regulate corporate economic power. The belatedness of such efforts is apparent in the fact that in the United States there were no laws prohibiting child labor in mines and factories until after 1900.

At the level of international political organization, the potential for destructive military conflict, thanks to the new industrial tools of war and the new demands for resources, met with equally slow response, even though many individuals perceived the threats. Immediately after World War I, in which nearly 13 million soldiers were killed, there were tentative efforts to regulate international conflict, but it was not until World War II brought perhaps 30 million civilian and military deaths that more effective international regulatory organizations were established.

Industrial society's impact on the environment has been a more subtle crisis, and its full potential for catastrophe has only recently become widely recognized. The general feeling that a rapidly evolving technology could overcome any environmental limitations seems to have blinded most scientists, economists, and government planners to the need for accommodating to the world's physical boundaries until those limits were undeniably obvious. In the United States a group of scientists representing the American Association for the Advancement of Science petitioned Congress as early as 1873 for resource conservation measures; but the first forest reserve was not even established until 1891, nearly 20 years later (Gustafson et al. 1939:7); and it was not until "Earth Day," 1970, almost a century later, that Americans generally began to acknowledge that industrial progress might not be fully compatible with nature.

The general pattern that is apparent so far in the response of modern nations to crises is a considerable delay from the time that the factors that will lead to a crisis are set in motion until anyone perceives the potential problem; further delay until the problem is *widely* perceived; and still further delay until corrective action is taken. For example, DDT was "discovered" in 1934, was first used as an insecticide in 1943, was killing birds by the late 1950s and fish by the early 1960s, appeared as a contaminant of milk in 1963, but was not even partially banned until 1972. In this case, nearly 30 years' lag time was required before a biologically disastrous technology was regulated, even though its harmful aspects had been apparent to many scientists for some two decades.

Unfortunately, DDT is still being applied on a vast scale throughout the "underdeveloped" world, and the potential for global damage is still enormous. For a cultural type that seems to value changes so highly, and which has indeed achieved a very high rate of change, such a correspondingly slow capacity for adjustment to obviously detrimental change seems incredibly maladaptive.

This poor response to crisis lends support to those who hold out such gloomy prospects for human survival. Aside from religious transformative movements that have periodically predicted the end of all things, it has only been in recent decades that a significant percentage of the members of any culture have ever had reason seriously to question the fate of humanity. This increasing doubt about the future is itself an important cultural fact that serves to highlight the gravity of the present crisis.

Anthropology's Contribution

> I hope to demonstrate that a clear understanding of the principles
> of anthropology illuminates the social processes of our times and
> may show us, if we are ready to listen to its teachings, what to do
> and what to avoid. (Boas 1928:11)

We have defined the general nature of the world crisis and suggested some of the possible dangers and difficulties inherent in the slow response that is occurring—now we must argue that anthropology has something important to say to these issues.

The problems facing us are unmistakable but complex, and acceptable solutions are still neither obvious nor easily implemented. In recent years, there has been an enormous outpouring of crisis-related literature. Specialists in many disciplines have attacked isolated problems; unfortunately, however, overall results have been limited. For example, far more has been written on pollution alone over the past five years than any single reader could master in a lifetime, yet pollution remains a problem of crisis proportions. Such apparent ineffectiveness, in spite of intense activity, is partly due to a redundancy and extreme specialization in research effort and to the complexity and interrelatedness of underlying causes, but perhaps more importantly, to a lack of genuine overview on the part of the problem solvers. It is time to divert at least some of our research energies away from the minutiae of diverse problems and to focus on their broader context. What has been missing is *perspective*—a combination of detachment, a predilection for viewing the total picture in the widest spatial-temporal frame, and a clear recognition of the interrelatedness of social, cultural, biological, and psychological factors. Anthropology appears to be a discipline that is uniquely qualified to offer just such an overview. An anthropological overview might not provide all the answers we seek, nor even many easily acceptable solutions, but it can show us how we got where we are and suggest how we might get out.

In a sense, anthropology has been remarkably "preadapted" to serve a sort of early-warning, equilibrium feedback function for cultures such as our own that are obviously slipping out of balance. From its first establishment as a professional discipline, anthropology has been defined in terms of its holistic, cross-cultural, and evolutionary approaches. These methodological specialties provide the very perspectives that now are most needed. Each of these viewpoints offers special advantages in the present crisis and deserves to be discussed individually.

The Holistic Approach of Anthropology

Anthropology calls itself *the study of humanity* and is clearly the broadest in scope and most generalizing of the disciplines. With a little organizational shuffle, virtually every other social science, the humanities, and portions of the physical sciences could easily be accommodated as subdisciplines of anthropology. Anthropologists ordinarily receive general training in—or are concerned with—the biological, cultural, social, and psychological aspects of humans, but they may *specialize* in any of these subfields. Those researchers emphasizing the sociocultural areas must constantly deal with the interaction of economic, social, and ideological systems, and must place these systems in relation to the natural environment. Only this kind of overview can hope to place the present problems in their full context.

The holistic approach leads naturally to the broad kinds of questions that must be asked if the modern crisis is to be adequately understood. For example, only an anthropologist might be expected to examine the psychobiological limits of our ability to adapt to a rapidly changing culture, or to explore systematically the interrelationships between symbolic religious systems and a culture's adaptation to nature. This freedom to jump readily between subsystems and to follow research leads even across disciplinary barriers is a marvelously adaptive quality in a time when solutions must be found rapidly. In anthropology, the *research problem* is what often determines one's subdisciplinary orientation. Specialist expertise and methodology are problem-solving tools, not ends in themselves. In many other disciplines the opposite situation seems to be too often true.

If it is true, as ecologist Barry Commoner (1971) persuasively argues, that *overspecialization* is one of the primary reasons for our lack of response to crises, then any discipline that is willing to lower its disciplinary boundaries should offer special advantages. Clearly, the recent formation of interdisciplinary environmental science programs, in which the problem defines the specialties, is a hopeful move in the right direction. Anthropologists should fit comfortably into such programs.

The Cross-Cultural Approach
No approach to our present crises can hope to be successful if it restricts itself to a single culture or even to a single cultural type. We cannot be certain that the problems we see are unique to industrial civilization or to specific subtypes of industrial civilization; but more importantly, other cultures might well have successfully avoided certain problems that we now find insurmountable.

Cross-cultural research also has certain other advantages. It requires a degree of objectivity and detachment that is often difficult to achieve when one deals with one's own culture. Relationships may stand out far more clearly in an exotic culture merely because they occur in an unfamiliar setting, and an outside observer may be more willing to draw conclusions that might conflict with comfortable patterns of thought. The fieldwork experience itself also encourages researchers to view their own culture through outsiders' eyes.

The Evolutionary Approach
Biological and cultural evolution affords a remarkable time perspective on our present condition. Without such a viewpoint, we would lack any

clear picture of our own origins. In its broadest sense, evolution implies change; and evolutionary change is what brought human beings as a species from the tribe, to the state, and finally to industrial civilization. It should be clear that understanding this process of change will be a vital step toward directing our own fate.

The Significance of Tribal Cultures

Anthropology's eclectic combination of holistic, cross-cultural, and evolutionary approaches emerges most clearly when anthropologists focus on tribal, or nonstate cultures. These cultures constitute anthropology's traditional specialty. They represent the way of life of humanity before the emergence of urban civilization and stratified kingdoms 5,000 years ago. Nonstate, or tribal, cultures still occupied much of the world until industrial nations began to expand a mere 200 years ago, and tribal cultures still persist in remote areas. Perhaps the most striking and relevant generalization that anthropology has revealed concerning tribal cultures is that they are totally different from our own culture and that, in a very real sense, they are the only proven cultural systems that humanity has ever known. They have existed since the dawn of humanity, perhaps 3 million years ago, and they successfuly satisfied basic human needs without the aid of cities or states and without high levels of energy consumption or elaborate technology. In fact, tribal cultures represent an almost total contrast in adaptive strategy and basic cultural design to our own unproven cultural experiment. We can certainly learn a great deal about the nature of present world crises by carefully comparing our own situation with related aspects of tribal cultures. Such a comparison will be one of this book's primary objectives.

Until recently it was fashionable to call these cultures "primitive," "savage," or "uncivilized," but most of these terms have now been dropped because they carried negative connotations for many people. Unfortunately, there is as yet no fully acceptable term for nonstate, tribal cultures. The term *nonstate* is also negative, and *tribal* has sometimes been applied to only certain nonstate peoples (Service 1962) and can be considered derogatory in some contexts. However, in spite of possible objections, I will use the term *tribal* to refer to basically self-sufficient cultures living largely outside of effective control by political states.

The Uniqueness of Tribal Cultures

> Authentically primitive and maximally civilized traits are, I believe, as antithetical as it is possible for cultural attributes to become within the limits of an established human condition.
> (Diamond 1968:110–11)

Several significant contrasts are immediately apparent when the socio-economic organizations of tribal and industrial cultures are compared. Primitive societies are quite small in scale, with densities of seldom more than one person per square kilometer, and maximum total population sizes of seldom over a thousand people divided into basically self-sufficient, kinship-based bands or villages of from 25 to a few hundred people. In comparison, industrial societies consist of millions of people organized into highly interdependent nation-states. This contrast in scale undoubtedly contributes to the obvious differences in degree of stratification and the corresponding differences in distribution of wealth, power, and opportunity between the different social systems. Within tribal cultures, status is normally a matter of sex, age, and personal qualities; and there is generally free access for all individuals to natural resources, food, and shelter. Historically, social stratification and inequality first become apparent with chiefdom-level societies; but even here, low rank does not deprive individuals of basic necessities. However, in an industrial culture, social stratification and inequality are developed to a high degree, and all individuals do not necessarily have free access to the same opportunities. On the basis of these differences, it might be assumed that personal and social problems related to inequality, such as poverty, powerlessness, and alienation, are not characteristic of tribal cultures, but they may be intrinsic aspects of industrial civilization.

Extreme contrasts also exist between tribal and industrial forms of economic organization, and these differences have obvious implications for the differential impact of these two cultural systems on the environment. Most significant here is the fact that tribal economies are locally self-sufficient, subsistence-based systems characterized by reciprocal exchanges and built-in limits to growth. Industrial economies are extremely specialized systems in which local areas generally do not consume the products they produce and in which market exchanges occur with individual profit as the primary motive.

Writers on cultural evolution (Morgan 1877; White 1959; Redfield 1953; Service 1962) have emphasized the contrasts between tribal cultures and civilization outlined here, and have stressed the *qualitative* transformation that has occurred with the development of civilization. It seems clear that in their general configurations, at least, tribal and civilized cultures lie at opposite and incompatible poles. Tribal cultures are so unique that they can only minimally interact with states and still retain their full identity. There is no way for a tribal culture successfully to participate in an industrial system without first surrendering local self-reliance for dependence on the world market economy and deemphasizing kinship to allow the profit system to operate freely. These changes will open the door to inequality of wealth and social stratification, and a chain reaction of further changes that will mean the complete transformation of the original tribal culture.

The Dangerous Spirit of Rousseau

Anthropologists who acknowledge any particular admiration or respect for tribal cultures, or who compare civilization unfavorably with a tribal people and suggest that we might learn from them, are likely to be accused of "Rousseauean Romanticism." In general, Romanticism seems to rank alongside ethnocentrism as the weakness to be most avoided by scientific anthropologists, and apologies are in order whenever tribal peoples are described in a favorable light. Edward Sapir (1964:96–97), for example, tells us that a sensitive ethnologist who has had firsthand field experience with a "primitive" society simply cannot help but admire the "well-rounded life" that the average member of that society leads. Even Ruth Benedict felt compelled to point out in her famous book *Patterns of Culture* that she is not using "primitive" case materials with any intention of "poeticizing the simpler peoples;" and explicitly rejects as "romantic Utopianism" the possibility that "primitives" have qualities that we might profitably consider as alternatives to our own "maladies": "But it is not in a return to ideals preserved for us by primitive peoples that our society will heal itself of its maladies. The romantic Utopianism that reaches out toward the simpler primitive, attractive as it sometimes may be, is as often, in ethnological study, a hindrance as a help" (Benedict 1959: 31–32).

Even more recent writers who actually have pointed out some specific advantages of tribal cultures are still apologizing. When Carleton S. Coon (1971:10) praises hunting peoples for having lived harmoniously with their environments, he hastens to add that he is not trying to follow Jean Jacques Rousseau's tradition by drawing a "glowing picture of the noble savage"; instead, he is interested in basic questions such as our own survival. In a similar manner, when physical anthropologist V. Neel suggested a number of important principles, derived from research among tribal Brazilian and Venezuelan Indians, that modern society might follow to improve the genetic quality of its population, he was careful to include the disclaimer: "These suggestions do not stem from any romanticism concerning the noble savage" (1970:820).

Romanticism: Why Not?

The earliest accounts of South American Indians to reach Europeans often contained obvious Romantic distortions. The first explorers quickly and correctly recognized the relative equality of many Amazonian societies, the ease of subsistence, the deemphasis on accumulation of wealth and property rights, and were especially impressed by the unselfconscious nudity and physical vitality of the people. However, the accuracy of these observations was easily ignored because they were unfortunately embellished with outrageous claims that the Indians were "noble savages" living in an earthly paradise. For example, Pietro Martire d'Anghiera reported in 1500 that the Indians "naturally follow goodness and consider odious anyone who corrupts himself by practicing evil" (Hemming 1978:15). Another early observer claimed that "in every house they all live together in harmony, with no dissension between them . . ." (Hemming 1978:15).

One need not be an anthropologist to know such perfection is simply fantasy, and that no people live together in total harmony. People who live together, whether in tribes or states, do quarrel and occasionally even kill each other. It is important to recognize that anthropologists who emphasize what might be considered "positive" elements of tribal cultures are not fantasizing about "noble savages."

In a television interview (Charbonnier 1969:21–37) in which the famous French anthropologist Claude Levi-Strauss was asked to discuss the fundamental contrasts between tribal societies and civilization, he emphasized that tribal societies are like clocks in that they strive for stability, unanimity, and equality, whereas modern society could be compared to a steam engine because its hierarchical structure assumes a built-in disharmony and antagonism. The interviewer was amazed at this apparent violation of a familiar anthropological taboo, and incredulously said to the great man: "I seem to detect an echo of Rousseau's ideas in what you are saying."

Levi-Strauss responded simply: "Why not?"

This seems a fair question. Exploring the contrasts between civilization and tribal cultures is certainly a legitimate and even critical activity for anthropologists, whether or not it is considered Romanticism. Actually, the term *Romanticism* is somewhat misleading when applied to the kind of emphasis on tribal culture we are concerned with here. By definition, *Romanticism* can mean a preoccupation with the picturesque and imaginary or unreal. Certainly, tribal cultures are often picturesque and even exotic when compared with our own, but they are *real*. Their exotic qualities have never been presented as a reason for *not* studying tribal cultures; and in fact, studying such qualities has often been thought to be anthropology's principal reason for being. Of course, an overidentification with tribals resulting in erroneous data on exotic cultures could justifiably be labeled Romanticism, but Rousseau himself has not often been accused of that. Instead, at least one authority observes that Rousseau "simply admires them [tribals] for qualities which they admittedly possess" (Fairchild 1928:133).

Overall, the validity of the specific ethnographic qualities we are attributing to tribals has never been seriously challenged by careful field research. What in fact the "Romanticist anthropologists" seem to be doing is critically investigating tribal cultures, finding them in many respects superior to our own, and expressing regrets that we have destroyed these cultures instead of learning from them. This kind of Romanticism is clear in Coon's confession of admiration for tribal hunters: "I respect and admire them . . . they led full and satisfactory lives, and it will do us no harm to reflect on the advantages of some of their age-old ways of dealing with nature and with each other" (Coon 1971:xix).

But why should there be such concern over this apparently innocuous kind of Romanticism? It is evident that the possibility that overinvolvement with tribals may bias ethnographic data is not the principal fear; rather, the real danger is that Romanticism might threaten the position of applied anthropologists in the culture modification–economic development field, and even more serious is the danger that an anthropology overidentified with tribals will disappear with them.

In spite of their general reluctance to engage in "Romanticism," it is fortunate that at least some anthropologists have explored these areas and reached some startling conclusions. For example, the work of Neel, the physical anthropologist referred to earlier, sheds interesting light on the problem of how well individual potential may be achieved in tribal society. After an eight-year interdisciplinary, team-conducted field study of some of the most isolated Amazonian Indians, Neel concluded: "It is a sobering thought that the relatively egalitarian structures of most primitive societies, plus the absence of large individual differences in material wealth seems to ensure that, within the culturally imposed boundaries, each individual in primitive society leads a life (and enjoys reproductive success) more in accord with his innate capabilities than in our present democracy" (Neel 1970: 821).

At this point, it would be appropriate to examine some of the qualities that other "Romanticist" anthropologists consider to be characteristic of tribal societies.

The Original Affluent Society

In 1965, 75 anthropologists assembled in Chicago* to examine the latest research findings on the world's last remaining tribal hunting peoples,

---

*The Wenner Gren–sponsored symposium on "Man the Hunter."

who were expected soon to become extinct. The result (Lee and DeVore 1968) was a new description of life in these simplest of ethnographically known societies, showing their existence to be stable, satisfying, and ecologically sound, and not at all "solitary, poore, nasty, brutish, and short," as Thomas Hobbes had proclaimed in *Leviathan* in 1651. It was learned, for example, that even remnant hunters such as the Bushmen, who survived in extreme and marginal environments, were not eking out a precarious existence, constantly on the edge of famine, as was thought; instead, they devoted only a few hours a week to subsistence and suffered no seasonal scarcity. When uncontaminated by outsiders, tribal hunters seemed to enjoy good health and long lives, while they had the good sense to maintain their wants at levels that could be fully and continuously satisfied without jeopardizing their environment. One researcher even suggested that this was, after all, the original "affluent society."

Most significantly, when the discussions ended, it was concluded that the hunting way of life, which had dominated perhaps 99 percent of humanity's cultural life span, had been "the most successful and persistent adaptation man has ever achieved" (Sahlins 1968); in comparison, newly arrived industrial civilization was in a precarious situation with the "exceedingly complex and unstable ecological conditions" it had created. At least one distinguished participant even felt that we should study why hunters were so successful, and that our civilization might actually learn something from them. These were remarkable conclusions to come from members of a profession that was vigorously disassociating itself from its long-exclusive identification with tribal peoples and that rigorously avoided any hint of Romanticism whenever it studied these so-called preliterate or preindustrial peoples. Hard ethnographic facts were forcing anthropologists to reconsider Rousseau's position.

Our Tribal Superiors

Rousseau was perhaps one of the earliest modern observers to comment on the success of tribal cultures when in the 18th century, at the very beginning of the Industrial Revolution, he observed that the period of human history dominated by tribal cultures "must have been the happiest and most durable of epochs. The more we reflect on it, the more we shall find that this state was the least subject to revolutions, and altogether the very best man could experience . . . all subsequent advances have been apparently so many steps towards the perfection of the individual, but in reality towards the decrepitude of the species" (Rousseau in Fairchild 1928:33).

A few widely known anthropologists have unabashedly followed Rousseau in this assessment of tribal cultures. Leslie A. White, for example, called nonagricultural, hunting societies "the most satisfying kind of social environment that man has ever lived in" and further elaborated: "[T]heir social systems . . . were unquestionably more congenial to the human primate's nature, and more compatible with his psychic needs and aspirations than any other of the cultures subsequent to the Agricultural Revolution, including our own society today" (White 1959:277–278).

Numerous other writers have also praised tribal cultures for successfully satisfying basic human needs. The evidence for this apparent success of tribal culture seems undeniable, especially when one considers the many thousands of years they have endured, their generally slow and conservative patterns of change, and the reluctance of surviving tribal peoples to abandon their life-styles.

The Antiprimitivists

Although most anthropologists have either abandoned the term *primitive* or cautiously retain the concept under new, less derogatory labels, a small minority have portrayed primitive or tribal culture in openly negative terms. Hallpike (1979) for example, argues that tribal peoples are really mental children. He suggests that in developmental terms they are like 12-year-olds, incapable of formal logical thought. If this view were to be substantiated, it would certainly have important implications for our understanding of tribal culture; however, Hallpike has found little support among other anthropologists (see, for example, Shweder 1982). It seems that many of the apparent differences in the mental processes of tribal peoples are actually related to the absence of writing and tell us little about their real capabilities (Goody 1976).

A more extreme antiprimitivist stance is taken by psychological anthropologist Arthur Hippler, who states emphatically that tribal cultures are inferior to modern civilization. Hippler argues that many anthropologists simply prefer tribal cultures to civilization and choose to ignore the negative aspects of the former. He of course labels this Rousseauean Romanticism, but goes beyond that to suggest that anyone who sees positive aspects of tribal cultures is actually suffering from a "pathological rebelliousness" against civilization (Hippler 1979a:510), or even an "irrational anthropological hatred of Euro-American . . . society" (Hippler 1979b:494). Hippler, on the other hand, emphatically prefers civilization and goes to the opposite extreme to totally deprecate tribal cultures. In his view, ". . . there is no question that Euro-American culture is vastly superior . . . to any primitive society extant" (Hippler 1981:395). In contrast, tribal cultures are "transparently, clearly, patently less adequately organized expressions of human beliefs and actions . . ." (Hippler 1979a:510). Hippler feels that Romantic anthropologists have systematically ignored the "often outrageous intrusions on individual capacities or crushing of human personality so common in primitive communities" (Hippler 1979c:294). Hippler uses a long list of deprecatory terms to describe tribal cultures. For example, he finds them rigid and unattractive, incredibly repressive, inadequate, and personally destructive. He believes that they stunt child development and create terrified, emotionally and cognitively deficient adults.

Hippler's underlying theory (1977) is that tribal cultures do an inferior job of childrearing and thus create inferior adults. He presents his own analysis of traditional Eskimo and Australian aboriginal culture as support for his argument. According to Hippler (1974), traditional Eskimo society in north Alaska was characterized by virtual anarchy and lawlessness. Thievery and murder were common, women were treated cruelly, and the "dangerously low level of social control" was maintained precariously by local "bullies" through bribery, coercion, and fear. Conditions were so bad that "there was no security of life, limb, or property." These brutal conditions were only improved by the arrival of missionaries, who "fearlessly faced down the shamans," and by the United States marshalls and the Coast Guard, who were able to enforce an end to the "terror." Hippler asserts that the causes of all this were faulty childrearing practices that produced a typically egocentric and selfish adult personality. The basic problem, according to Hippler, was that children were at first "massively indulged" and later teased and frustrated. This treatment retarded the normal development of the ability to distinguish self from others, and therefore adults could not separate the supernatural from the real world and fell easy prey to the manipulations of shamans.

Hippler's (1981) portrayal of Australian aboriginal culture is, if any-thing, more negative. He describes aboriginal parents as selfish, thought-less, very harsh, neglectful, infantile, and inconsistent; as a result adults are emotionally and cognitively scarred and have difficulty separating fantasy from reality.

What Hippler presents is not a pretty picture. It is also a gross exaggeration and misrepresentation of the ethnographic data. Anthro-pologists who are well acquainted with the peoples that Hippler describes have strongly rejected his interpretations (see, for example, Hamilton 1979; Berndt 1981; Reser 1981). Hippler's critics point out serious de-ficiencies in his fieldwork and his failure to adequately take into account the social problems created by detribalization and cultural change. No one would deny that cases of poor childrearing practices can be found in tribal societies, or in any society, but it is clear that Hippler's description is an inaccurate caricature. Furthermore, he draws a dubious connection between childrearing practices and adult culture.

Although I emphatically reject both the antiprimitivist approach and the "noble savage" fantasy, in the following pages I will deliberately emphasize certain aspects of tribal culture to highlight the problems that our own culture has created. In my view, our problems are cultural problems; they are not problems of human nature.

2
ADAPTATION, TRIBAL CULTURE, AND THE ENVIRONMENTAL CRISIS

> Nor are those cultures that we might consider higher
> in general evolutionary standing necessarily more
> perfectly adapted to their environments than lower.
> Many great civilizations have fallen in the last 2,000
> years, even in the midst of material plenty, while the
> Eskimos tenaciously maintained themselves in an
> incomparably more difficult habitat. The race is not to
> the swift, nor the battle to the strong.

Marshall Sahlins and Elman R. Service (eds.), *Evolution and Culture*

Many general conclusions of direct relevance to our own environmental situation emerge from the cultural ecological data that anthropologists have compiled over the years. Perhaps the most important conclusion to be drawn is that tribal cultures did indeed tend to mesh harmoniously with their environments. Although tribal peoples certainly did modify their environments and manage their resources, there was clearly a pattern in which long-term, relatively stable balances were established between the human population and natural communities. These balances were often disturbed for a variety of reasons, but even so, the contrast with the scale of disruption and the degree of instability characteristic of the industrial world is truly striking. If culture had never "advanced" beyond the hunting stage, it is likely that an environmental crisis of the magnitude we are now experiencing would never have arisen, except perhaps through some natural catastrophe. Even tribal food producers have been relatively more successful at avoiding environmental problems than most state-level cultures. Tribal cultures are clearly more stable and better suited to long-run survival than any more highly evolved cultures. These facts challenge many widely accepted interpretations of such basic anthropological concepts as cultural evolution and adaptation, and raise important questions concerning our own ability to survive.

Cultural Evolution and Adaptation

Among the widely held misconceptions regarding cultural evolution and adaptation is the view that evolutionary progress has meant greater security, greater freedom from environmental limitations, and greater efficiency of energy use. In many minds, higher levels of evolutionary development have also been equated with greater adaptive success. If theories of cultural evolution are to be harmonized with what is known about the obvious ability of tribal cultures to avoid environmental catastrophes, then these theories and their interpretations must be examined more closely.

The principal pioneer of modern cultural evolutionary theory, Leslie A. White (1949), defined evolutionary progress largely in terms of increasing per capita utilization of energy. A culture that consumed more energy per capita was simply more highly evolved. Other writers (Sahlins and Service 1960) have elaborated on this theory, arguing that two kinds of cultural evolution can be distinguished, *general* and *specific*. General evolution is concerned with levels of evolutionary progress, the more "advanced" forms that interested White. These higher forms are defined in terms of energy consumption, organizational complexity, and the ability to exploit a wider range of environments and to replace cultures at "lower" levels. Specific evolution means *adaptation to local environments*, and it is clear that cultures at low levels of evolutionary progress, as defined above, may be far more *efficient* in terms of energy input-output ratios, and far more stable and successfully adapted to their environments, than more "advanced" cultures. Cultural progress, in terms of general evolution, may actually reduce security, diversity, and energy efficiency, and dramatically *increase* the likelihood of environmental crisis. Furthermore, it may increase the work load of individuals.

Many of these points seem to have been missed by those anthropologists who have been particularly impressed with the material accomplishments of industrial civilization, and who have not paid close attention to the differences between general and specific evolution. For example, in an attempt to describe general levels of cultural evolution in terms of adaptation, Yehudi Cohen (1974:45–68) states that at each stage (hunting-gathering, cultivation, industrialism), people become better adapted for survival, more secure, freer from the environment, and more energy-efficient. In Cohen's view, cultural evolution has been achieved because people have sought to gain mastery over nature, and it has been inhibited in certain areas through ignorance of basic technologies. Recent research on such critical evolutionary advances as food production and state organizations suggests that the role of invention and discovery has been greatly overemphasized. It is more likely that such changes were gradually forced on reluctant people as a result of unintended demographic imbalances. In this sense, "mastery over nature" has not been something eagerly sought by inventive minds; rather, people have been compelled to accept certain burdens and assume new adaptive risks by the grim need to readjust to altered circumstances.

Progress can indeed open more habitat types to exploitation by a given cultural type, but such progress is not escaping the limits of nature, and it may prove highly maladaptive. Cohen devotes considerable attention to the "freedom from environmental limitations" concept and reaches some surprisingly shortsighted conclusions that directly conflict with more realistic assessments of the adaptive shortcomings of industrial culture. He argues, for example, that increasing mastery over nature leads to an increasingly secure food supply, and points to supermarkets and the ability to eat fresh fruit out of season as great triumphs over nature. Strawberries at Christmastime are, in this regard, "perhaps one of man's greatest achievements. . . ." However, if viewed in wider perspective, supermarkets and Christmas strawberries are incredibly wasteful of resources, and they are likely to be short-lived institutions as industrial civilization reaches the limits of its global environment.

Many writers confidently measure the "higher" adaptive success of industrial culture in terms of its apparent reproductive success and because of its ability to displace and destroy "lower," "less effective" cultures. What such assessments overlook is the time factor. As Sahlins points out in the quotation introducing this chapter, real adaptive success can only be measured in terms of survival—over the long run. If we insist on considering short-term reproductive success, or proliferation of people, an indication of adaptive achievement, then perhaps a new "law" of cultural evolution can be formulated: *Culture evolves as the global biomass becomes increasingly converted to the human sector.*

Certainly, a clear trend in cultural evolution to date has been toward a remarkable increase in the human sector of the global biomass (humans, and domestic plants and animals) and a corresponding reduction in the earth's natural biomass. This reduction in the nonhuman sector is necessary because of the simple ecological fact that a fixed amount of solar energy fuels the planet's primary producers (green plants); consequently, there are absolute limits to how many consumers can exist (biologist Isaac Asimov [1971] places the actual limit of consumers at about 2 million million tons of biomass). As human consumers increase, natural consumers must decrease. The ultimate pinnacle of evolutionary achievement, then, should be the point when every gram of living material on earth has been transferred to the human sector and man's every natural "competitor" has been eliminated. At present rates of progress, it is estimated (Asimov 1971) that we could reach such a point by A.D. 2436.

Nature and Scope of the Environmental Crisis

In its most basic sense, the environmental crisis is a deterioration of environmental quality with a corresponding reduction in carrying capacity due to human intervention in natural processes. At the present time, given the existing global social order, we are clearly running up against basic limits to the earth's ability to supply the resources that we consume and to absorb our industrial by-products. Later chapters will treat the specific environmental problems of food, energy, population, and resources in more detail; but first, it may be useful to consider the general implications of man's intervention in the biosphere.

The environmental crisis is not new; it has developed as general cultural evolution has given humans greater ability to influence nature, increased population and per capita consumption rates, and altered distribution patterns. Tribal hunters have contributed to the creation of grasslands; pastoral nomads have overgrazed their lands; peasant farmers have caused deforestation and erosion. From archaeological evidence, it is clear that tribal cultures and early civilization at times faced their own local environmental crises as imbalances occurred, and were forced to abandon certain regions or drastically alter their cultures. However, the scope and quality of the changes that global industrialization has set in motion over the past 200 years make these earlier problems seem quite insignificant. We now have the potential for disrupting basic life support processes and may already be inadvertently reducing our own prospects for survival. The following examples should make this point clear.

Death of the Tropical Rain Forests
In an article in *Scientific American*, Paul W. Richards, the world's leading authority on tropical rain forests, very calmly and objectively, with only a slight trace of bitterness, made the following announcement: "It appears likely that all of the world's tropical rain forests, with the exception of a few small, conserved relics, will be destroyed in the next 20 to 30 years. This destruction will inevitably have important consequences for life on the earth, although the nature and magnitude of these consequences cannot be foreseen with precision" (Richards 1973:66). Five years later the United Nations published a report estimating that the Amazon rain forest, the largest uninterrupted tract of tropical rain forest

in the world, was being destroyed at the rate of 4 percent a year (UNESCO 1978:475). If that pattern were to continue, the most reasonable prediction is that the rate of destruction would steadily increase. The rain forest of Amazonia would be reduced to a third of its 1978 size by A.D. 2005 and would be virtually eliminated within another 50 years. The actual percentage rate of global rain forest destruction is quite problematic, because the experts do not agree on baseline data. Some authorities suggest global rates ranging from 1 to 2.6 percent a year (Grainger 1980). Whatever the current rate, it can be expected to increase in the future.

Scattered populations of tribal farmers, hunters, and fishermen have lived successfully in Amazonia for several thousands of years by relying on shifting cultivation (Lathrap 1970; Meggers 1971). Their adaptation rested on their ability to maintain fallow periods of sufficient length to allow regrowth of the primary forest before a new garden was opened. In recent years, outsiders have attempted to introduce permanent agricultural development schemes and have thus permanently destroyed the forest, leaving rain-leached, impoverished, rock-hard soils and scrub thorn forests in their place. As populations expand and governments look to the tropical forests for new lands to open to colonization, this destruction is accelerating throughout the tropical world.

Richards remarked that the destruction of the tropical rain forests will be a "major event in the earth's history" and that it will irreversibly alter the course of biological evolution. The tropical rain forests have existed continuously for more than 60 million years and have been the source of most of the plants and animals, including humans, that have moved out from them to pioneer the more difficult temperate zones. The rain forest is the most stable and complex ecosystem in the world and is characterized by a diversity of species that is unsurpassed by any other natural community. For all of its richness in plants and animals, the rain forest is remarkably poor in soil nutrients. Critical nutrients are stored largely in living plants, not in the soil, and are then quickly and efficiently recycled when plants die.

It has sometimes been predicted that the clearing of these forests will lead to serious depletion of the global oxygen supply, but Richards feels that this is unlikely. He is not so certain, however, that their removal will not upset global climate patterns. In his estimation the destruction of rain forests will clearly be a major loss for humanity in terms of potential human experience and scientific knowledge.

Death of the Oceans

> The end of the ocean came late in the summer of 1979, and it came even more rapidly than the biologists had expected. There had been signs for more than a decade, commencing with the discovery in 1968 that DDT slows down photosynthesis in marine plant life. It was announced in a short paper in the technical journal, *Science*, but to ecologists it smacked of doomsday. (Ehrlich 1969)

Perhaps the most serious environmental crisis, which has already been predicted by biologists and oceanographers, is the death of the oceans. The above quotation is from a fictional scenario of such an event. In this case, it is assumed that pesticide pollution and overfishing will simplify the marine ecosystem to such an extent that toxic forms of marine plankton suddenly will expand, killing all other forms of marine life. There are many other possibilities. Oil pollution from spills, offshore drilling, and dumping may in itself become serious enough to kill off all marine plankton, particularly because oil on water concentrates chlorinated hydrocarbon residues.

Whatever the cause, the death of the oceans will be a far greater "event" in earth history than the destruction of the tropical rain forests. Marine phytoplankton supplies approximately 70 percent of the atmosphere's free oxygen—their destruction would almost certainly mean the disappearance of most higher life forms on the planet. Such an ecocatastrophe is now clearly within our capability, and indeed seems to be shaping up, "if present trends continue."

Since Ehrlich published his scenario in 1969, increasing data have been compiled, emphasizing the extent of the damage that has already occurred. Several fisheries have already been eliminated; the great whales have been systematically exterminated; and coastal marine ecosystems have already been seriously disrupted or destroyed by overuse, dumping, unintended pollution, and "reclamation" projects. Even the midocean has become a cesspool of plastic and oil in some areas, and smaller, enclosed seas such as the Baltic are seriously threatened. The danger is unmistakable, but experts disagree over the details. A more recent assessment of the marine environment (Goldberg 1976; Barney 1980) suggests that, whereas coastal regions can be expected to deteriorate further over the coming decades with continued serious disruption of fisheries, the oceans will be neither dead nor dying by the year 2000. In the longer run, however, the future of the oceans remains in doubt. Much depends on the international response.

Environmental Crisis and Cultural Change

In the broadest sense, an environmental crisis is any imbalance between a human population and its resource base in which the ability of the natural environment to meet human demands is diminished. Such a crisis could be initiated naturally by a climatic fluctuation that caused a reduction in available resources. It could also be caused by an increase in the human population or in its technology or consumption rates. This kind of environmental crisis has been a factor in cultural change perhaps throughout human evolution. However, the present environmental crisis is very different from any in the past, not only because of its scope but because it is primarily caused by cultural features that never existed in the past.

The environmental changes associated with tribal societies tend to unfold gradually and are much more likely to lead to new, relatively stable balances. In contrast, stratified societies are associated with rapid, often catastrophic environmental crises that arise more and more frequently. Prehistoric Europe provides an example of gradual change introduced by tribal cultures.

In Europe, following the arrival of Neolithic shifting cultivators, the limits of their subsistence adaptation were reached within a few thousand years. Forest fallow periods were shortened as population pressure increased, and domestic grazing animals further inhibited the regeneration of forest. Eventually, permanent open country and heath lands appeared over large areas of what had formerly been a vast expanse of virtually unbroken forest that hunting peoples had kept intact for tens of thousands of years (Clark 1952). As a result of this environmental crisis, shifting cultivation became all but impossible; the natural fertility of the forest soils was being exhausted; and a period of population movement, warfare, and dramatic culture change ensued. When conditions finally stabilized, it was at a higher population density and with an entirely different social and ecological basis. This is not the place to attempt an analysis of exactly how this imbalance in Neolithic Europe occurred. The important point is that it did occur, it was an imbalance, and it precipitated an environmental crisis and culture change in response.

Numerous other examples of similar environmental crises can be cited. There is clear evidence that agricultural practices in ancient Mesopotamia, where irrigation favored the gradual accumulation of salts in the soil, were contributing factors in the fall of Sumerian civilization after 2000 B.C. (Jacobsen and Adams 1958). In the New World, some have suggested that the "mysterious" sudden collapse of the classic Mayan civilization in Yucatan after A.D. 790 was at least partly a result of increasing demographic pressures on a limited resource base and that some kind of "environmental crisis" either occurred or was developing (Willey and Shimkin 1971; Culbert 1974). However, there are other possible explanations for the collapse (Hamblin and Pitcher 1980), and the issue is not clear. Detailed archaeological data are available to document the collapse of a stratified, chiefdom-level culture on Marajó Island at the mouth of the Amazon River just prior to the arrival of Europeans, again as a result of overwhelming pressures on a limited resource base (Meggers and Evans 1957).

Such collapses and transformations must have occurred many times, and would seem to be the inevitable fate of any expansive, disequilibrium culture. However, on the basis of present anthropological data, it can be stated that, in general, hunter-gatherers only infrequently and gradually accelerate their population and consumption rates to the point that environmental deterioration and a reduced carrying capacity result. Tribal food producers, with a similar economic organization, have somewhat more difficulty, but still tend to enjoy environmental equilibrium. Social stratification, inequality, urbanization, and state organization, however, set in motion a system that is almost inherently unstable. When expansive market systems and industrialization are added, disequilibrium is assured, and environmental problems become a certainty. The most critical difference now, however, is that the disequilibrium culture is a global culture, and we are seeing a global environmental crisis unfolding. The

predictable transformation or collapse of industrial culture will, like the
passing of the tropical rain forests, be a "major event in earth history."

Global Disequilibrium: "The Limits to Growth"

> We can thus say with some confidence that, under the assumption of no
> major change in the present system, population and industrial growth will
> certainly stop within the next century, at the latest. (Meadows 1972:126)

> The basic behavior mode of the world system is exponential growth of
> population and capital, followed by collapse. . . . [T]his behavior mode
> occurs if we assume no change in the present system or if we assume
> any number of technological changes in the system.
> (Meadows 1972:142)

On the very eve of the Industrial Revolution, in 1798, Thomas R.
Malthus, a British economist, warned of population's potential for exponential growth and pointed out that, if unchecked, population would
outstrip the ability of a country or the world to produce food. He revised
and refined his basic argument several times in the face of a barrage of
criticism that held that there was no such tendency, or that the potential
of the earth was virtually limitless. Many critics, particularly economists
and social planners, argued that population growth was essential for
industrial growth, and that together these would assure continued hap-
piness and prosperity for humanity. This growth concept has certainly
been a central theme in the world view of industrial civilization; and
perpetual expansion, whether in population or consumption, has in fact
been the distinguishing feature of industrial economic systems. Malthus
was not alone in his pessimism over growth. Other early economists,
including Adam Smith and David Ricardo, also felt that continual economic growth would not be possible forever because of ultimate limits
and inevitable diminishing returns from a dwindling resource base. Any
stabilization of the industrial economic system was thought to be so far
in the future that no one need worry about planning for it. Only in
recent years have significant numbers of scientists begun to doubt that

continual growth can be sustained by a finite planet long into the foreseeable future.

In 1864, an American scholar, George P. Marsh, published a massive indictment of the deterioration of the natural environments of Europe and America that had already occurred because of human intervention, and boldly warned that a "shattered" earth and the extinction of the species might result from further human "crimes" against nature.

Over the next 100 years after these early warnings, the hazards of constant growth in a finite world were largely ignored, thanks to the dramatic achievements of science and technology in increasing production. Few people seemed to worry that a sudden switch to nonrenewable new energy sources (coal and oil) and the imperialist expansion into Africa and Asia might only increase the disequilibrium and temporarily delay a stabilization while greatly raising the cost of readjustment and heightening the potential dangers.

In 1954, as the great effort for global economic development gained momentum, the combined problems of population growth, industrial expansion, and the limitations of the world to support such developments were posed as serious threats to the future survival of humanity in a provocative book by Harrison Brown entitled *The Challenge of Man's Future*. Brown suggested that the most likely outcome would be the irreversible collapse of industrial civilization due to its own instabilities and the destruction of its resource base through inadequately regulated exploitation. The only other likely outcome that Brown could imagine that would permit the limited survival of industrial civilization would be careful planning and rigid restriction of individual freedom by authoritarian governments. In effect, new mechanisms of social integration would need to evolve. Similar pessimism and warnings were raised in 1974 by Robert L. Heilbroner, an economist who a short time earlier was an optimistic champion of worldwide industrialization.

One of the most ambitious and authoritative attempts to examine the probable implications of the present instability of industrial civilization is *The Limits to Growth* study (Meadows et al.), published in 1972. This study is the result of some two years of research by a 17-member international team of experts working with a complex computer model of the "global system" devised by Jay Forrester of the Massachusetts Institute of Technology. Starting from certain basic assumptions about the interrelatedness of population, agricultural production, resource depletion, industrial production, and pollution, the team set out to estimate how these factors might interact to set limits on the future expansion of industrial civilization (see Figure 2-1). The results of this research were surprising to many people and distressing to everyone. No matter how the variables were manipulated (i.e., by technological solutions, assuming twice as many natural resources, solving the problem of pollution, and so on), the system collapses before A.D. 2100 because of basic environmental limits. Figure 2-2 illustrates how a collapse might occur if present trends continue. Stabilizing population extends the system somewhat, but collapse still occurs because resources are exhausted. According to these projections, the only feasible solution for maintaining industrial civilization as a viable adaptation is to stabilize both population and industrial production as quickly as possible.

The M.I.T. *Limits to Growth* study has prompted severe criticism from technological optimists, who imply that the long-run limitations are still far in the future and at present undefinable (see especially Cole 1973). The world model has been criticized as imprecise, too complex for wide understanding, and oversimplified. It has been suggested by such critics that it might be dangerous to attempt to bring economic growth to a halt, and those desiring stability are accused of being elitists who only wish to maintain the status quo in their favor. For their part, the critics have yet to present more adequate models or to show convincingly that present economic systems and values and future technologies will deal with the problems that both pessimists and optimists agree already exist.

If the basic trends and the relationships between trends shown in the world model are valid, then perhaps it is time for anthropologists to reconsider seriously their own position on the question of economic growth. Certainly, anthropologists have been actively engaged in the promotion of economic development throughout the world. Now, perhaps, many will wish to explore the relationship between such growth and the increasing environmental crisis and the instabilities of our present industrial adaptation. Anthropologists may well want to join the rising debate over how industrial growth might end and how a transition to a steady-state economy might be achieved.

Global 2000

The most knowledgeable professional analysts in the executive
branch of the U.S. Government have reported to the President that,
if public policies around the world continue unchanged through the
end of the century, a number of serious world problems will become
worse, not better . . . the world in 2000 will be more crowded,
more polluted, less stable ecologically, and more vulnerable to
disruption. . . . Serious stresses involving population, resources, and
environment are clearly visible ahead . . . the world's people will be
poorer. . . . (Barney, *Global 2000 Report*, 1977, vol. 1:xvi,1)

In 1977 President Carter commissioned a special study of global trends
in population, resources, and environment up to the year 2000, to fa-
cilitate long-range planning by United States government agencies. The
work was over two years in preparation and ultimately involved a budget
of nearly $1 million, 13 government agencies, and scores of advisors and
researchers. In general this study was similar to the *Limits to Growth* study
in that it was attempting to project the future outcome of present trends
at a global level. However, *Global 2000* is much more cautious than the
Limits to Growth in that some of the subsections of the study, such as
food production, do not always take into account losses caused by activities in other sections, such as industrial pollution. Furthermore, the
Global 2000 study looks only to the year 2000, whereas the *Limits to
Growth* looks much further ahead. The *Global 2000* study is also quite
conservative; it assumes continued technological progress, no major

F I G U R E 2 - 1 The Global System. The entire world model is represented
on the following pages by a flow diagram in formal System Dynamics notation.
Levels, or physical quantities that can be measured directly, are indicated by rectangles; rates that influence those levels, by values; and auxiliary variables that
influence the rate equations, by circles. Time delays are indicated by sections within
rectangles. Real flows of people, goods, money, etc. are shown by solid arrows; and
causal relationships, by broken arrows. Clouds represent sources or sinks that are
not important to the model behavior.

Source: Donella H. Meadows et al., *The Limits to Growth* (New York: Universe Books, 1972),
102–3.

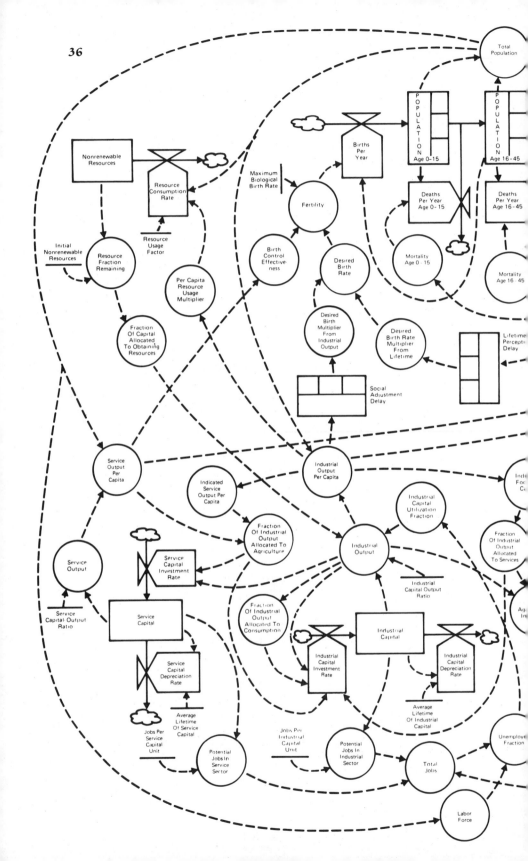

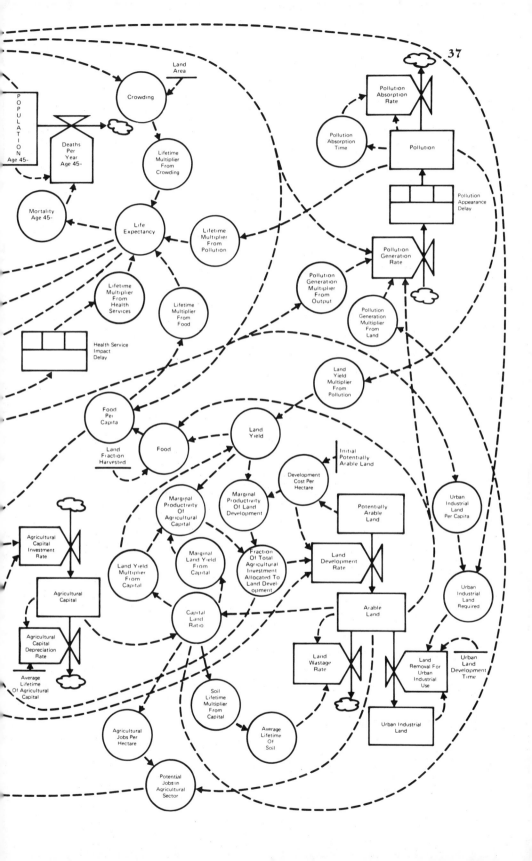

political upheavals, and a continuation of the present world political system. In view of all these conservative elements, it is perhaps remarkable that the conclusions of Global 2000 still contain ominous warnings of serious problems in the near future, as indicated in the summary quote cited above. Although no catastrophic collapse of the world system is foreseen in the next few decades, the report warns that population will continue to increase, and there could be serious water shortages, major deforestation, deterioration of agricultural lands, increased desertification, and massive plant and animal extinctions, together with more poverty, human suffering, and international tension—all this assuming that present trends continue.

The Global 2000 study also has generated widespread criticism from those who prefer a more optimistic viewpoint, and there are certainly many weaknesses in the projections. The authors of the report, however, feel that they have deliberately erred on the side of optimism, and that the outcome will be considerably bleaker if the problems are not corrected. This is not the place to review all the conclusions of Global 2000, but it should be clear that the study's many findings do emphasize the continued seriousness of the environmental crisis, as well as many other closely related areas of concern.

At this point, it will be useful to examine some of the explanations that have been offered for our present envrionmental difficulties before moving to the perspectives that can be gained from tribal cultures.

"Roots" of the Environmental Crisis

Whether the environmental crisis will lead to a collapse of industrial civilization within the lifetime of many persons now living, as some scholars believe, its basic causes are still best understood as an imbalance between pressures on the environment and the environment's ability to meet them. Resources are being consumed at a rate greater than they are being produced by natural biological or geological processes, and wastes are being created that disrupt existing natural cycles. This imbalance may conveniently be considered a problem of *overconsumption* in order to emphasize that more is involved than an absolute increase in population. Overconsumption may be defined as consumption in a given area that exceeds the rates at which natural resources are produced by natural processes, to such an extent that the long-run stability of the culture involved is threatened. Every culture certainly has the potential for overconsumption, and this potential could be realized by a simple increase in population over the carrying capacity of a given region. However, this overconsumption seldom occurs in primitive cultures because negative feedback systems are activated to reduce population, or because cultural mechanisms to promote better distribution are used. Unusual increases in per capita consumption rates could also initiate overconsumption; but again such an outcome is normally prevented by negative feedback mechanisms. Unfortunately, industrial civilization has short-circuited the normal cultural feedback mechanisms that prevent overconsumption in at least four critical ways:

1. Dependence on nonrenewable resources
2. Dependence on imports
3. Urbanization
4. Institutionalized inequality

Perhaps the most critical turning point in the development of industrial civilization was its shift away from renewable resources to overwhelming dependence on stored fossil fuels, which have become substitutes for both solar energy and natural products such as fibers. These resources have been "banked" in the earth over millions of years and, in fact, represent stored solar energy; yet they are now being used to support temporarily a tremendous overgrowth of consumption far beyond what could ever be supported by local renewable resources. The danger in this case is that by the time these stored resources have become significantly depleted, we shall have "overshot" our renewable resource base to such an extent that collapse will be assured. A culture relying largely on local renewable resources would feel an impending shortage much sooner and could make corrective adjustments, either by intensifying its productive technology or, more wisely, by reducing its population or consumption, or both.

A second critical way in which industrial civilization has temporarily escaped an inevitable balancing with resource limitations has been through its enormous reliance on extraterritorial resources—i.e., imports.

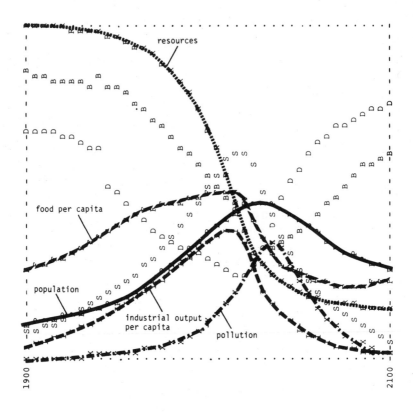

FIGURE 2-2 World Model, Standard Run. The "standard" world model run assumes no major change in the physical, economic, or social relationships that have historically governed the development of the world system. All variables plotted here follow historical values from 1900 to 1970. Food, industrial output, and population grow exponentially until the rapidly diminishing resource base forces a slowdown in industrial growth. Because of natural delays in the system, both population and pollution continue to increase for some time after the peak of industrialization. Population growth is finally halted by a rise in the death rate due to decreased food and medical services. B = crude birthrate (births per 1,000 persons per year). D = crude death rate (deaths per 1,000 persons per year). S = services per capita (dollar equivalent per person per year).

Source: Donella H. Meadows et al., *The Limits to Growth* (New York: Universe Books, 1972), 124.

Intercultural trade or exchanges of resources are perhaps universals, but it is unusual to find cultures totally dependent on such exchanges for survival. In the past, energy sources have probably never been imported; trade was often limited to ritual items, or it may have served as a special means of maintaining peaceful intercultural relations. Reliance on imported resources to support otherwise unsupportable growth and consumption is an obvious source of instability and carries the same danger of overshoot and collapse as does reliance on stored nonrenewable resources.

Urbanization creates a similar problem because urban populations must be supported by internal "imports" from rural areas. The urban consumers are far removed from their resources and are unlikely to become immediately aware of impending shortages or of any other environmental impact of their consumption patterns.

Institutionalized inequality is normally defined by differential consumption patterns and serves to promote overconsumption while diverting much of its adverse impact onto "lower" classes who must first pay the real costs. Again, this process merely serves to divert and thereby delay the mechanisms that would otherwise maintain consumption within environmental limits.

In addition to overconsumption, industrial civilization has greatly increased the probability that it will cause environmental crises by disrupting natural cycles and simplifying ecosystems on a vast scale. Natural cycles have been disrupted by the introduction of new synthetic materials (such as plastics), which, as we have seen, have been used to support overconsumption artifically, but which also cannot be readily broken down by the environment to their constituent parts for reuse. Furthermore, even "natural" wastes have been created and concentrated in ways that have blocked their effective recycling or that have made them biologically destructive. In this regard, we have consistently violated what ecologist Barry Commoner has called the basic "laws" of ecology (1971). Simplification of ecosystems is best exemplified by the industrial factory farm, in which an attempt is made to exclude all but one or two "desirable" species. This process greatly lowers the biological productivity and stability of an ecosystem, and can only be maintained at enormous cost in imported energy, and by increased use of pesticides and synthetic fertilizers, which in turn deplete nonrenewable resources and disrupt natural cycles.

Thus, our present environmental crisis is the direct result of over-consumption, disruption of natural cycles, and simplification of ecosystems. Since all cultures seem to have the potential for degrading their environments by such means, it remains to be explained why states—and industrial states in particular—have been much greater culprits in this regard than tribal cultures. Many writers point out a single basic cause, such as misuse of technology, overpopulation, or misplaced values, and emphasize it almost to the exclusion of other factors. Their arguments run as follows: if we can simply develop better technology, achieve zero population growth, or invent a new value system, our environmental problems will be over. The population and technology arguments will be examined later, but for now the values argument may profitably be examined.

Ideological Roots

Much of the discussion of the need for a value change stems from an article published by historian Lynn White, Jr., in 1967.* The author points out that religion promotes certain attitudes toward nature that are in turn reflected in ecological processes. Christianity is held responsible for our present crisis because in Genesis, God gave man dominion over nature, thereby initiating our victorious battle with nature. On the other hand, it is argued that tribal animism, which makes man part of nature, prevents such a battle and avoids the crisis. This viewpoint has much to recommend it, and it does emphasize important differences between tribal religions and Christianity; however, it confuses *association* with *causation* and may divert attention from the more fundamental changes that are needed. Anthropologists generally see religion in a *support* role, helping to maintain socioeconomic systems rather than directly causing them. Religious ideologies *reflect* economic adaptations and are more likely to change with them rather than vice versa. White concludes: "Since the roots of our trouble are so largely religious, the remedy must also be essentially religious. . . ." This approach might be going at the

---

*See also Anderson 1969.

problem backwards. More direct results could be achieved through a socioeconomic reorganization, and then religious ideology would swing in line.

Herders, Self-Interest, and Tragic Commons

Biologist Garrett Hardin (1968) sees the environmental crisis as a failure to define maximum good and considers it to be the inevitable outgrowth of individuals seeking their own self-interest in combination with a failure of appeals to conscience and social responsibility. He calls for mutually agreed on coercive restraints to maintain population and pollution within safe limits and suggests that these problems, strictly speaking, have no technical solutions. Like Lynn White, Jr., he feels that a change in values is required, but adds the important additional qualification that political regulations must be strengthened.

It is clearly not possible to optimize both population and consumption, because limiting consumption will allow a larger population, and vice versa. Cultures must, in effect, define "maximum good" and then adjust population levels in conformity with the ability of specific environments to supply that "good" on a sustainable basis. Hardin correctly sees the solution of this problem, either implicitly or explicitly, as critical to the stability and survival of any cultural group, but fails to recognize that the problem has already been solved by tribal cultures without direct coercion. Regarding maximum good, Harden asks: "Has any cultural group solved this practical problem at the present time, even on an intuitive level? One simple fact proves that none has: there is no prosperous population in the world today that has, and has had for some time, a growth rate of zero" (Hardin 1968).

This of course overlooks the fact, discussed in Chapter 1, that tribal cultures have maintained their stability by defining maximum good at easily satisfied levels, and in their own terms have achieved both "affluence" and environmental balance. At the same time, they have done so without the coercive restraints that Hardin feels will be needed to control the dangers of the pursuit of self-interest.

The example Hardin uses to illustrate why the pursuit of self-interest in the exploitation of a "commons" or public resource will not work is misleading because it fails to consider anthropological data. He assumes that a traditional herding society is kept in balance with its resources only because of warfare, poaching, and disease, which prevent individual herders from expanding their herds. When these controls are eliminated, Hardin supposes that individual herdsmen will continue to add extra animals to their own herds even beyond the point at which environmental damage results from overgrazing, because they will receive full advantage for each additional animal, whereas the costs of overgrazing will be shared by all herders. Each herdsman is thus caught in a conflict between social responsibility and personal self-interest, and only coercive force would make it obviously in his best interest to refrain from expanding his herd.

Anthropological research has shown that the actual situation in traditional herding societies is quite different, however. There is seldom any conflict between individual self-interest and social responsibility. Where self-sufficient individual households or small household groups must depend on herd animals for their primary subsistence, maximum herd size is determined by the number of animals a given herder can safely handle, quality of pasture, and daily grazing requirements of the animals, in addition to sociopolitical considerations. A large herd of large animals in an area of poor pastures would quickly become impractical, because the herd would need to move so rapidly to get enough to eat that productivity would decline (Spooner 1973).

The successful adaptation of herding societies is clearly illustrated by the traditional herders of southwest Asia and the Middle East. Nomadic pastoralism emerged in these regions as a means of exploiting the vast steppe areas that were created by climatic changes beginning some 10,000 years ago. Given the particular mix of poor rainfall, poor soil, and rugged topography, these regions are unsuitable for any form of permanent agriculture but can support herds of grazing animals such as sheep and goats. Recent data collected during a two-year study of herders in Afghanistan (Casimir, Winter, and Glatzer 1980) using ground surveys together with satellite pictures showed convincingly that traditional herders do not overgraze their pastures under normal climatic conditions. The researchers measured the biological productivity of all major plant communities in the region and calculated the food requirements of the animals. They found that, during the study, the herders were using only 23-32 percent of the available sustained yield forage production of the natural pastures.

Other researchers have used dynamic mathematical models to explore the relationship between soil moisture, grass and shrub biomass, and grazing pressure in the semiarid savannas of South and East Africa (Walker et al. 1981). Their work suggests that traditional cattle herders maintained a very resilient balance between grassland and shrubs, because their grazing system was "irregular and opportunistic" and the human population remained relatively low. Herd productivity was also relatively low, but perfectly adequate for domestic needs in a nonmarket subsistence economy. Under these conditions the natural pastures tolerated even intense grazing because it was only periodic. Traditional herders thus actually favored the growth of a wide variety of grass types, and these wild pastures became more productive. However, settled peasant farmers and commercial ranchers replaced many of the tribesmen after 1800, when the colonial period began, and introduced a much less variable grazing system that has proven less stable. The result is that now there is often serious overgrazing, leading to reduction in the water-absorbing capacity of the topsoil, and a replacement of grass by less productive woody shrubs. Overall, there is often a striking reduction in the ability of the natural pastures to support grazing animals.

On marginal grazing lands in many parts of the world, overgrazing is often encouraged when outside energy sources are introduced, making it possible to concentrate animals by drilling wells and hauling feed, and when animals are raised for the market rather than for direct subsistence. Many such developments have been promoted by governments interested in increasing the productivity of pastoral nomads, and have often included settlement schemes. Unfortunately, the result has often been serious overgrazing as traditional negative feedback mechanisms have been subverted. Only then does self-interest come into conflict with social responsibility.

Pleistocene Extinctions

In spite of overwhelming evidence to the contrary, some people still maintain that tribal culture had no special advantages over industrial civilization in its relationship to the environment. Friedman (1979:262),

for example, in his zeal to purge anthropology of "Romanticist" tend-
encies, asserts that "social systems have never been adaptive." Some
writers even reverse the argument and suggest that tribal cultures abused
the environment more than have modern states. Martin (1967), for
example, maintains that 10 thousand years ago primitive hunters over-
hunted and destroyed hundreds of species. He concludes:

> The thought that prehistoric hunters . . . exterminated far more
> large animals than has modern man with modern weapons and
> advanced technology is certainly provocative and perhaps even
> deeply disturbing. (Martin 1967:115)

This view of early hunting cultures quickly found its way into introductory anthropology texts. For example, Marvin Harris stressed the
"basic insecurity" of hunting and gathering cultures and called their
potential for overhunting a "basic weakness" that could "easily result in
the extinction of the natural biota." Echoing Martin, he specifically
charged that the "unprecendented efficiency" of upper Paleolithic technology contributed to the ecological catastrophe of the extinction of the
Pleistocene megafauna (Harris 1975:186).

The "Pleistocene overkill" argument is certainly dramatic and, if it
could be substantiated, would clearly temper our view of tribal culture
and its relationship to the environment. The implications of this problem
are certainly serious enough to merit careful examination. The undisputed
facts are briefly as follows: Throughout the world during the late Pleistocene, some 200 genera rather suddenly disappeared. These extinctions
involved many large animals, such as the mastodon and mammoth, giant
birds, giant kangaroos, and other "mega" forms, and they were not
replaced by related species. Although the chronology of these extinctions
is not precise, early human populations were colonizing new portions of
the globe and improving their hunting technologies during roughly the
same time period.

When Martin first presented his argument, it was based largely on
circumstantial evidence and the absence of equally plausible counter-
evidence. More recent research has challenged many of Martin's basic
assumptions (see Webster 1981), and it now seems likely that, if humans
had any role in Pleistocene extinctions, it was very indirect. For example,
it is now suggested that in some cases the extinctions actually preceded

the arrival of humans with advanced hunting technologies, and they involved more than merely big game species (Webster 1981). There is now also more evidence that climatic change and associated shifts in vegetation probably were important factors contributing to the extinctions of the late Pleistocene. Furthermore, recent interpretations of traditional hunting cultures suggest that overkill to the point of exterminating major prey species is theoretically very unlikely (Lee and DeVore 1968; Hayden 1981b; Webster 1981). In the first place, "hunters" rarely relied exclusively on a single prey species, and often the bulk of their diet was based on plant foods. Furthermore, hunting systems stressed predictability and energetic efficiency. Any subsistence system based on deliberately hunting key prey species to extinction would have been extremely unreliable, wasteful of time and energy, and disastrous in the long run. This is of course not to say that tribal hunters never wasted game animals, because even though there was often a strong ethic against wasteful overhunting, certainly in many cases full utilization of game killed was impossible or impractical. It is also now generally appreciated that tribal hunters maintained low population densities and low growth rates. The general pattern was to maintain long-term balances with their resource base.

Impressive evidence for such long-term balances is represented by the archaeological record left by middle and late Stone Age peoples in southern Africa, covering a time span from the recent past to over 130,000 years B.P. Richard Klein (1979, 1981) made a careful study of the age and sex distribution of the game animals taken by Stone Age hunters, based on an analysis of the bones left in their camps. He discovered that the pattern of human predation on large, dangerous game animals such as buffalo closely resembled that of natural predators such as lions. Human hunters took only the very young or very old individuals. He concluded that "the age distribution of buffalo in the archaeological kill samples is what one might expect if the Stone Age hunters were to enjoy a lasting, stable relationship with prey populations of buffalo" (Klein 1979:158). Furthermore, he found no evidence of a decline in the buffalo population, even though they were hunted for tens of thousands of years. Klein found that even species of docile or small antelope, such as the eland and steenbok, which were easily driven or trapped, showed no evidence of any significant decline in numbers, even though they were utilized relatively intensively. Extinctions of game animals did occur during the period of human occupation, however, and Klein raises the possibility that improved hunting technology may have been a factor in some of these cases.

It is important to keep the issue of Pleistocene extinctions in perspective. Even if it can be demonstrated that tribal hunters did play a significant, albeit indirect, role in these extinctions, these losses are quite trivial when compared with the scale of extinctions underway today. Modest predictions of future extinctions, which assume that present trends in global deforestation will continue at modest rates, estimate that perhaps 20 percent of existing life forms will be exterminated by the year 2000 (Barney 1980, vol. 2:327–32). Such losses will be catastrophic, and in this case the human role will be clear.

Tribal Cultures and the Environment

The narrow range of environments that individual tribal cultures exploit is one of the most striking features of their adaptation when compared with an "industrial" adaptation. This contrast is an aspect of the "import" factor discussed earlier. It was recently highlighted in the distinction drawn by the distinguished ecologist and conservationist Raymond Dasmann (1976) between "Ecosystem" and "Biosphere" peoples. Dasmann's definition stresses the fact that "Biosphere" or tribal peoples depend on the resources supplied by local ecosystems and know immediately if their exploitation patterns are damaging. Biosphere peoples extract resources from throughout the globe and may not even be aware of, or immediately affected by, the local destruction of ecosystems that they might cause. If too wide a range is exploited, a culture might escape the ecological constraints of a given local environment and become unresponsive to natural equilibrium mechanisms and thus ignore its own detrimental impact on that environment. Industrial nations are dependent on resources from throughout the world and can bring overwhelming external forces to bear on particular local environments; in the short run, however, they remain immune to whatever damage they may cause. For example, at the present time the Amazon rain forest ecosystem is being syste-

matically destroyed by remote forces ultimately deriving from the industrial capitals of the world, while the tribal cultures occupying the area
remain dependent on their local environments and respond immediately
to detrimental changes within them (Meggers 1971). Roy Rappaport
(1971) makes the same point using a New Guinea example.

Environmental modifications occurring as a result of the intervention
of tribal cultures in general appear to be much more gradual and more
akin to "natural" environmental processes than the modifications caused
by industrial civilization, which are often extremely rapid and qualitatively unusual. Industrial civilization introduces completely new environmental pollutants that disrupt natural biochemical processes. At the
same time, ecosystems modified by industrial civilization become much
simpler, less efficient, and more unstable than those affected by tribal
cultures. Such differences sometimes result directly from contrasting subsistence systems. For example, the ecological advantages of traditional,
root crop shifting cultivation over intensive monocrop systems in tropical
areas have frequently been noted (Geertz 1963; Rappaport 1971). In
their crop diversity and organization, swidden plots structurally resemble
the rain forest ecosystem, and thereby utilize solar energy with great
efficiency and minimize the hazards of pests and disease. This point is
discussed more fully in Chapter 4.

It is obvious that most experts on economic development do not
understand the significance of these differences, because they usually
argue that "primitive," "pretechnological" cultures have little knowledge
of their environment and no control over it. Yet the data of cultural
ecology indicate that tribal cultures actually possess deep and highly
practical knowledge of their environments, based on intimate experience
accumulated over many generations. For example, Nelson (1969) reports
that Eskimos in north Alaska who hunt on sea ice employ an elaborate
vocabulary with dozens of special terms to describe the thickness or age
of ice, conditions related to ice movement, and ice topography. Indians
in interior Canada, who must travel over frozen lakes and rivers, distinguish 13 categories of ice according to eight dimensions. Their labels
distinguish whether the ice is solid, melting, or cracked, details of water
under the ice and on its surface, ice texture, thickness, clarity, color,
and stages of cracks (Basso 1972). Tribal knowledge of the complex and
varied tropical rain forest environment is even more impressive. The

Hanunoo of Mindoro Island in the Philippines are tribal peoples practicing shifting cultivation. Conklin (1954) found that they distinguish ten basic soil types and 30 subtypes, 450 animal types, and more than 1,600 plants, including some 400 types not recognized by botanists. They cultivated 430 plant varieties. In the Brazilian Amazon rain forest, Carneiro (1978) found that the Kuikuru Indians could name at least 187 different tree species. They identified every specimen he tested them on, including tiny seedlings and dead leaves plucked from the forest floor.

The notion that tribal cultures have no control over their environment is based on a misunderstanding of what constitutes control. If "control" were understood to mean a stable and predictable exploitation of the environment, then tribal cultures might well have exercised greater real environmental control. The basic difference here seems to be that whereas industrial culture prides itself on its apparent ability to defy nature and struggles constantly to subdue it to its own ends, tribal cultures are designed to work within the natural limits of their environments. In this regard, long centuries of success would suggest that the tribal approach to control is far more knowledgeable.

Fire and Tribal Resource Management

I have stressed that tribal cultures tended to maintain balances with the natural environment, but it is also important to emphasize again that tribals were not living in some passive "state of nature." They were not surrounded by an undisturbed wilderness. There is abundant evidence to show that tribal peoples deliberately managed local ecosystems, often on a large scale, to increase "natural" biological productivity for human benefit. Perhaps the most striking example of such resource management is the use of selective burning by hunting and gathering peoples to deliberately create and maintain "game parks." Although the earliest European explorers often recorded that tribal peoples regularly burned vast areas of forest, brushland, and savanna, the significance of these practices was largely overlooked. Today, foresters and range management scientists generally recognize that carefully controlled, frequent burning can dramatically increase ecosystem productivity. For example, as Mellars

(1976) shows, burning in forests can improve soil fertility; favor the growth of herbaceous plants; promote vigorous growth of trees and shrubs by "pruning"; and induce germination of fire-dependent species. The effect of such burning is an increase in both the quantity and the nutritional quality of the forage available to game animals. This elevates the game-carrying capacity three to sevenfold, and means that there will be more animals that are healthier and that reproduce faster. Hunting is also facilitated because it is easier to move through the forest and the game is easier to see. Furthermore, frequent burning reduces the accumulation of combustible material and makes natural fires less destructive.

Anthropologist Henry Lewis (1982) recently investigated the use of fire by traditional Indians in northern Alberta. He found that they clearly understood the ecological effects of burning and carefully timed their burning to speed the growth of forage in the early spring. This was also the time when fire was most easily controlled, because prairie soils were still frozen and snow was still on the ground in the forest. The Indians deliberately burned the grassland to increase the populations of bison, elk, and deer, and to control their movements. They were also interested in increasing the production of wild berries, reducing noxious insects, and creating supplies of dry firewood. They burned lakeshores to improve nesting and feeding habitats for waterfowl and to increase the food supply for muskrats. Within the forest they used fire to create and maintain small prairies, and to extend the microenvironment along streamsides that were favored by moose.

There are documented examples of similar uses of fire by tribal peoples in many other parts of the world, including Australia (Gould 1971; Hallam 1975; Lewis 1982). In all these cases, the timing and frequency of burning are critical factors, and the success of the technique depends on a detailed knowledge of a wide range of environmental variables. This type of resource management resembles agriculture in some respects, but selective burning involves much less human manipulation of natural systems and is less expensive in energy terms.

Tribal Economics

Given the critical role that economics must play in any culture, some of the most important contrasts between tribal and industrial cultures should be expected here. Unfortunately, attempts by earlier anthropologists to describe tribal economic systems as if they merely represented simplified cash economies have resulted in widespread misunderstanding of such systems. In the older anthropolitical literature, it is not uncommon to find such inappropriate terms as *investment* and *interest* applied to tribal ceremonial exchanges, a bow and arrow called *capital*, and a shell necklace labeled *money*. At least one major classical economic analysis throughout, assuming, in spite of obvious difficulties, that tribal systems merely display modern economic institutions in a blurred and generalized fashion. This viewpoint, in a more refined form, continues to be represented in anthropology. It has been called the "formalist approach," and stresses that people everywhere are driven by self-interest and ever expanding wants, and always seek to maximize ends and minimize means (see especially Dowling 1979). Unfortunately, such interpretations have obscured both the significant accomplishments and the unique qualities of tribal economic systems.

In the mid-19th century Karl Marx identified some of the important contrasts between tribal and market economies when he coined the terms *use value* and *exchange value* (Caulfield 1981). According to Marx, tribal, or what he called primitive, communal, economies, were based on use value because people produced for their own use. In capitalist economies, people produced not primarily for their own use, but rather for sale or exchange. Of course, goods are both used and exchanged in both types of economy. However, in a tribal, or use value economy, producers are directly involved in production decision making and are immediately concerned with both the environmental and social consequences of production. Today, the economic anthropologists who emphasize these contrasting features of tribal and market economies identify themselves as "substantivists," as opposed to "formalists." The substantivist view of tribal economic systems is well represented in the works of Dalton (1961, 1965) and Sahlins (1972). Certainly the most significant contrast between tribal and market economies hinges on the presence or absence of markets and multipurpose money and on the role of kinship. Dalton presents a substantivist definition of a nonmarket, tribal economy as follows:

> In marketless communities, land and labour are not transacted by purchase and sale but are allocated as expressions of kinship right or

tribal affiliation. There are no formal market-place sites where indigenously produced items are bought and sold. These are subsistence economies in the sense that livelihood does not depend on production for sale. The transactional modes to allocate resources and labour as well as produced items and services are reciprocity and redistribution. (Dalton 1965:51)

Other substantivist writers such as Redfield (1947) have emphasized the relative technological simplicity of tribal economies, the fact that there is a minimal division of labor, or that everyone has equal access to the means of production, and that tribal societies are basically economically self-sufficient. Radin (1971) argues that tribal economies are distinguished most remarkably by their emphasis on a concept of an "irreducible minimum." According to Radin, tribal economies operate on the principal that "every human being has the inalienable right to an irreducible minimum, consisting of adequate food, shelter and clothing" (1971:106). In other words, tribal economies are designed to satisfy basic human needs, and this imperative overrides individual concerns for profit making.

Whereas tribal economies are often correctly described as cashless, subsistence based, and simple in technology, these obvious contrasts alone do not explain their achievements. More important are the built-in limits to economic growth that characterize tribal cultures, and the fact that they explicitly recognize their dependency on the natural environment. In this respect, one of the key concepts in tribal economics is *limited good*, described by George Foster (1969:83) as the assumption that "*all* desired things in life . . . exist in finite and unexpandable quantities." Tribals made this principle central to their economic system, whereas industrial people operate their economy on the diametrically opposed principle of *unlimited good*, which assumes that "with each passing generation people on average will have more of the good things of life." Within a tribal economy, several specific attributes, such as wealth-leveling devices, absolute property ceilings, fixed wants (Henry 1963), and the complementarity of production and needs, all center on the principle of limited good and contribute directly toward the maintenance of a basically stable, no-growth economy.

In a tribal society, wants are not considered open to infinite expansion, and the economy is designed to fill existing wants by producing exactly what is culturally recognized as a need. Wealth inequalities are often considered direct threats to the stability of a tribal community, and individual overacquisitiveness may be countered with public censure, expulsion, or charges of witchcraft. At the same time, individuals may obtain prestige through generosity, and the redistribution or destruction of excess goods is accomplished through kinship and ceremonial obligations, feasting, and gambling. In contrast, our economy operates on the assumption that wants must be continually expanded. Specific mechanisms, such as advertising agencies, are employed to increase wants, while individual acquisitiveness and increased consumption gain prestige.

Many anthropologists seem to miss the significance of growth-curbing mechanisms in tribal economies, and instead mistakenly represent as cultural universals the unlimited acquisitiveness characteristic of our economic system and the parallel inability to satisfy all of society's wants: "We have seen that the scarcity of goods in the face of the wants of a given people at a given time is a universal fact of human experience; that no economy has been discovered wherein enough goods are produced in enough variety to satisfy all the wants of all the members of any society" (Herskovits 1952:17).

Cultural devices to curb wants in tribal societies are also sometimes attributed to unavoidable circumstances, such as the fact that any accumulation of unessential goods would merely be an undesirable and impossible burden for nomadic peoples. This explanation may be partly valid in some instances, but it does not apply to primitive sedentary villages in which limits on property accumulation are just as widespread. To explain their apparently self-imposed limits on economic growth, such villagers often simply state that property must not be allowed to threaten their basically egalitarian social systems. This is a significant point, for tribal economies with their careful limits on material wealth do in fact occur with egalitarian societies. In contrast, fundamentally nonegalitarian societies are characteristic of market systems. Clearly, if we want to understand the stability of tribal economies, we must look to other explanations.

Some ethnocentric economic development writers have suggested that the only reason tribal societies curb their wants is because their technologies cannot fill them, the implication being that more productive techniques would free people's innate capacity for unlimited wants: "[People] in every culture harbor unexpressed wishes to have more in order to be more. Once it becomes evident to them that it is possible to desire more, they will, by and large want more" (Goulet 1971:76).

Indeed, anthropologists have sometimes dramatically overemphasized the supposed technological deficiencies of tribal economies.* Tribal systems have been described as if they were barely able to meet subsistence needs, and it has been assumed that tribal peoples faced a daily threat of starvation that forced them to devote virtually all their waking moments to the food quest. This traditional view remained almost unchallenged until careful studies of productivity and time-energy expenditure in tribal societies revealed that even the most technologically simple peoples were able to satisfy all their subsistence requirements with relatively little effort.** It has been shown, in fact, that many of these societies could have produced far more food if they had been so inclined; instead, they preferred to spend their time at other activities, such as socializing and leisure. It was discovered that hunters such as the Bushmen (Lee 1968) and certain Australian aborigines (McCarthy and McArthur 1960), who were thought to be among those groups closest to the starvation level, put in on the average of no more than a 20-hour workweek getting food. Other researchers (Carneiro 1960; Rappaport 1971) have shown that primitive farming systems offer a reliable subsistence base that may actually be more efficient than the "factory farm" techniques replacing them.

On the basis of this kind of evidence, it can now be assumed that primitive cultures did not deliberately curb their wants and operate stable economies merely because they were incapable of either producing or desiring more, or because circumstances automatically prevented the accumulation of goods. Rather, it would appear that such systems survived and proliferated because of their greater long-run adaptive value.

---

*For example: Herskovits (1952:16); Levin and Potapov (1964:488–499); Nash (1966:22); Dalton (1971:27).

**Much of this data has been reviewed by Sahlins (1972).

Nature in Tribal Ideology

Numerous anthropologists have emphasized the fundamental contrasts in values, religion, and world view existing between tribal and industrial cultures in relation to the natural environment.* The most remarkable general difference is that tribal ideological systems often express humanity's dependence on nature and tend to place nature in a revered, sacred category. As Lynn White, Jr., and others have noted, the notion of a constant struggle to conquer nature, which is so characteristic of industrial civilization, where it is supported by biblical injunction, is notably absent in tribal cultures. Indeed, tribals generally consider themselves to be part of nature in the sense that they may name themselves after animals, impute souls to plants and animals, acknowledge ritual kinship with certain species, conduct rituals designed to help propagate particularly valued species, and offer ritual apologies when animals must be killed. Animals also abound in tribal origin myths; and at death, one's soul is often believed to be transformed into an animal. Careful research has shown that many of these seemingly irrational beliefs may actually contribute directly to the stability of tribal cultures by contributing to the regulation of both population size and levels of resource consumption. Population growth, for example, is curbed by beliefs calling for sexual abstinence, abortion, infanticide, and ritual warfare, and various taboos control the exploitation of specific food resources. McDonald (1977) has shown that in Amazonia special taboos restricting the consumption of specific game animals by certain categories of people are most often applied to the animals that would be most vulnerable to overhunting. In highland New Guinea, it has been argued that ceremonial cycles help maintain a balance between the human population, pig herds, and the natural environment (see Chapter 6; Rappaport 1968). Other writers (Bartlett 1956) have pointed out that sacred groves in many parts of the world have maintained forest remnants and reduced soil erosion, while under Christian influence the forests have been chopped down, with unfortunate results. It is significant that these belief systems often disintegrate under the impact of industrial civilization, and are replaced by other beliefs that accelerate environmental disequilibrium.

---

*See, for example, Gutkind (1956) and Spoehr (1956).

The Desana Equilibrium Model

The case of the Desana Indians of the Colombian Amazon will now be examined in order to illustrate, in reference to a specific example, how the unique characteristics of tribal cultures operate to maintain a balance with the resource base, and to show how this balance may be disturbed by industrial civilization. The Desana are a tribal society of some 1,000 hunters and manioc farmers living in the Vaupés region of Colombia. According to the in-depth research of Colombian anthropologist Gerardo Reichel-Dolmatoff (1971: 219), their culture "has formulated a series of very strict norms to assure the maintenance of a biotic equilibrium."

Perhaps the most exciting aspect of Desana culture is that its norms are explicitly based on such fundamental ecological principles as the energy cycle and the interdependence of life forms. The Desana assume that the fertility of both man and animals is dependent on the same finite circuit of recycling solar energy, and it is recognized that uncontrolled human population growth would unbalance the entire energy system through overhunting. Various cultural mechanisms are employed to prevent disequilibrium, including contraceptive herbs, used to support the stated norm of no more than two to three children per family, and a variety of sexual taboos and specific ritual observances that limit the frequency of hunting. It is understood that the availability of game animals is under the control of a supernatural being, the "keeper of game," who can restrict supply or cause illness if the norms regulating hunting and sexual activity are not observed. A key role is played by the shaman, who must mediate between the demands of society for meat and the limited resources available. In order to carry out this duty, he communicates with the "keeper of game" by using hallucinogenic drugs and attempts to gain his favor while keeping the hunters informed of his demands.

The entire Desana culture is supported by its creation myth and is constantly reinforced by daily ritual activities, by periodic ceremonies, and, more importantly, by its obvious success. The system is designed to operate indefinitely into the future, and archaeological evidence indicates that the Amazon tropical forest cultural adaptation, which the Desana represent, has already existed for at least 4,000 years (Lathrap 1970). Unfortunately, however, missionaries are now seeking to replace

Desana beliefs with opposing Christian beliefs, and settlers are arriving to "share" Desana resources. These outside pressures have already begun to upset the delicate balances Desana culture evolved.

Tribal Conservation in the Pacific

This chapter may be concluded with a description by anthropologist George P. Murdock of the condition of the high tropical islands of the Pacific after long years of undisturbed occupation by tribal cultures:

> There was no destruction of forests by reckless lumbering with resultant reduction in water retention. There was no wholesale replacement of natural cover by cultivated crops such as occurs with modern sugar or copra plantations or intensive rice cultivation. There was no pollution of streams or coastal waters by sewage or chemical plants; no flooding of valleys by artificial lakes constructed for irrigation or hydroelectric power; no ruining of land surfaces through strip mining or slag piles; no massive earth removal for roads or air strips. There was no extensive soil erosion initiated by careless plowing or by overgrazing. The indigenous pig does not compare with the goat or the sheep as a conservationist's nightmare. (Murdock 1963)

3
NATURAL RESOURCES
AND THE CULTURE
OF CONSUMPTION

The biosphere with industrial man suddenly added is like a balanced aquarium into which large animals are introduced. Consumption temporarily exceeds production, the balance is upset, the products of respiration accumulate, and the fuels for consumption become scarcer and scarcer until production is sufficiently accelerated and respiration is balanced. In some experimental systems balance is achieved only after the large consumers which originally started the imbalance are dead. Will this happen to man?

Howard T. Odum, *Environment, Power, and Society*

In the previous chapter, two specific aspects of the environmental crisis—resource depletion and pollution—were related to overconsumption. The present chapter will explore further the problem of overconsumption, because it appears to be the critical defining feature of industrial culture in contrast with tribal culture, and because it is the feature that most contributes to the present instability of the industrial adaptation. Here, we shall be concerned specifically with how industrial cultures extract and utilize energy and other natural resources in comparison with patterns typical of tribal cultures, and how these patterns relate to the environmental crisis.

Energy and Culture: Basic Considerations

It becomes the primary function of culture, therefore, to harness and control energy so that it may be put to work in man's service. . . . The functioning of culture as a whole therefore rests upon and is determined by the amount of energy harnessed and by the way in which it is put to work. (White 1949:367–68)

Culture evolves as the amount of energy harnessed per capita per year is increased, or as the efficiency of the instrumental means of putting the energy to work is increased. (White 1949:368–69)

Anthropologist Leslie A. White has elaborated a theory of the evolution of culture based largely on energy utilization. In his view, culture is an extrasomatic, superorganic mechanism for harnessing energy. The earliest human cultures necessarily remained at a very low level of evolution as long as they were restricted to their own energy and minimal use of wind, rain, and fire. The additional control of solar energy through domesticated plants and animals released vast amounts of energy and made possible higher levels of social complexity, greater productivity per unit of area, and greater population density. These developments culminated with the appearance of state organization.

Since White developed this evolutionary scheme in 1949, other researchers have shown that the theory is quite misleading. In fact, until the use of fossil fuel energy sources, *per capita* use has not increased significantly—humans have remained the basic source of mechanical energy. The real difference was that domestication permitted larger populations, and thus larger *total energy* was available for building culture (Sahlins 1972:5–6). That state organization can arise without domestication, or with only minimal use of domesticates, is demonstrated by the evolution of civilization in Peru by 1000 B.C. on a marine fishing base (Mosely 1975).

White feels that the full potential for cultural evolutionary advance on the basis of agriculture alone was realized before the Christian Era, and that further advance into industrial civilization was only made possible by the *fuel revolution*, his term for the utilization of fossil fuels. With the discovery of nuclear energy, White felt, culture was poised on the verge of a major new energy revolution that could lead to even higher levels of evolutionary progress. Brazilian anthropologist Darcy Ribeiro (1968) confidently applied the term *thermonuclear revolution* to this new era, but it is not at all certain that culture will survive such a revolution.

It is certainly reasonable and useful to describe general evolutionary progress in terms of energy utilization; but if we are concerned with the environmental crisis and with achieving a successful and sustainable cultural adaptation, it might be more useful to compare cultures in terms of the rate at which energy resources are consumed—and the rate at which they are being depleted may be far more meaningful. The global energy sources that are most significant for human use can be divided into three categories:

1. Solar radiation
2. Fossil fuels
3. Nuclear energy

Solar radiation can be considered a steady "income" source of energy that may be renewed daily or annually and may be converted by green plants through photosynthesis into usable forms of energy, or through the movement of water and wind; or some of this energy may be concentrated and converted directly to heat for human use. Only a very small, relatively constant quantity of energy can ever be available through these sources, and because of the Second Law of Thermodynamics, the amount of energy available for use is constantly reduced at each con-

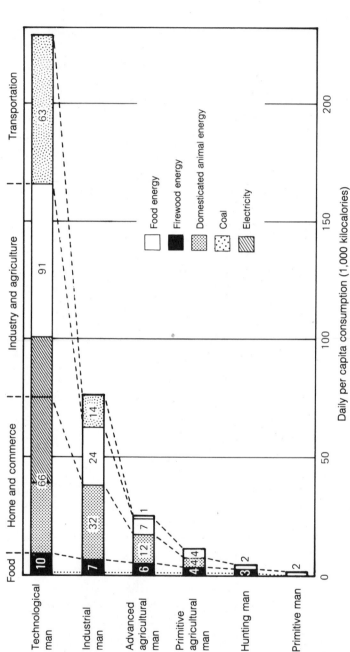

FIGURE 3·1 Daily Consumption of Energy per Capita for Six Stages in Human Development. Daily consumption of energy per capita was calculated by the author for six stages in human development (and with an accuracy that decreases with antiquity). Primitive man (East Africa about 1,000,000 years ago), without the use of fire, had only the energy of the food he ate. Hunting man (Europe about 100,000 years ago) had more food and also burned wood for heat and cooking. Primitive agricultural man (Fertile Crescent in 5000 B.C.) was growing crops and had gained animal energy. Advanced agricultural man (northwestern Europe in A.D. 1400) had some coal for heating, some water power, wind power, and animal transport. Industrial man (in England in 1875) had the steam engine. In 1970, technological man (in the U.S.) consumed 230,000 kilocalories per day, much of it in the form of electricity (*hatched area*). Food is divided into plant foods (*far left*) and animal foods (or foods fed to animals). *Source:* Earl Cook, "The Flow of Energy in an Industrial Society," *Scientific American* 224, no. 3 (1971):136. Copyright © 1971 by Scientific American, Inc. All rights reserved.

version. Fossil fuels supply solar energy that has been trapped by green plants and stored in the earth through incomplete oxidation over the past 600 million years and represent only a minute fraction of the globe's annual energy budget. The process of fossil fuel formation is presumably still under way but at a rate too slow in human terms for this energy source to be considered anything other than nonrenewable. Any use of this stored energy must then be considered a withdrawal from a steadily dwindling stock. Nuclear energy can be released from its storage within the atomic structure; but the most easily utilized radioactive fuels are in limited supply, and all controlled releases of nuclear energy require enormous inputs of energy to be safely maintained and to deal with the waste heat and radioactive materials produced. Nuclear energy also must be converted to electrical energy and thus seems an unlikely replacement for all present uses of fossil fuels in industrial civilization.

In terms of energy use, cultures may easily be divided into "high-energy cultures" and "low-energy cultures," and these categories have immediate implications for both evolutionary progress and adaptive success. The quantitative differences between high- and low-energy cultures can be seen easily in terms of their per capita levels of energy consumption. Prior to the fuel revolution, it has been estimated, no state-organized cultures utilized more than 26,000 kilocalories per capita daily, whereas tribal nonstate hunters and farmers utilized between 4,000 and 12,000 kilocalories per capita daily (see Figure 3-1). These cultures might all qualify as low-energy cultures, and might theoretically be stable adaptations. In contrast, early industrial cultures utilizing fossil fuels consumed approximately 70,000 kilocalories per capita daily, and Americans by 1970 had elevated the rate to 230,000 (Cook 1971). Projections for 1990 would place the rate at 273,000 kilocalories (Barney 1980, vol. 2:162). These high-energy industrial cultures clearly represent a qualitative difference in energy consumption that merits a special terminological distinction.

Given the apparently immutable laws of thermodynamics and the physical limitations of the global energy budget, any culture that taps renewable solar energy sources must necessarily remain a low-energy culture relative to those drawing on stored, depletable sources. Theoretically, low-energy cultures could exist another five billion years until the sun burns out, whereas high-energy cultures must be transformed to low-energy cultures when their depleted energy stores are burned up, or perhaps be destroyed by the waste heat they unavoidably produce through energy conversion. High-energy cultures thus have life spans that can easily be predicted for comparison with the 5-billion-year life expectancy of low-energy cultures.

Estimates for the depletion of fossil fuels vary slightly, depending on accepted rates of utilization and the total reserves estimated, but the general magnitude of the figures is clear. One of the most pessimistic estimates, recently presented by *The Limits to Growth* study (Meadows et al. 1972), suggests that, at present exponential rates of consumption, all known reserves of oil will be gone in 20 years, natural gas in 22 years, and coal in 111 years (see Figure 3-2 for another estimate for oil depletion). More recent projections based on constant production rates at 1976 levels would show oil depleted within 77 years, natural gas in 170 years, and coal in 212 years (Barney 1980, vol. 2:189–93). We should stress that all these projections are based on differing assumptions concerning future economic conditions, population growth, the amount of a given resource that remains to be found, political considerations, and the technological and economic feasibility of resource recovery. However, it is significant that, even given these variables, the overall magnitude of the resource depletion problem does not change significantly. More recent research has often tended to substantiate earlier projects. For example, estimates for the life cycle of petroleum production in the world originally proposed by geologist Hubert King in 1969 (see Figure 3-2) are still considered basically correct.

If we assume that oil and natural gas are indeed depleted so quickly, then a switch to full reliance on coal would greatly accelerate its depletion. The most optimistic estimates would give us perhaps 100 years' worth of oil and 500 or 600 years' worth of coal. High-grade uranium ores needed to support our present nuclear fission technology will be in very short supply, and a switch to vastly more costly and unproven systems such as "breeder" and fusion reactors will be urgently needed if a high-energy culture is to be sustained. * Even if this transition is successfully achieved,

---

*There has been a tremendous outpouring of energy-related works in recent years. I have drawn primarily on the 1969 *Resources and Man* study sponsored by the National Academy of Sciences, the *Scientific American* special issue for September 1971 (vol. 224, no. 3), and the collected papers in Finkel (1974).

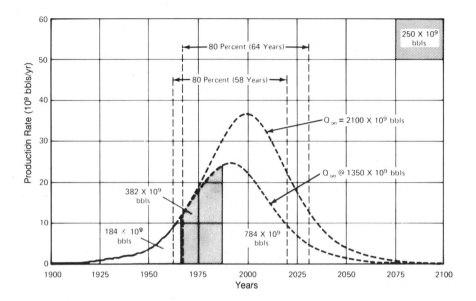

F I G U R E   3 - 2   Complete Cycles of World Crude Oil Production. Values of shaded areas represent cumulative production; each full box = 250 billion barrels. Q_∞ = the ultimate amount of oil to be produced. 10^9 bbls = billion barrels. Two estimates of the total production cycle of oil in the world are illustrated, optimistically assuming that either 2,100 billion barrels will be produced or, more conservatively, that only 1,350 billion barrels will be produced. It is remarkable in either case that the bulk of this production (80 percent) will cover only some 60 years, either 64 years in the optimistic case or, in the conservative projection, a mere 58 years.

Source: M. King Hubert, "Energy Resources," in National Academy of Sciences, Resources and Man (San Francisco: W. H. Freeman, 1969), 157–242.

continued progress appears unlikely because even at the present rate of increases in energy utilization it is estimated that waste heat may adversely alter world climate within 30 to 50 years beause of the "greenhouse effect" caused by atmospheric carbon dioxide holding in heat. Within 200 years of a mere 5 percent annual increase in world energy production, the waste heat produced would equal that received from the sun, and all life on earth would cease to exist (Luten 1974). Long before such a "Sun Day" could possibly arrive, however, the polar ice caps would melt, flooding out most of the world's urban centers, and enormous adverse changes in world vegetation would occur.

Thus a continually expanding high-energy culture will be self-terminating, and its maximum life expectancy can be no more than a few hundred years. Furthermore, it is doubtful that relatively high levels of energy utilization can be stabilized at safely sustainable levels with nuclear technology, because of its unknown risks, and because of the uncertainty that unstable high-energy cultures will evolve the social mechanisms needed to achieve such a transition, and finally because of the operation of Justus von Liebig's Law of the Minimum.

More than energy alone is necessary to sustain a high-energy culture—because if that energy is used to produce what Leslie A. White calls "human need-serving goods and services," other raw materials must be consumed. Liebig's law states that an organism's growth and survival will be limited by the essential material that is present in the lowest quantity. If this law is applied to cultures, and if we assume that specifiable annual quantities of iron, copper, and aluminum are essential for the continued existence of a high-energy industrial culture, then its life expectancy could be even shorter than its potential energy base would permit. *The Limits to Growth* study (Meadows et al. 1972) indicates that, at present exponential use rates, presently exploitable world iron ore reserves will be extinguished within 173 years, aluminum within 55 years, and copper within 48 years. The availability of mineral resources could be extended by recycling and more costly exploitation technologies; but their quantity will inevitably diminish through use, and any culture entirely dependent on them will not outlast the shortest-lived critical mineral resource. Although it is not possible to estimate precisely the life expectancy of a high-energy culture, it can confidently be stated that it will never be as successful as low-energy cultures, which might have enjoyed a 5-billion-year existence if they had not been destroyed by high-energy cultures. Evolutionary progress beyond low-energy cultures may thus only be possible through self-limiting overconsumption that will otherwise initiate environmental crises and ultimately destroy a culture's ability to adapt.

The Culture of Consumption Defined

Industrial civilization has developed into something totally unique in the evolution of culture—a *culture of consumption* (Bodley 1975:4-5), a culture whose major economic, social, and ideological systems are geared to nonsustainable levels of resource consumption and to continual, ever-higher elevation of those levels on a per capita basis. This is *overconsumption*, not only in terms of reduced cultural viability, but also in a strictly biological sense, as ecologist Howard Odum explains:

> In the industrial system with man living off a fuel, he manages all his affairs with industrial machinery, all parts of which are metabolically consumers. . . . The system of man has consumption in excess of production. The products of respiration—carbon dioxide, metabolic water, and mineralized inorganic wastes—are discharged in rates in excess of their incorporation into organic matter by photosynthesis. If the industrialized urban system were enclosed in a chamber with only the air above it at the time, it would quickly exhaust its oxygen, be stifled with waste, and destroy itself since it does not have the recycling pattern of the agrarian system. (Odum 1971:17)

Odum estimates that on a global scale "human industries add about a 5 percent excess of consumption over production."

Growth through increased consumption is so much a part of our present economy that most economists find it difficult to imagine any other state, even though perpetual growth is only possible in an infinite environment. Some writers (Boulding 1966) have characterized the present economy of growth as a "frontier" or "cowboy" economy, meaning that it is the type of economic system that might be appropriate to a particular period of expansion into a new environment, but it becomes inappropriate when that historical period has passed and further expansion threatens to become destructive. A more descriptive term might be simply "consumption economy"; the important point is that such a system is defined by a continual increase in "throughput," i.e., production and consumption measured in terms of gross national product. There is little account made of the unintended by-products of the process. Waste, depletion, pollution, and various indirect social costs or "externalities" do not immediately detract from the gross national product (GNP) and may actually be a positive aspect of it. For example, accidents and diseases caused by the production and consumption process contribute to economic growth because further output of goods and services must deal with them. Adverse side effects of growth will be certain to make growth self-limiting in the long run; but because of the investment process, a consumption economy is focused only on the immediate furture and disregards impacts even 25 to 50 years into the future.

Perpetual economic growth is firmly entrenched in the culture of consumption and has become a solution to maintaining a grossly stratified, nonegalitarian social system. Disruptive dissatisfaction among the lowest classes due to poverty and unemployment can be prevented without the most wealthy sacrificing their positions if the total volume of wealth can be steadily increased. In this way the poor gradually become "wealthy" while their relative position remains constant. The same principle operates at the world level. "Poor" nations might be prevented from warring against rich nations if certain minimal levels of economic growth can be maintained.

In the ideological system of the culture of consumption, predictably, the primary focus seems to be on increasing consumption, although this is defined as "progress" or "economic growth." An elaborate mythology of unquestioned "truths" supports the economic system and helps convince individual members of the consumption culture that they are well served by the system. Unfortunately, however, many of these cultural myths can be easily shattered by careful examination. For example, higher standards of living or improved quality of life is not a necessary correlate of progress, whether progress is measured in terms of ever-increasing per capita consumption of energy, GNP, or national income statistics, as shown clearly by the Physical Quality of Life Index (PQLI) developed by Morris (1979). This index averages national-level data on infant mortality rates, life expectancy at age one, and literacy rates into a single index value. The PQLI is considered to be a simple, comprehensive, and relatively nonethnocentric measure of overall quality of life, at least for literate national societies. The PQLI demonstrates that there is no absolute relationship between quality of life and GNP. There are nations with low GNP that have high life-quality indices, such as Sri Lanka, Cuba, and Western Samoa, and nations with high GNP and low life quality, such as Libya and Saudi Arabia. Cross-national surveys (Mazur and Rosa 1974) suggest that only up to a certain point do increases in energy use correspond with rises in commonly accepted measures of quality of life in industrial cultures, such as health care, education, and "cultural" activities. Very high energy levels are part of evolutionary progress, but they make little contribution to improving the quality of life. There are even indications that very high energy use rates are related to such negative qualities as high suicide and divorce rates, but the causal relationships have not been fully explored.

It is also firmly believed that the ever-increasing output of household appliance consumer goods has meant a steady reduction in housework and an increase in leisure time. Consumer appliances thus become principle indicators of a high standard of living. Anthropological research among tribal hunters, however, has shown that they worked far less at household tasks, and indeed less at all subsistence pursuits, than any modern populations. Aboriginal Australian women, for example, were found to devote an average of approximately 20 hours per week to collecting and preparing food (McCarthy and McArthur 1960), whereas women in rural America in the 1920s, without the benefit of laborsaving appliances, devoted approximately 52 hours a week to their housework (Vanek 1974). Some 50 years later, contrary to all expectations, urban, nonworking women were putting in 55 hours a week at their housework, in spite of all their new "laborsaving" dishwashers, washing machines, vacuum cleaners, and electric mixers. This actual *increase* in work time shows how illusory the idea of an increased standard of living may be when judged according to the consumption culture's traditionally accepted measures. Some of this increased work load is probably due partly to the fact that more time is now required for such consumption-related tasks as shopping and caring for an increased volume of clothing. The economic value of a woman's household work is also so poorly defined that women may feel compelled to make their contribution more conspicuous.

The relationship between a culture of consumption and the natural environment can be seen more clearly through the examination of specific examples. The following sections will deal primarily with the United States in an effort to illustrate special principles that may be valid for all consumption cultures and that clearly show how serious environmental crises may be precipitated by overconsumption.

Resource Consumption in America

The United States is without question the leading example of a culture of consumption. Within a few decades, it has suddenly become the world's major consumer of nonrenewable resources on both an absolute and a per capita basis. Estimates vary widely, but it appears that by 1970, although their population constituted only about 6 percent of the world total, Americans consumed some 40 percent of the world's total annual production, and 35 percent of the world's energy (Cook 1971). The historic pattern of this consumption illustrates important trends that may be generally characteristic of consumption cultures.

High and rapidly increasing rates of energy consumption have been made possible by switches from primary dependence on theoretically renewable "income" sources such as fuel wood to nonrenewable "capital stock" resources such as coal. In 1850, approximately 90 percent of America's energy was derived from fuel wood; but by 1890, over 50 percent was supplied by coal. By 1960, nearly 70 percent came from oil and natural gas, and optimists hoped that in the near future nuclear energy would replace depleted fossil fuels (Landsberg 1964). In a mere 100 years, Americans have tripled their per capita use of energy and multiplied their total use 30 times. They have already made two major shifts in their basic energy sources and now face shortages and further adjustments in the foreseeable future. Much of this increased use has been at enormous environmental cost due to air pollution from burning the fuels, and from disturbances caused by drilling and mining operations and accidents such as oil spills. As more easily exploited energy resources have become depleted, higher extraction costs have forced the United States to rely heavily on imported energy sources; the result has been increasing political uncertainties and economic instabilities due to high rates of inflation.

Certainly, one critical question to ask is how a culture of consumption responds to the impact of its own consumption on what must be an ever-dwindling resource base. Tribal cultures, as noted earlier, tend to respond quickly to adverse impacts on their resource base because they are immediately dependent on local resources. Industrial cultures, however, lack this instant responsiveness because of their complexity and specialization. They are especially vulnerable to overgrowth and collapse because of the rapidity with which they are expanding. More importantly, they lack substitute response mechanisms, and the market system seems to thrive on resource depletion. Governments have occasionally stockpiled certain critical resources as strategic reserves as a military preparedness measure; but in general, present political institutions and leaders seem quite unwilling or unable to prepare in advance for inevitable shortages. The only specialized mechanisms for anticipating critical resource shortages that industrial cultures have so far evolved are the teams of experts that have periodically taken stock of resources and advised governments of potential problems. Characteristically, however, these assessments have been surprisingly shortsighted and optimistic, or else their warnings have been simply disregarded. The consumption culture seems unable to imagine its own demise.

Taking Stock

> Our nation, looking toward a future of continuing economic progress, is well-advised to take stock of its natural resources. Industry can expand only so far as raw materials are available. (Dewhurst 1955:754)

After World War II, in 1949, the United Nations brought together in New York over 700 scientists from over 50 nations to exchange information on world problems of conservation and resource utilization. In assessing the world mineral situation, H. L. Keenleyside, Canada's deputy minister of mines and resources, noted that between 1900 and 1949 more world mineral resources had been consumed than during all of humanity's previous existence. He felt that there were as yet no critical mineral shortages developing, but recognized future limitations: "Thus it is quite

clear that the combination of an increasing population and rising standards of living will place a strain on our metal resources which will almost
certainly in the end prove beyond the capacity of man and nature to
supply" (Keenleyside 1950:38).

To postpone the inevitable, Keenleyside recommended increased
exploration for minerals, improved extraction and processing technology,
conservation, and substitution. Given increasing demands, his warning
was clear: "[Unless] there is a fundamental change in the economic fabric
of human society we will ultimately be faced with the exhaustion of many
of our mineral resources."

In the United States, no comprehensive inventory of natural resources was ever undertaken until 1908. There were early moves toward
conservation, but little concern that serious problems might arise. A
major study published in 1947, entitled *America's Needs and Resources*
(Dewhurst 1947), attempted to project national requirements for resources for 1960. It reported that no real resource exhaustion was likely
within 20 years, although high-grade zinc, lead, and bauxite ores might
be exhausted by that time and oil shortages might occur somewhat later.
The report recognized that domestic mineral resources would ultimately
be depleted; but it was felt that, given free access to foreign resources,
an "expanding American economy" could be supported for "many decades
to come." Curiously, the report suggested that even if imports were
unavailable, there was no reason for believing that reliance on domestic
resources would be a necessary barrier to continued economic growth.

Eight years later, the *America's Needs and Resources* study was updated
with the publication of a new edition (Dewhurst 1955) that displayed a
greater appreciation for the incredible consumption rates that Americans
were developing, but this awareness was more than overshadowed by an
even greater confidence in the country's ability to solve any problem. It
was noted that, by 1950, Americans were consuming some 18 tons of
raw materials per capita, and that the United States consumed as much
of many important minerals as the rest of the world combined. In spite
of these staggering facts, the authors of the report were certain that there
would be no insurmountable problems that would limit further growth:
"Despite man's seemingly devastating exploitation, he has merely
scratched a small segment of this gigantic ball of resources on which he
lives. Our power to use the materials in nature is growing rather than

diminishing, through favorable technology and economic organization" (Dewhurst 1955:754–55).

While, perhaps, in 1955 we were only scratching the surface of the globe's resources, the suddenly increased extent of this scratching on the part of Americans is perhaps seen in greater perspective by the observation published in President Truman's *Resources for Freedom* study (United States, President's Materials Policy Commission 1952), which pointed out that, just since 1914, American consumption of most minerals and fuels exceeded total world consumption for all previous time. Furthermore, other projections show how quickly this minor scratching could have a serious impact on a finite earth. In 1956, geochemist Harrison Brown calculated that a world population of 30 billion (which some experts feel would be the maximum conceivable human population and which might be reached at present rates by 2075), with nuclear breeder technology and the capability of extracting all needed mineral resources directly from ordinary rock and seawater, would literally eat up the continents. The crust of the earth would be skimmed off at the rate of 3.3 millimeters a year, or over 3 meters every thousand years.

In 1963 a third major assessment of American resources was published by the Resources for the Future (RFF) corporation supported by the Ford Foundation. The 1,000-page report, entitled *Resources in America's Future* (Landsberg et al. 1963), attempted to project supply and demand for natural resources up to the year 2000. The authors of the study recognized the general difficulty of any such projections but felt they were essential for decision making. They recommended that such studies be conducted or updated every five years by a government agency, perhaps through computer simulation techniques. This study, like earlier assessments, could foresee no immediate critical general shortages. Although the authors felt that some specific problems might arise, they assumed that any problems would be solvable. New technology, world trade, and careful utilization would maintain continued high consumption rates. On the basis of careful projections, which considered the interrelatedness of population, technology, and "demand" levels, and assuming continued imports, no major wars or economic depressions, the RFF report concluded that within 40 years the United States would triple its annual consumption of energy, metals, and timber. Resource shortages would be no major handicap to progress. According to the major summary of the RFF report by Landsberg:

> Neither a long view of the past, nor current trends, nor our most careful estimates of future possibilities suggest any general running out of resources in this country during the remainder of this century. The possibilities of using lower grades of raw material, of substituting plentiful materials for scarce ones, of getting more use out of given amounts, of importing things from other countries, and of making multiple use of land and water resources seem to be sufficient guarantee against across-the-board shortage. (Landsberg 1964:13)

This optimistic view was quite in agreement with earlier studies on this point:

> On the whole, it seems clear that we shall not be hampered in meeting future needs by a shortage of raw materials.
> (Dewhurst 1955:939)

The RFF projections optimistically assumed continued technological advances, greater efficiency, and continued substitution of synthetics for natural materials. Without constant technological "advance," it is clear that the culture of consumption would rapidly be faced with what the RFF report called "inconvenient and perhaps critical material limitations." For example, it was estimated that 64 percent of the fibers consumed in the year 2000 would be synthetics drawn largely from fossil fuel stocks. The report noted that by 1952, western softwood forests were already being cut at over their replacement rate and warned that unless we wished to be extremely optimistic we could expect a continued depletion of western forests. Eastern hardwood forests would be "on the way to extinction" by the end of the century. Annual demand for forest products by 2000 was expected to be double the annual rate of forest growth now; and it seemed that short of technological miracles that would produce synthetic hybrid trees capable of growing twice as fast, only substitution of plastics and consumption of the world's tropical rain forests would support continued American "needs." Unfortunately, we see now that the tropical forests and the oil for the substitute plastics will quite likely both be gone by the year 2000. Presumably, if the culture of consumption does find itself still intact by 2000, we can hope for further miracles to carry us to 2050, and so on.

It is difficult to escape the conclusion that the consumption culture is fighting a losing battle to support a rising level of consumption that must ultimately be unsupportable. At any given moment the culture seems poised on the edge of total collapse but somehow manages to put forth greater effort to keep the system functioning a little longer through any means short of reduced consumption.

Shortly after publication of the RFF study, the National Academy of Sciences conducted its own two-year study, which took a much broader approach to the resources and consumption question. This work, entitled *Resources and Man*, was completed in 1968 and published in 1969. It was concerned with the entire globe and looked beyond the year 2000. The outlook was far more sober and raised serious questions about the long-range viability of an ever-expanding industrial culture. It warned that the earth's supply of oil might be gone in 70–80 years, coal in 200–300 years, and that in the not-distant future the high-energy cultures will only be supportable by nuclear breeder technology. Some authors even felt that there were serious possibilities that certain critical mineral shortages might arise before 2000. Mercury, tin, tungsten, and helium were minerals for which true shortages were either already occurring or threatened. The report was also clear on one point—even given technological breakthroughs, continued expansion in consumption rates cannot be supported indefinitely. The report holds out the hope that, if population and consumption can be stabilized at reasonable levels, industrial society may last for centuries or millennia.

The National Academy of Sciences 1975 report entitled *Mineral Resources and the Environment* (National Research Council 1975) carries the most pessimistic warning of all: "Man faces the prospect of a series of shocks of varying severity as shortages occur in one material after another, with the first real shortages perhaps only a matter of a few years away. . . ." This report suggests that world oil supplies may be gone within 50 years and, for the first time ever, calls for a massive conservation program and an actual reduction in consumption:

> Because of the limits to natural resources as well as to means of
> alleviating these limits, it is recommended that the federal
> government proclaim and deliberately pursue a national policy of
> conservation of material, energy and environmental resources,
> informing the public and the private sectors fully about the needs
> and techniques for reducing energy consumption, the development

of substitute materials, increasing the durability and maintainability of products, and reclamation and recycling.

According to these findings, the world's leading culture of consumption went from just scratching the surface of world resources to almost quite literally the "bottom of the barrel" in a mere 20 years. Since then our increasing dependency on foreign resources has further confirmed the pessimistic projections. Perhaps Americans deserve a special trophy for evolutionary progress.

The Economics of Resource Depletion

> Sooner or later, the market price will get high enough to choke off the demand entirely. At that moment production falls to zero. . . . the last ton produced will also be the last ton in the ground. The resource will be exhausted at the instant it has priced itself out of the market. The Age of Oil or Zinc or Whatever It Is will have come to an end. (Solow 1974:3)

The culture of consumption has clearly developed within the framework of an economic system that advances systematically from one resource to another, supported by theoretical assumptions that deny that "real" scarcity or limits to further growth can exist. We have already seen how industrial society has moved rapidly through several alternative energy sources as they become depleted or inadequate. This process occurs with different grades of ore and virtually every other depletable resource from whales to timber, and represents the predictable operation of market principles in combination with continuing technological advances.

To orthodox economists, the simple solution to the obvious incompatability between an ever-expanding economy and a finite world is to "redefine" *resource*. When, for example, as was the case in the whaling industry in the 1940s (Payne 1968), blue whales are being exterminated, then fin whales may be declared a replacement resource, then Sei whales, and then sperm whales. When the whales die out, we can save the whaling industry by converting it into a krill-catching industry. Krill are an Antarctic shrimp eaten by whales. Indeed, by 1984, Krill were labeled an "untapped bounty" and their commercial exploitation was under way (Nicklin 1984).

Theoretical support for such a process of self-perpetuating depletion and never-ending technical progress has been clearly spelled out by economists Harold Barnett and Chandler Morse in their influential study *Scarcity and Growth: The Economics of Natural Resource Availability*, published in 1963 for the Resources for the Future Corporation. The primary objective of the *Scarcity and Growth* study seems to be to disprove the notion of the classical economists, such as Thomas R. Malthus, David Ricardo, and John Stuart Mill, that resource scarcity will halt economic growth. Such an outcome, according to Barnett and Morse, would only be possible in a world without progress, and is quite unrealistic in today's world. What they are saying, of course, is that progress will end when progress ends, but they cannot conceive of such a contingency: "The notion of an absolute limit to natural resource availability is untenable when the definition of resources changes drastically and unpredictably over time" (Barnett and Morse 1963:7).

In other words, today trees and whales, tomorrow plastic and granite. According to these enthusiastic consumption economists, depletion of resources will make way for economic alternatives of equal or even *superior* qualities and at reduced cost. Industrial technology is now virtually "turning the tables on nature, making her subservient to man." Whatever resource scarcity may exist is always *relative*, never absolute, and substitution always solves it. Resource limits cannot be defined in economic terms, so the argument goes, and therefore must not exist. Attempting to conserve resources now might actually reduce the "heritage" of future generations because it could preclude future technological advances. The authors mistakenly assume that tribal cultures failed to expand their economic systems because they neglected to control their populations and were too ignorant to redefine their resources technologically.

Barnett and Morse represent the superoptimistic orthodox view. The process of relative scarcity and substitution they describe typifies the operation of the consumption economy thus far, but there is no solid evidence that it will be able to continue operating this way or that it would even be desirable for it to do so. Some unorthodox economists have recently characterized these theories as pure "growthmania," simply absurd, and contrary to the Second Law of Thermodynamics. It has been pointed out that the assumptions of Barnett and Morse were based largely on trends in the mining industry between 1870 and 1957, and that they ignored clear cases of increased costs and diminishing returns. New theories of a steady-state economy are beginning to emerge.

The Consumption Culture's Environmental Cost: Western Coal

Any culture that continues to accelerate consumption in a fixed environment will eventually be forced into making trade-offs between environmental quality and a continuation of its consumption pattern. The fossil fuel base of the present consumption culture in the United States is now seriously threatened as domestic sources of petroleum and natural gas have fallen short of domestic consumption in recent years. Nuclear technology, a short time ago hailed as a source of unlimited energy, is an unlikely solution because it is proving far more costly and hazardous than previously supposed. Instead, the nation is now preparing to strip the coal reserves of the western states in an effort to meet the ever-expanding energy "needs" of the country. As the new federal coal-leasing program is initiated, vast areas of the West, which were left in almost pristine condition after supporting Native American cultures for perhaps 20,000 years, will be deliberately devastated on a massive scale to perpetuate the culture of consumption for a few short years.

The 1974 *Draft Environmental Impact Statement* (U.S. Department of the Interior), dealing with the coal-leasing program and written by the Bureau of Land Management, makes the rationale for the coal stripping clear, and concisely summarizes the costs. The entire procedure is a remarkable example of the extremity to which overconsumption can drive a culture. The fundamental assumption underlying the proposed stripping program is simply that economic growth cannot be sustained without it: "We assume the first principal demand pressure for coal development will be from the physical and economic inability of the United States to obtain sufficient oil supplies to meet the demand generated by normal growth rates of the national economy" (Part 1:8).

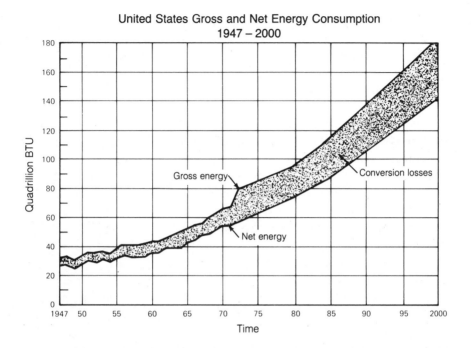

FIGURE 3-3 **United States Energy Consumption.** Gross energy = total amount of energy produced for the economy. Net energy does not include loss caused by converting the primary source to the secondary form, as for example in oil refining.

Source: United States Department of the Interior, Bureau of Land Management, *Draft Environmental Impact Statement: Proposed Federal Coal Leasing Program* (Washington, D.C.: U.S. Government Printing Office, 1974), 1: pt. 1: 26.

"Normal growth rates" means that by the year 2000 the population will have increased by less than 50 percent, but total energy consumption will have nearly doubled (see Figure 3-3). If we were having difficulties meeting our energy needs in 1974, it should be no surprise that, if total consumption more than doubled by the year 2000, it would be at an enormous cost.

Strip mining coal involves simply removing all the overlying surface material, placing it to one side, and extracting the coal. Federal regulations require "rehabilitation" of the site, but this term must be broadly interpreted. The impact statement carefully understates the immediate effects of surface mines in the following terms: "The operation completely eliminates existing vegetation, disrupts soil structure, alters current land uses, and to some extent changes the general topography of the area" (U.S. Department of the Interior BLM 1974, pt. 3:33).

The report makes it clear that surface drainage patterns may be disrupted; water sources might be eliminated; streams may be silted in and contaminated with toxic materials; big game wintering grounds and migration routes, and wildlife habitat in general, would be destroyed; archaeological sites would be destroyed; geological features and scenic resources would be destroyed or "disrupted"; and miles of impassable "high walls" might be left. Where undergound mining takes place, surface collapses might occur. Contamination by radioactive fly ash would occur in the vicinity of the coal-fired electric plants. Local communities would be disrupted by a temporary influx of outsiders. A variety of other detrimental impacts can be predicted. In summary, the "grand scale of the operation impacts significantly on the environment."

In 1978 President Carter confirmed in a speech to Congress that a major expansion in American coal production would indeed be pursued as a way of coping with the "energy crisis" and the country's increasing dependence on foreign oil. He asked for an increase in coal production by more than two-thirds by 1985. Of course the bulk of the targeted coal reserves in the West are on Native American lands, and as the new energy development programs have been implemented, there has been widespread protest by affected Native American communities angered over the potential destruction of their grazing land, the pollution, and the loss of critical irrigation water (Anthropology Resource Center 1978).

"Restoration" of stripped areas is expected to require from 20 to 30 years, but the statement is concerned only with the period before 1985. "More lengthy projections" are considered to be "impractical." The statement glibly notes, however, that "man cannot immediately restore natural biotic communities." Experience with strip mining in Appalachia indicates that the worst erosion and pollution problems may occur as much as 25 years after mining; in some cases, spoil piles are still eroding 65 years after the coal was extracted. Some researchers estimate that 800 to 3,000 years may be needed before toxic wastes will leach away (Spaulding and Ogden 1968). We know for certain that the leased areas will never be the same again, but the total cost is incalculable. What is most important for the culture of consumption is that the coal will be destroyed, too! It will again be time to look for another energy source to carry us to the next crisis.

Consumption Culture Versus Tribal Culture: Bougainville Copper

Overconsumption by the industrial nations not only destroys the physical environment, but it has also been the primary cause of the almost total destruction of tribal cultures over the past 150 years. Throughout the world, tribal cultures have been devastated along with their environments as the resources they controlled have become necessary components of industrial growth. This subject has been dealt with at length elsewhere (Bodley 1975); but here, a single example may be presented to illustrate how the consumption culture's need for a critical mineral resource can totally overwhelm small-scale cultures thousands of miles away.

Copper is one of industry's primary raw materials and is being consumed in such enormous quantities by the industrialized nations that if present trends continue, the world's supply of ore will be exhausted within 20 to 50 years (Meadows et al. 1972, table 4). Nearly 60 percent of the world's annual copper production is consumed by three of the most highly industrialized nations—the United States, Japan, and the Soviet Union. By itself, the United States consumes 33 percent of the world's total production—substantially more than it can produce. In fact, in 1968, Americans were consuming the equivalent of 15 pounds of copper per person per year, much of it in the form of copper electrical wiring. Even though copper ore has become progressively more difficult to find and the quality of the ore is steadily decreasing, and even though production costs have steadily risen, there has been no effort to limit consumption (Lovering 1968). Instead, copper ore is being exploited for the short-run benefit of the richest industrial nations—wherever in the world it can be found and regardless of the impact on local populations and their environments.

In 1963 the Australian administration of the Trust Territory of New Guinea gave an Australian mining corporation, Conzinc Riotinto Australia, Ltd., permission to prospect for minerals in the center of Bougainville Island in an area occupied by subsistence-farming tribal peoples. Major deposits of copper ore were discovered, and a gigantic project was soon under way that was described as "perhaps one of the most ambitious mining ventures ever undertaken" (Mining Magazine 1971). When production began in 1972, some $400 million had been invested, and a company-owned town for 3,000 people had been established at the mine site, which was connected by a pipeline and a 16-mile highway to a specially constructed public port town for 8,000 people built on the coast.

The environment posed seemingly insurmountable problems for the engineers because of the island's rugged topography, loose soil, and heavy rainfall. Constant slumping made road building in the area "a major engineering achievement" requiring constant relocation and the excavation of some 13 million cubic yards of material. When conventional underground mining techniques proved economically unfeasible, the company burned off the tropical forest cover and resorted to open-pit, stripping techniques on an immense scale. The problem of disposing of the enormous quantity of tailings had not been solved when production was begun, and there was no discussion of the environmental impact of the project or possible plans for restoration of the region.

Whereas the physical environment posed a serious enough problem for the successful development of the mine, the company encountered "social barriers" that were even more difficult to solve. From the time prospecting began, there were serious difficulties in securing the approval and goodwill of the local tribal population. As one report euphemistically explained, "The company encountered many difficulties in establishing its presence satisfactorily" (Ryan 1972). In the first place, under the existing tribal system of land tenure, no one had the right to transfer land to outsiders, and many people were very reluctant to accept any form of compensation or rent for use of their land because they feared they might thereby lose it completely (Dakeyne 1967). Not surprisingly, the company had a difficult time explaining to the indigenous people why it was necessary for them to move aside so that their homesites and gardens could be totally destroyed. In compensation, the Australian administration negotiated an agreement with the company in which the local people were to receive a rent of $2 an acre for their land, which they were to provide to meet the "reasonable needs" of the company.

In exchange for their traditional homes, which were destroyed, the people were to receive "durable" buildings. Royalties would accrue to the administration to be used for the further "progress" of all the people in the territory, and various other inducements were offered to secure their cooperation, including employment opportunities, provision for resettlement, and opportunities to buy shares in the company.

The company reportedly (Ryan 1972) attempted to minimize the "inevitable" disturbances to the local people and, apparently making good use of applied anthropology, was bringing "experience, sound personnel and community management and enlightened policies" to bear on the problem of satisfactorily establishing its presence. Plans called for the integration of the people into the company's operation, and they were to feel that they would have some choice: "Policy seeks social integration which gives a local person some option on how fast he wants to go along this course." It is not clear what option was open to those who chose not to approve the "integration" course, but there was certainly no way for the people to resist the $400-million operation effectively. This lack of real choice was apparent when, during the company's negotiations for tribal land, it refused to halt construction because the company considered the expense involved in any work stoppage to be unacceptable. The people merely had to make the best of an unfortunate situation.

United Nations visiting missions to the area in 1968 and 1971 (United Nations, Trusteeship Council) found many local people disturbed over their treatment by the company and reported that violent disputes had occurred. However, the district police and the Australian administration sided with the company, and violent resistance was clearly not a solution. The UN mission acknolwedged that "mistakes" had been made, but felt that the islanders were being presented with a unique opportunity to raise their living standards. From the company's view, the whole problem was due to the natives' strong emotional ties to their land, and the natives' misunderstanding and "difficulty in comprehending the project" due to their having been "quite sheltered from contact with a western-type industrial society." The local people realized perfectly well what was happening to them, but they were powerless to do anything about it. Douglas Oliver summarized the native viewpoint in 1973:

Most of them however appear to have become resigned more or less disconsolately to what they regard as another example of the white men's cupidity, deceit and irresistible power. (Oliver 1973:162)

Perhaps the most critical anthropological question to ask is: What cultural forces drive the present consumption patterns of the consumption culture? We *can* say that overconsumption is not an innate human trait; it *is* culturally determined. It is also clear that high rates of consumption, or a lack of cultural controls on consumption, relate to social stratification within a culture; but there are many stratified societies that have set limits to consumption. The presence of specialized institutions to increase consumption, such as advertising agencies, must play an especially critical role, but why do they exist? The only reasonable explanation seems to lie in the structure of the modern market economy itself—it is uniquely geared toward expanding consumption, but *why* this is so is still unclear. The following two chapters will explore further the problem of overconsumption by focusing on the food systems of tribal and industrial cultures.

4
WORLD HUNGER AND THE EVOLUTION OF FOOD SYSTEMS

(The) power of obtaining an additional quantity of food from the earth by proper management and in a certain time has the most remote relation imaginable to the power of keeping pace with an unrestricted increase of population.

Thomas R. Malthus, *An Essay on the Principle of Population*

As long as food is something bought and sold in a society with great income differences, the degree of hunger tells us nothing about the density of the population.

Frances Moore Lappé and Joseph Collins, *Food First: Beyond the Myth of Scarcity*

Food systems are cultural mechanisms for meeting basic human nutritional needs. Every food system must confront two general problems if it is to continue to perform satisfactorily: (1) it must avoid long-term depletion of the natural resource base; and (2) it must equitably distribute essential nutrients to people. The existence of widespread hunger in the modern world indicates that many food systems are not performing adequately, but concerned observers have not always agreed on either the causes or the best treatment of the problem. Since the Paleolithic, production techniques have steadily intensified as human populations have increased, but it seems clear, as British economist Thomas R. Malthus observed, that population always has the potential of increasing more rapidly than production techniques.

The Malthusian Dilemma

> The power of the earth to produce subsistence is certainly not
> unlimited, but it is strictly speaking indefinite; that is, its limits are
> not defined, and the time will probably never arrive when we shall
> be able to say that no further labour or ingenuity of man could make
> further additions to it. But the power of obtaining an additional
> quantity of food from the earth by proper management and in a
> certain time, has the most remote relation imaginable to the power
> of keeping pace with an unrestricted increase of population.
> (Malthus 1895:110)

Malthus was certainly the most influential early writer to raise the fundamental question of the relationship between population growth and food production. Writing first in 1798, he argued that, if unchecked, human population has the natural capacity to expand at a geometrical or exponential rate, where over the long run, food production could only be expected to increase at an arithmetical or *linear* rate. The capacity for population growth is largely an empirical question, and Malthus had data to support the view that a doubling every 25 years was possible. Reliable data on food production through time were unfortunately not available, but Malthus merely assumed that there were in fact ultimate limits and that whatever those limits were, food production could not long be expected to keep pace with a doubling population. He felt that as population began to press on the subsistence base, "misery," in the form of poverty, would tend to reduce population growth, while greater efforts would be made to increase production through opening new land and improved techniques until eventually a balance would be restored. Malthus was convinced that these principles were self-evident laws of nature.

In many respects cultural evolution has been related to peoples' efforts to avoid hunger by maintaining a secure subsistence base, while minimizing the pain of regulating population. This is the Malthusian dilemma, and in a general sense Malthus was quite right. Tribal societies can often be reasonably viewed in these terms; but in nations in which large segments of the population are denied access to the resources needed to feed themselves because of basic social inequalities, it is a mistake to base assistance policies on the assumption that Malthusian limits are being exceeded. Unfortunately, until recently, most aid programs assumed that world hunger was caused solely by overpopulation and inadequate production. Instead, it now seems obvious that hunger is caused by poverty and landlessness, which in turn can encourage population growth. Hunger will best be eliminated by changes in social and economic policies to better provide people with the resources to feed themselves.

To illustrate the operation of his "laws," Malthus projected population and food production trends for Britain and the world, and showed how quickly an exponentially growing population would surpass a linearly expanding food production system. Many writers have misunderstood him on this point. He did not make specific *predictions* for future demographic patterns, but merely tried to show how unchecked population growth would compare with what he felt were optimistic projections for increases in food production. Malthus certainly did not anticipate the enormous population expansion that has in fact occurred, but these later developments have actually mirrored very closely the models of unregulated growth that he constructed. Figures 4-1 and 4-2 graph the population and food production curves for the world and for Britain that Malthus projected on the basis of his theoretical maximum population growth (doubling every 25 years) and simple linear growth in food production. His starting point of one billion people for the world is precisely the

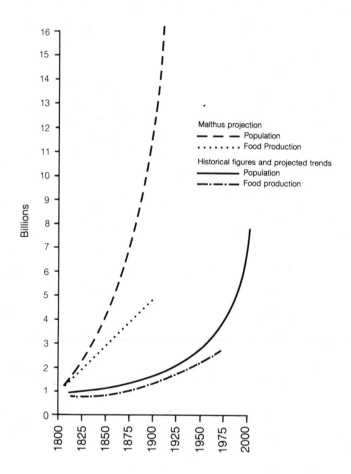

FIGURE 4 - 1 Population and Food Production (World).

Sources: The gap between world population and food production is based on the estimate of 50 million hungry made by the editors of *Time* (Nov. 11, 1974, "The World Food Crisis," 66–80) and data from Malthus, 1895.

world estimate for 1800 presently accepted by many demographers; however, at that time the world population was doubling only every 172 years. By 1950, the doubling time had dropped to just over 80 years. According to the *Global 2000* projections (Barney 1980, vol. 2:231), the

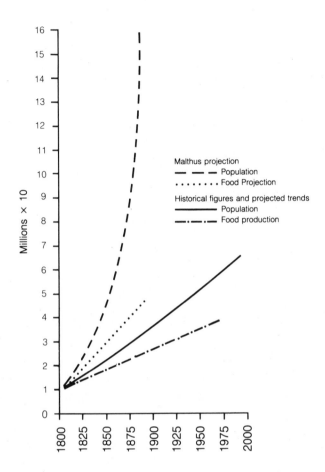

F I G U R E 4 - 2   Population and Food Production (Britain).
Source: Data from Malthus, 1895.

average global doubling time from 1975 to the year 2000 will be approximately 39 years, based on an average rate of annual increase of 1.8 percent. Thanks to recent technological developments and enormous subsidies of fossil fuels, overall world food production has just kept pace with population; but distributional problems have already created an unmistakable hunger gap, and it is not at all clear how much longer food production can be successfully increased. In a general sense the world is now experiencing the very problem that Malthus projected, but it is happening 150 years later than his model indicated. Unfortunately, these global trends have shifted attention away from the sociocultural aspects of food systems—how actual families produce, distribute, and consume food—to the strictly technological limits of production. There is no doubt that there are real physical limits to food production, and exceeding limits with specific technologies has been a serious cause of resource depletion and ecosystem destruction. However, social inequality within and between nations significantly accelerates the appearance of Malthusian symptoms.

Britain has followed the predicted Malthusian pattern quite closely. However, viewing the trend only in these terms masks the enormous internal inequality and poverty of the country, and seems to justify the colonialist expansion that helped maintain the system. Since 1798, the apparent gap between domestic food production and population growth has widened very much as might be expected given basic Malthusian assumptions, although both have grown much slower than the Malthus projection. In 1970, Britain was only producing about two-thirds of its basic requirements in grain and meat, and made up the deficiency through imports (Cooke 1970). This gap was about what Malthus expected after 50 years of exponential population growth in Britain. He suggested that food production in England might keep pace with the first doubling of population during the first 25 years by opening up more land and offering "great encouragements" to agriculture, but he was certain that domestic production would be unable to cope with the second doubling. The second doubling of population actually occurred shortly after 1900, some 50 years later than in the model, but food production still did not keep up with it. In fact, while total acreage has varied only slightly through time, British wheat production per acre required 150 years to achieve its first doubling. Significant advances beyond the first doubling were only possible through enormous applications of chemical fertilizers and the use of new high-yield varieties. Per-acre wheat production actually doubled again between 1948 and 1980, but further increases will be extremely costly (Great Britain 1982:253). Fortunately, the population of Britain seems to have stabilized in about 1968 at approximately 55 million people, and by 1982 it had even experienced a slight decrease. Even with the increases in domestic food production, however, by 1980 it was officially estimated that Britain produced only 60 percent of its total food supplies (Great Britain 1982:253). If Britain were to support the 100 million people that technological optimists foresaw as a realistic possibility in the late 1960s (Cooke 1970), this could only be accomplished under vastly different cultural conditions. Surely the *optimum* population for Britain would be very different.

The Evolution of Food Systems

In a sense, the Malthusian dilemma—the problem of balancing the power of population with the power of food production—is the most basic adaptive test that any culture must successfully solve if it is long to survive. Anthropologists have devoted a large share of their research effort to examining subsistence systems in various cultures, and archaeologists in particular have focused on the evolution of food-producing systems as one of their primary research topics. The major findings of this research are of special relevance to a better understanding of today's food systems.

Much of the early theoretical literature on the evolution of food systems has been cluttered by a consistent tendency to view each change in subsistence as a hard-won major improvement that was only achieved through some brilliant invention. Furthermore, "advances" in food production have traditionally been considered prerequisites for increases in population and other forms of evolutionary progress. These views apparently reflect the popular tendency to view all problems as simple technological issues and to underrate the intelligence of tribal peoples. More recent approaches to food systems have been more balanced. At least three different interpretations of the causal factors underlying changes in subsistence technologies have been recently proposed. The first approach, the *Population Pressure Model*, argues that increases in population mean that more food must be produced per unit of space (see, for example, Boserup 1965). This model reverses the earlier view that new inventions allowed population to increase. The issue involves a number of complex arguments and will be examined more fully in later sections. A second approach, the *Optimization Model*, assumes that people are striving for the most energy-efficient production techniques that will satisfy basic nutritional needs (see Winterhalder and Smith 1981; Johnson and Behrens 1982). This interpretation meshes well with the Population Pressure Model and allows one to predict what new techniques might be adopted if efficiency declines as population increases. However, efficiency analyses are usually based on average production rates and might not adequately consider long-term fluctuation in resource availability. Finally, the *Risk Minimizing, Subsistence Security Model* (Gould 1981; Hayden 1981a) argues that people are always most concerned with the long-run security of subsistence. This argument is not a revival of the earlier view that tribal peoples were always on the brink of starvation; instead it calls attention to the diverse measures that were successfully applied to maintain long-term subsistence reliability. Certainly all these factors—population stress, energy efficiency, and overall security—have in varying degrees shaped the food systems of tribal societies for thousands of years. State organization, particularly industrial systems, and global economic structures have largely distorted and displaced these processes in such a way that today famine and malnutrition are commonplace and food systems are very fragile.

Anthropologist Brian Hayden (1981a) has presented an overview of subsistence strategies from earliest times to the beginnings of farming, following the Risk Minimizing or Subsistence Security approach. Throughout, it appears that people have consistently sought to maintain maximum subsistence security and stability at the lowest possible cost. A successfully balanced food system could be disturbed by either natural decline in the resource base (caused perhaps by climatic changes) or by a relative increase in the human population. Regulating population involved costs, as we will discuss later, but it certainly contributed to subsistence security. Increased subsistence effort and regional exchange networks also meant greater security.

According to Hayden (1981a), during the Lower Paleolithic, protohumans were probably able only to scavenge and opportunistically capture a few species of small animals. As both organizational and physical abilities increased during the Middle Paleolithic, subsistence diversified to include larger herbivores. Since a wider range of food sources was available, presumably subsistence became more reliable. During the Upper Paleolithic, beginning perhaps 35 thousand years ago, highly effective hunting techniques were developed, including spear-throwers and finely made stone projectile points. During this period, virtually all game animals, including carnivores, were possible prey. This wide inventory of food resources would have helped minimize the stress caused by the large-scale climatic and vegetational fluctuations that occurred throughout the Pleistocene.

Further increases in subsistence reliability during the Mesolithic beginning about 14,000 years ago involved significant use of small, rapidly reproducing, short-lived species (that biologists have called "r-species"), such as insects, fish, shellfish, and grasses, which were available in relative abundance but which required special techniques to harvest and process efficiently. Thus, during this time, grinding tools, nets, hooks, baskets, the bow and arrow, hunting dogs, and boiling all become common. These new methods certainly expanded the available range of food and would have provided a greater cushion against resource shortages, but they also involved greater effort and reduced energetic efficiency. Wild grass seeds, for example, may be seasonally very abundant, but they are not easy to harvest in quantity, and then they must be threshed, winnowed, milled, and cooked before they can be consumed. It seems unlikely that people would have included grass seeds in their diet unless they significantly increased subsistence security.

Since even the most reliable local system of food production might still be vulnerable to unpredictable environmental factors such as periodic drought, tribal peoples evolved mechanisms for maintaining permanent home territories while encouraging use of their resources by outsiders. Kinship ties and ritual practices provided opportunities for widespread sharing of resources, thereby providing an extra margin of security.

It appears that, during the Mesolithic, people began to culturally manipulate their food resources, by such methods as selective burning, as discussed earlier, but also by replanting roots, scattering seeds, and diverting water to increase wild plant productivity. Campbell (1965) discusses some of these practices by Australian hunter-gatherers. The productivity of game would be further increased by selectively killing certain age or sex categories, removing competing predators, holding and breeding captives, etc., as discussed by Hecker (1982). The result of these practices may ultimately be "domestication" as it is usually conceived. Ironically, although the drive to maintain subsistence security may have ultimately resulted in domesticaton, it is not totally clear that settled farm life was such an obvious improvement over nomadic or seminomadic hunting and gathering. However, it may be that given greater population density, for whatever reason, farming necessarily becomes more reliable, even though reducing population density and returning to hunting and gathering would be more reliable yet. Hunters and gatherers generally have a convenient cushion against food shortages, because their subsistence depends on collecting food from a diverse range of species drawn from complex and stable natural or only partially modified ecosystems. Hunters can easily switch and choose among a variety of wild foods in the event that specific food sources fail, and if local conditions become very bad they may temporarily join kin in more favorable areas. Farmers, however, must rely on a few domestic species grown in artificial, highly simplified, and relatively unstable ecosystems. Such systems are quite vulnerable to many kinds of disruptions. When crop failures occur, famine is almost certain to follow when peoples do not have access to alternative resources, or when elites remove storable surpluses. Even regular seasonal scarcity, such as that preceding harvest, may be more exaggerated among farmers. For example, Lee (1979:294–302) found no significant weight loss for the Bushmen during the severest season of the year, whereas West African farmers showed losses of 6 percent of body weight before harvest. Clear testimony to the greater overall security of hunting adaptations is also afforded by the cases on record of farming peoples joining neighboring hunters in order to weather out droughts (Woodburn 1968a; Colson 1979), and by the common tendency of hunters to reject farming until it is absolutely forced on them. There are also cases of farmers who turned hunters when the right conditions presented themselves. This is of course not to argue that occasional hungry times never occurred before farming; rather it seems that they were less frequent and less devastating.

Not only is farming less *secure* than food collecting; it often involves longer, more monotonous work, and a loss of independence and mobility. In some cases, it has even meant a switch to nutritionally inferior foods. Given so many disadvantages, it seems remarkable that people ever bothered with domestication. Indeed, the origin of domestication has become one of the major theoretical debates in anthropology.

It has become increasingly apparent that domestication was not a sudden or unique technological discovery. At best, it was a long process of transformation that occurred independently in perhaps five or more major areas of the world. Theories that stress the "invention" aspect of the process are quite misleading, because there is no reason to believe that peoples with the accumulated knowledge of many thousands of years of plant collecting would not realize that plants grew from seeds and cuttings. There are also many examples of food gatherers who maintained trade contacts with food producers and were well acquainted with the basics of farm life but had no desire to emulate it.*

The most reasonable theories are those that assume some kind of disequilibrium between population and food production in specific areas that made greater productivity per square mile necessary.

The transition from hunting to farming has been intensively investigated in the Tehuacan Valley of central Mexico since 1961 by archaeologist Richard S. MacNeish (1971). After several years of work and examination of some 454 sites, a detailed cultural history covering the period from 10,000 B.C. to A.D. 1520 has been reconstructed. This work reveals a gradual shift during the first 3,000 years from small nomadic bands depending primarily on extensive hunting of game to more careful scheduling of subsistence activities and a greater dependence on wild plant foods as gradual climatic changes brought environmental modifications that reduced the frequency of game. It appears that these changes set in motion another gradual process of sedentarization, increasing concentration of population, and increasing dependence on plant food. By approximately 4,000 B.C., 14 percent of subsistence was derived from cultivated plants; and by about 1000 B.C., they accounted for 40 percent.

In the Near East a very similar picture is beginning to emerge (Flannery 1969). In that area, somewhat prior to 20,000 B.C. and up to about 10,000 B.C., a gradual intensification in subsistence began, which represented a shift away from large game to a "broad spectrum" of wild foods. These wild foods included wild cereal grasses and small invertebrates, and the subsistence shift occurred together with the adoption of sedentary life. It has been suggested that this change was a consequence of local population disequilibriums in game-poor areas caused in turn by

---

*The Australian aborigines maintained contacts with New Guinea agricultural peoples, but did not themselves take up farming.

overflow population from the richest hunting zones. Unfortunately, it is not yet clear what caused the initial overpopulation in the optimum hunting areas. A later climatic shift toward a warmer and wetter period may have accelerated the process, however. Sedentariness may have encouraged further population growth by disrupting prior checks on fertility and may have led to increasing pressure on marginal areas, where full domestication and farming eventually became a necessity. The slowness of the transformation process is apparent when it is realized that early dry farming was not well established in the Near East until around 7,000 B.C. Thus, perhaps 10,000 years of gradually increasing population in very specific environmental zones caused an intensification in food collecting and ultimately forced people into domestication. The domestication process in that area was of course much more complex and probably would not have occurred at all without a series of intervening variables, such as peculiarities of climate and soil conditions that suited dense stands of wild cereal grasses, and cultural "preadaptations," such as grinding stone technology and storage pits.

The early dry-farming technique in the Middle East afforded a subsistence system that was relatively insecure because total harvests of wheat might fluctuate widely, depending on weather conditions. Some of the domesticates even displaced wild foods of higher protein and caloric content. The only clear advantage of farming over hunting was that it supported a much denser population. Thus an initial "victory" was scored in the struggle to keep food production in line with an expanding population; but as we shall see, the ultimate costs were high. One immediate, undoubtedly unexpected side effect of the change was that cultivated grains quickly displaced wild legumes and grasses, which were greatly valued as wild foods but could not compete successfully with the domesticates. These desirable wild plants were replaced by relatively useless weeds such as ryegrass, and a major alteration of the native flora ensued. Early cultivators almost literally burned their bridges behind them and thus made a return to wild-plant gathering very unlikely. It is of course probable that the entire process took place so gradually that no one would have realized the full implications.

It has been suggested that in tropical areas, early moves toward domestication occurred within a framework of careful ecosystem manipulation in which mixed communities of desirable food plants replaced less useful species in what became small domestic garden plots in the immediate vicinity of households (Harris 1972; Lathrap 1977). Such a process of domestication might have occurred in a few specific zones of high biological productivity and seasonal variation in resource availability in connection with sedentarization. Fixed-plot horticulture was readily suited to sedentary living because the rich organic wastes that tended to accumulate about house sites provided an ideal environment, and such gardens could be easily tended and protected from competitors. As population density increased, it became necessary to increase productivity by opening larger gardens further from the house, but these new gardens had to be periodically moved because of the invasion of weeds, decline of soil fertility, and a variety of other reasons. The result was a new form of cultivation, commonly called swidden, slash-and-burn, or shifting cultivation, which proved to be a highly productive, very adaptive subsistence strategy. In this system a garden site is cleared in the forest with the aid of fire or axes; the slashings are burned, providing a dressing of fertile ashes and debris; and a garden is maintained for a year or two. A new garden is then opened elsewhere, and the old plot is allowed to return to forest. Such a pattern can greatly elevate the carrying capacity of a region over what could be supported by hunting and gathering; and as long as the fallow periods allow regrowth of the forest, the system can be quite stable.

Two distinct forms of shifting cultivation apparently evolved separately, each with quite different implications for ecological stability and cultural evolution. In the more humid zones, swidden systems based on vegetative reproduction of root crops such as yams and manioc developed, whereas in the drier zones the emphasis was on seed crops such as corn, beans, rice, and millet.

Root-crop gardens are characterized by greater species diversity, and the plants are usually arranged in a mixed pattern of overlapping layers resembling the structure of the unmodified tropical rain forest (Beckerman 1983). The result is the creation of a fairly stable ecosystem and a dense leafy canopy that maximizes incoming solar radiation for photosynthesis, and minimizes potential erosion and leaching of nutrients from heavy rainfall. At the same time the crops utilized make only light demands on the soil. The primary disadvantage of this system is that the typical crops are usually poor sources of protein and heavy reliance is placed on wild fish and game.

Seed-crop gardens, in contrast, are not diverse; they do not form a protective canopy; they make greater demands on the soil, and are thus more vulnerable to soil erosion, depletion of nutrients, fluctuation in weather, and invasion of weeds and insects. These problems are compensated for by the fact that seed crops tend to be much richer in protein and thus open a wider range of habitats because there is less need to depend on animal protein. Cultures relying on seed-crop swidden cultivation, as a result of some of these differences, tend to expand more readily into new environments and have even replaced more stable root-crop cultivators in several cases.

The transformation from food-*collecting*, hunting and gathering subsistence systems to food-*producing*, cultivating systems was without question an enormously significant event in the evolution of culture.* It can be viewed as an expansion of the subsistence base in response to population pressure, and in a sense represents the failure of the previously successful homeostatic control mechanisms of hunting societies, which may never be fully explained. Food production was not a necessary or even desirable improvement over food collecting. It was a major evolutionary advance, however, in that it was related to increased population density, which quickly meant new forms of social organization and higher levels of integration. It must be emphasized that this assessment of the process is a reversal of the more traditional view, which held that food production was "discovered" and then population grew. It is also quite likely, as we shall see, that the state itself had a hand in promoting further population growth and technological advance.

Food production has been widely acclaimed as a dramatic new source of energy and a laborsaving device that increased leisure and left people free to build culture. This does not seem to have been the case. Even with domesticated plants and animals, people still remained the basic source of mechanical energy until much later. What actually happened in the transformation was that more people worked longer hours than ever before to produce more food in a smaller area. Careful comparison of the inputs of labor and outputs of calories between contemporary hunters and shifting cultivators reveals that increases in efficiency with early farming were not significant enough to encourage hunters to adopt

---

*Smith (1972) presents a general survey of the consequences of food production.

T A B L E 4 - 1 Labor per one million calories in tribal hunting and shifting-cultivation cultures

Subsistence	Culture	Hours of labor
Hunting	Bushmen[a]	694
	Australians[b]	631
	Amahuaka[c]	795
	Miskito[d]	787
Shifting	Amahuaka	603
cultivation	Tsembaga[e]	720
	Machiguenga[f]	694
	Shipibo[g]	1025

Sources: Data from (a) Lee 1969, (b) McCarthy and McArthur 1960, (c) Carneiro 1968, (d) Nietschmann 1973, (e) Rappaport 1971, (f) Johnson and Behrens 1982, (g) Bergman 1974.

it for that reason alone.[*] Table 4-1, which presents the number of hours required to produce one million calories of food (enough to sustain an average person for one year)[**] for several different cultures, shows that some hunting cultures may even get by with a lighter total work load than some shifting cultivators. The comparison is more striking in Table 4-2, which compares the Bushmen and the Tsembaga of New Guinea. The Bushmen are hunter-gatherers in the harsh Kalahari desert of southern Africa; yet, even with their seemingly difficult environment, they

T A B L E 4 - 2 Labor, dependency ratio, and population density in hunting and shifting-cultivation cultures

Subsistence	Culture	Hours of labor per worker annually	Workers per 100 persons	Population density per km²
Hunting	Bushmen[a]	805	61	0.25
Cultivating	Tsembaga[b]	820	70	25.00

Sources: (a) Data from Lee 1969, (b) Rappaport 1971.

---

[*]Carneiro (1968) argues for precisely this viewpoint using data from the Amazon basin.

[**]A comparative figure used by Carneiro (1968).

work fewer hours per worker and are able to maintain a smaller percentage of their population in the work force than the shifting cultivators. The Tsembaga, who work harder to maintain their gardens and domesticated animals and occupy a much richer environment, are able to support a population 100 times denser than that of the Bushmen. Clearly, the only gain is in population, and that gain is at a cost.

The Domestic Mode of Food Production

While in many cases there are obvious technological differences, food production in tribal cultures differs in other, very important respects from any food systems found in state-level cultures. Many of these critical differences have been outlined in a study by Marshall Sahlins, entitled *Stone Age Economics* (1972, chapters 2 and 3), and they are valid for both tribal hunters and cultivators. According to Sahlins, when food production is for local, household, or village domestic consumption, as in all tribal cultures, actual production tends to be far below the maximum that might be sustained, given the potential limitations of technology, labor force, and resources. The result of this *underproduction* is that the danger of a tribal culture ever exceeding the carrying capacity of its environment is greatly reduced, as is the likelihood of environmental deterioration and famine. On the other hand, as political advancement occurs, food production is accelerated, and so is the possibility of over-shooting carrying capacities, and the attendant famine and environmental deterioration.

Underproduction is an important concept, but it must be approached with caution. It does present an obvious contrast with the *overconsumption* of industrial cultures; but before the existence of underproduction can be established with certainty, some estimate of potential production or carrying capacity must be arrived at. The concept of carrying capacity must certainly be used with caution, because it is at best an extremely crude device for discussing the relationship between population, technology, and resource base. In theory, all these are in relative balance in tribal societies at any one time. However, we must stress that this balance is always *relative* and can be disrupted frequently and easily. The balance is also difficult to demonstrate empirically because, as Hayden (1975) points out, it might be impossible to realistically calculate the food production potential of any particular environment for a given tribal group, especially when cyclical fluctuation in resource availability is involved. Remember also that we are always dealing with a continuum of subtle changes in technology (i.e., intensification) that can increase subsistence output. Even resource deterioration, caused by exceeding the carrying capacity for a given technology, is not always easy to measure. It would certainly be ideal, as Hayden suggests, to measure increases in sickness and death related to resource shortages, but such data are rarely available for tribal societies. In spite of its theoretical limitations, the concept of carrying capacity will still be employed here as a rough impressionistic measure of the practical limits of particular subsistence systems.

Many estimates of the potential carrying capacity are available for specific shifting cultivators, derived from simple calculations of the amount of land needed to feed an individual per year, the length of time a garden was cropped, and the length of the fallow period. The Kuikuru in South America were found (Carneiro 1960) to be at a population density of only 7 percent of what their immediate locality would support in terms of garden produce, although the limited availability of fish and game as a protein source would be certain to reduce the total possible. Sahlins presents data from nine other traditional cultures practicing shifting cultivation in Africa, Asia, and New Guinea, showing that actual population densities ranged from as low as 8 percent of the carrying capacity to an average of 50 percent. In only one culture in the sample did local areas reach the full carrying capacity. Another study (Brown and Brookfield 1963) of 12 Chimbu subgroups in New Guinea found them ranging from 22 to 97 percent of maximum sustainable densities, and averaging just 64 percent of capacity. Precise figures on carrying capacity for hunters are more difficult to calculate, but J. B. Birdsell (1971) has suggested that Australian aborigines maintained themselves at an "optimum" carrying capacity that was 10 to 20 percent below the "maximum" capacity. Other researchers have frequently commented that hunters seem generally not to be exploiting their food resources to the maximum potential. Similar observations have been made for tribal pastoralists. The problem here, of course, is that it is difficult for a researcher at one point in time to estimate the extent of long-term fluctuation in the availability of resources. Cultures that do not store food must necessarily be restricted to the population that can be supported in the worst year.

Another approach to underproduction, which avoids the problem of carrying capacity, is simply to assess the labor potential of a given culture and evaluate how hard the population is working at food production (Sahlins 1972). There is actually very wide cross-cultural variation in the length of the average working life span, the sexual division of labor, seasonal labor, and the output of individual households within a given culture. For example, young adults are not commonly involved in food production, and tribal cultures often retire adults far sooner than may be the case in politically advanced cultures. Young Bushman males may be 25 years of age before they are actively involved in subsistence activities, and older men may retire by 60. It is quite characteristic in tribal cultures generally for labor to be irregular and intermittent. Particular tasks are easily and frequently postponed for what might seem the most trivial excuses—because of the weather, for a nap, for visiting, for feasting, or for no reason at all. Among agriculturalists, and in some cases even among hunters, there can be seasonal slack periods when virtually no hunting or farming may be done. There are also wide tolerances of individual variation in work load; some persons do far more than their "share," while others consistently loaf. Even the concept of "work" as opposed to "play" or "leisure" may not be an important distinction in all cultures. There seems little doubt that most tribal peoples could easily produce a "surplus" of food above their own immediate subsistence needs if they merely worked a little harder, put in a few more hours a week, or slightly reshuffled their labor force. The limitation on production, then, is not an inadequate technology or a scarcity of natural resources. It is the presence of a built-in cultural limit; or, phrased negatively, there is a cultural lack of incentive to raise production in tribal cultures in which production is essentially for domestic use.

It is a striking and well-verified fact that many households in tribal cultures do not actually produce enough to feed themselves and must depend on the overproduction of the most ambitious households to provide their needs. This variation in household productivity may result from normal stages in the domestic cycles when households may be more vulnerable, from chance variation in dependency ratios; it may be caused by random variation in success at hunting or farming, misfortune, or simply because some households choose not to work as hard as others.

Sahlins argues that what makes "Stone Age" or tribal economies unique in comparison with "more advanced" economies is that in tribal economies the basic production unit, the dominant institution, is the household. This creates a qualitatively very remarkable kind of economy, and its operation can only be understood in its own terms. Most importantly, within this domestic mode of production lies a major key to the adaptive success of tribal subsistence systems.

The domestic mode of production is based on marriage and a sexual division of labor, a simple technology that is available to all, and in which each household can perform all the technological functions itself. Individual households in a tribal culture are not economically autonomous, but the critical point is that the objective of production is domestic use. Food production goals are set by the individual food-consuming household. When the specific need—daily in the case of hunters, or annually in the case of garden planting—is met, then labor ceases. The system is not designed to produce a surplus above domestic needs. In a market economy, production is for exchange, for cash, for profit. There is no culturally recognized limit to production, because the need for wealth is infinitely expandable. The distinctive features of industrial food production will be examined below; but here, it may be noted that the contrasts between the tribal, domestic mode of production and the market mode of production are so great that much of the economic behavior of tribal peoples in contacts with market-oriented outsiders has been considered quite irrational. What has been interpreted as laziness or ignorance on the part of tribals is actually the operation of a very unique and very adaptive system of food production.

Equilibrium mechanisms within tribal cultures helping to maintain production at a low level relative to the maximum potential include the operation of "Chayanov's Rule." This basic labor principle was originally formulated by A. V. Chayanov (1966) in a study of Russian peasants. Chayanov noted that in larger households, in which there were more workers, each worker worked less than did the average worker in smaller households. Sahlins rephrases the rule as follows: "Intensity of labor in a system of domestic production for use varies inversely with the relative working capacity of the producing unit" (Sahlins 1972:91).

Thus the potentially most productive households automatically tend to slack off, whereas individuals in smaller households must work harder. In effect, household production norms are culturally set at average levels, not at the highest attainable. The maintenance of living standards by some households at a level significantly above that attainable by the majority would lead to social disorder in the absence of more elaborate forms of political control.

The general egalitarianness of tribal cultures is an obvious element in the success of tribal subsistence systems. In the first place, all households enjoy free access to the natural resources needed for their subsistence. Various redistributive mechanisms may be initiated when serious local imbalances result because of random fluctuations in demography or subsistence success. A further stabilizing factor is that reciprocal pooling of food and redistribution along kinship networks assure a relatively uniform distribution of nutrients. As a result, everyone enjoys the same nutritional standard.

Technological Advances in Food Production

If population densities are to rise, food production must be intensified either by increased labor or by technological improvements. How this might occur in a tribal culture is an interesting theoretical problem because, as we have seen, food production is relatively frozen by the shutoff factors inherent in the domestic mode of production, and population growth is normally minimized by the operation of the equilibrium mechanisms outlined in Chapter 6. In effect, there is normally no Malthusian dilemma in tribal cultures—the two forces are continuously kept in check. These facts place a new light on the traditional argument as to whether technological advances in food production cause population growth, or whether population growth itself causes advances in food production. The most basic determining factors would appear to lie in the actual arrangement of the social system. Tribal social systems are, as we have shown, structured to restrain both population and food production. They are, by definition, no-growth systems. Growth of either population or food production, or both, may, however, be deliberately promoted and even institutionalized within more complex social systems.

Within tribal cultures organized around the domestic mode of production, there is a constant struggle to balance the demands of the society at large, which extracts food from individual households by means of kinship obligations, with the immediate self-interest of each isolated household. If growth of either population or food production is to occur, a social system must develop that will tap the "underdeveloped" resources and transform the domestic mode of production into something else. Political authority must overcome the natural tendency of individual households to set their own production goals and to maintain their economic autonomy over and against the interests of the larger society. The political order must establish a *public* economy. "Big-man" leadership systems, segmentary lineage and clan systems, and hierarchical chiefdoms all represent different sociopolitical strategies for mobilizing productivity above the cutoff point normally operating in the domestic mode of production, but still remaining within the limitations of a kin-based, nonstate social system.

It does seem to be the case that certain cultures respond to the ever-present tendency of population to expand by increasing food production and at the same time developing more complex forms of social organization. These three variables—population growth, intensification of subsistence, and increasing social complexity—are so interrelated that it is not always reasonable to assign priority to any one of them, although a number of recent theorists place primary emphasis on population growth as the basic determinant. It can be assumed that technological improvements that demand greater intensification of labor will only come about in the presence of population pressure. Conversely, they may be facilitated by the prior existence of certain levels of sociopolitical organization. A complex irrigation system, for example, could probably not be initiated in a society that lacked effective supralocal forms of political control. For their part, more complex forms of social organization may often become necessary as disputes over access to resources begin to arise in situations of increasing population pressure.

Danish economist Ester Boserup (1965) argues that technological changes in primitive agriculture can all be viewed as responses to population pressure. Her approach is very similar to that of anthropologists in recent attempts to explain the transition from hunting to farming. She assumes that the earliest, simplest farming techniques, such as shifting cultivation, were more productive per hour of labor than the more advanced systems, but they were *less* productive per unit of land. People would automatically prefer such extensive methods; i.e., these methods simply required less work to produce food than more intensive methods. There is indeed a clear relationship between the frequency of cropping in a given unit of land and the density of population. Denser populations require more intensive land use. Fallow periods may well be shortened as a direct response to an increase of population in local areas, and this shortening of fallow periods or more intense land use will initiate ecological changes that force the use of new technology. Under a typical swidden or "forest fallow" system, a simple digging stick is all that is required for planting in newly cleared, virtually weed-free forest, However, when the fallow cycle is shortened because of the need to increase food production in a limited area, then the increasing appearance of weeds makes hoes necessary. Continued shortening of fallow periods will lead to grasses that can be easily cultivated with plows.

From this viewpoint, advances in food production can be seen not as simply brilliant inventions that in turn cause population growth; rather, they were forced on people by prior population growth. It would make no sense at all for shifting cultivators with adequate forest resources to invent a plow, because it would simply not fit their mode of land use and would not be an advantage. It must not be forgotten, however, that intensification in food production will of course reinforce the need for further itensification by supporting and amplifying the prior deviation from population equilibrium. This "deviation amplification" is a basic process of population growth, and population growth and subsistence intensification clearly constitutes a self-intensifying spiral.

As cultural evolution proceeds, the basic trend is for food production to become more and more intensive and for more food to be produced in a smaller and smaller area. Kent V. Flannery (1969) estimated that probably 35 percent of modern-day Iran would have provided a favorable habitat for Mesopotamian hunting cultures that were able to support 0.1 persons per square kilometer in the late Paleolithic period. Ten percent of Iran probably was suited for dry farming, and could have supported one or two persons per square kilometer. Highly intensive irrigation agriculture might have been possible over only 1 percent of the total area of the country; but with it, up to six or more persons per square kilometer could have been supported even in ancient Mesopotamia. This level of productivity implies both state organization and a totally different kind of food system.

State-Level Food Systems

The most intensive food production systems can apparently only be supported by state-level political systems. State-level food systems contrast strongly with patterns characteristic of tribal cultures. Through political coercion, states are able to exact food production from local villages and households in the form of taxes or tribute far above the levels that would be required for local needs. Specific data on highly productive wet-rice cultivators in China prior to the Communist government (Harris 1971:203–17) shows that 84 percent of their crop was an "exported surplus" beyond their immediate subsistence needs. With increases of this magnitude, it is not surprising that states may often be much closer to the maximum carrying capacity of their environments than tribal cultures.

Other important cultural features of state-level food systems are that access to productive resources such as land and water may be allocated according to social class and status, and that significant segments of the population may not be involved in food production at all. This arrangement makes it quite likely that nutrients will no longer be equally distributed in the society—some social classes may indeed be hungry, while other classes are "overnourished." This combination of differential access to subsistence resources and inequitable distribution of nutrients by social class is, as we have seen, one of the basic correlates of hunger in the modern world.

Thus, there are three aspects of the food problem that might be considered adverse side effects of evolutionary progress. On the one hand, the adoption of agriculture creates an ecologically less stable food system that is inherently more prone to famine-causing fluctuation. Secondly, as a deviation amplification, technological advances in food production tend to reinforce an accelerating spiral of population and further subsistence intensification that must inevitably place greater strains on the ecosystem and increase the likelihood of further environmental deterioration, and which results in an approach close to, if not beyond, the ultimate carrying capacity of the resource base. Finally, social stratification creates an imbalance in the availability of food to the population. It would appear from this analysis that many of the food problems that the world is now experiencing are merely predictable cultural evolution processes and intrinsic features of state-level organization. Many of these difficulties have been with us since the first appearance of agriculture around 10,000 years ago, but they were clearly intensified and enlarged by the evolution of states and urban civilization some 5,000 years ago. The fact that they are still unsolved suggests that these may be quite intractable problems that may well only be overcome through a drastic transformation process. This picture has been altered considerably over the past 200 years, however, by the emergence of the culture of consumption and its unique food system.

Famine in the Modern World

> [Despite] the enormous sums invested, the impressive technical
> progress we have made, and the extraordinary efforts by
> governments, by international bodies, and by scientific and technical
> communities—mankind has by and large failed in its supreme effort
> to feed adequately those billions of people *now* living on earth. Of
> these, at least one billion are undernourished, and the diets of an
> additional eight hundred million are deficient in one or several key
> nutrients. (Borgstrom 1967:xi)

Famine is not new. It has been, and continues to be, a chronic hazard of civilization. Famines of varying degrees and intensity were recorded in China at the rate of 1,828 over the 2,019 years up to 1911. Four million people may have died in China in 1920–21. Three million died in the Indian famine of 1769–70, 2 to 4 million in West Bengal in 1943. Five to 10 million may have died in Russian famines from 1918 to 1934.

Famines have ravaged Europe many times, and even England counted more than 200 famines between A.D. 10 and A.D. 1846 (Ehrlich and Ehrlich 1972). Since Malthus outlined the dangers in 1798, Europe has moved to the brink of famine, and sometimes beyond, several times. By the middle of the 19th century a general food crisis was developing in Europe, but it was alleviated by emigration and food imports from the United States. The most notable problem during this period was the Irish "potato famine" of 1845–46. The introduction of the potato to Ireland permitted rapid population growth up to some 8 million people by 1841; but a blight struck the monocrop, and more than a million people died and another million emigrated. The Irish population has since stabilized at half its preblight level. A second European food crisis developed early in this century but was averted when vast acreages in Australia, Argentina, and Canada were taken from aboriginal hunting peoples and put into production for the world market.

In 1905, Harvard geologist Nathaniel S. Shaler warned that the world was very near the limits of food production; he doubted that a threefold population expansion could be supported. World population then stood at well under 2 billion. Forty years later the United Nations declared that much of the World suffered from malnutrition and launched a major "freedom from hunger" campaign. In 1965, George Borgstrom, a food scientist with 20 years of experience, declared that the world had already failed in its effort to feed itself,and that hunger—"hunger rampant"—was now the great issue of our age. In 1967, William and Paul Paddock, brothers with long experience in tropical agriculture and national food systems in the underdeveloped world, published a major book in which they predicted that by 1975 United States grain surpluses would no longer be able to make up for world food shortages, and a period of disastrous famines would begin.

Recognizing the dangers, President Lyndon B. Johnson declared that the world food problem was"one of the foremost challenges of mankind today"; and in 1966, he directed his Science Advisory Committee to investigate the problem and look for solutions (United States, President's Science Advisory Committee 1967). The committee brought together 115 experts on all aspects of the problem from universities, industry, and government agencies. They worked for a year, with subpanels devoted to such topics as food supply, population, nutritional needs, plant and animal productivity, soils and climate, marketing, processing, and distribution. Finally, in 1967, the committee issued a three-volume, 1,200-page report, confirming all the dire predictions that had been made before. Their major conclusion was that: "the scale, severity, and duration of the world food problem are so great that a massive, long-range, innovative effort unprecedented in human history will be required to master it." (vol. 1:11).

The report dealt with the basic problem of the food crisis in the immediate future, the 20 years from 1965 to 1985, on the mistaken assumption, or at least the hope, that effective family planning programs would be initiated immediately and would stabilize the population by 1985. The panelists felt that if the food problem was solved by 1985, it would be manageable well into the future. By 1975, barely halfway to the 1985 safety target, the population problem had slight hope of being stabilized in the near future, and it appeared that the predictions of "Famine—1975!" are being fulfilled. At the United Nations World Food Conference, which met in Rome in November, 1974, it was reported that 460 million people were threatened with immediate famine and that 10 million would probably die before the year was out. In 1974, biologist Paul Ehrlich (Ehrlich and Ehrlich 1974) stated flatly that it was already too late for population programs to prevent famine, because the great famines were already under way. At the Rome food conference, one American agronomist was quoted as saying that unless something was done to provide better food security for the world, "we may be seeing the end of our civilization." By 1984 it was clear that the food problem was not going away; hunger was occurring throughout the world, although it was perhaps less dramatic than earlier predictions.

Measuring Hunger

There are several ways of determining the adequacy with which the world or any given region is meeting its nutritional needs. One obvious and apparently simple method is to estimate per capita calorie and protein requirements and to compare these figures with estimates of the availability or the actual consumption of nutrients. This is a very difficult method to work with, in fact, because it is not easy to establish a completely adequate basic nutritional standard for the world. In the first place, caloric requirements vary with age, sex, health status, body weight, quality of diet, physical activity, and climate. A world average might have little relevance in any particular area. Furthermore, low body weights in many countries, and their corresponding "adequate" levels af per capita caloric requirements, may be very misleading because these low weights may in turn be a result of nutritional deficiency in children that prevented the population from realizing its genetic growth potential. There may also be a large gap between calories available and calories consumed, because food may be lost in storage, shipping, and preparation, and a further gap between calories consumed and calories absorbed. It is well known that intestinal parasite infestations, which are common in tropical countries, can divert a significant proportion of the calories an infected individual consumes. Other difficulties involve distinguishing between whether specific applications of caloric requirements are concerned with minimum, average, or optimum allowances, and how these are defined.

The United Nations Food and Agriculture Organization (FAO 1963) has conducted three major world food surveys covering the periods 1934–38, 1948–52, and 1957–59, and more recently has prepared annual world food balance sheets. These data vary widely in quality and have serious limitations, but they remain one of the most useful assessments of the world food situation, and their conclusions merit careful consideration. The first survey, published in 1946, concluded that immediately before World War II, two-thirds of the world had less than a desirable quantity of food available at the retail level. They fell below a 2,750 daily per capita calorie availability level, which was then considered a reasonable minimum figure, it being assumed that probably 10 percent of that amount would be lost before being actually consumed. The postwar survey found that even fewer calories were available per capita than previously; however, a slight adjustment in the calculated average caloric requirements made the gap between adequate and inadequate appear somewhat smaller. A serious decline in the proportion of animal protein in calorie-poor areas was also noted. The third survey, published in 1967, found that calorie availability was only slightly above prewar levels and that much of the increase occurred in the already industrialized nations, leaving the rest of the world relatively further behind. It was concluded that 10 to

15 percent of the world was undernourished in terms of caloric quantity, and as much as half of the world was qualitatively malnourished in terms of protein availability. Considering these figures at the world level, of course, conceals where the real famine problems lie, because nutrients are very inequitably distributed in the world at large and within individual countries. The third FAO food survey indicated that at least 20 percent of the population in underdeveloped countries was undernourished, and for 60 percent the diet was qualitatively inadequate.

The extent to which a somewhat different interpretation of the caloric adequacy of the diet can yield a different picture of the world food situation is clear when the estimates by the U.S. Department of Argiculture, also published in 1963, are compared with UN estimates. In this report, Lester R. Brown estimated that nearly 80 percent of the underdeveloped world population, or 56 percent of the population of the entire world, was below acceptable caloric levels. Ninety-two percent of Asia was found to be deficient! Some writers scoff at such figures and argue that much lower average per capita requirements are really adequate. Others feel that these estimates may even be too low.

Whereas there may be honest dispute over the establishment of nutritional standards, there can be little dispute over certain other indicators of major world food problems. One particularly ominous change in the world food system occurred in the early 1950s, when the underdeveloped countries stopped exporting grain and became net importers (Brown 1963:76; Paddock and Paddock 1967:41-44). Many of these countries have become increasingly dependent on grain produced by the United States and Canada to make up periodic shortfalls or to supplement regular deficiencies. This dependency is a total reversal of the prior situation, in which these same countries were grain exporters.

Perhaps the most directly meaningful indication of food shortage is the occurrence of deficiency diseases and deaths related to malnutrition. Whereas deaths due to actual starvation are rarely recorded, it is certain that poor nutrition dramatically increases mortality rates from many other causes. It is well known, for example, that the elevated infant mortality rates in much of the world are to a considerable extent due to protein-calorie deficiency. Numerous studies have shown that infant deaths due to common childhood diseases that seldom are fatal in developed countries can be sharply reduced by provision of adequate diets. The most severe and most common protein-calorie deficiency diseases are kwashiorkor and marasmus, which largely affect children and involve a dramatic wasting away of body tissue (Trowell 1954). Protein deficiency is also clearly linked to mental retardation and growth impairment in children (Montagu 1972). The extent of such health problems is impossible to estimate precisely because of inadequate surveys and varying interpretations of clinical symptoms. However, these conditions are clearly reflected in the fact that infant mortality rates in underdeveloped countries are often 30 to 40 times higher than the rates of developed countries. Growth retardation related to malnutrition has been called "almost universal" in poor countries, and some writers have placed malnutrition rates at as high as 70 percent in these countries.

Many of the symptoms of chronic food deficiency are probably so common in hungry areas that they have become accepted as "normal" conditions. Reduced physical activity and a general physiological slowdown are basic adaptations to starvation (Young and Scrimshaw 1971), but these symptoms may not be immediately obvious when they characterize entire populations or segments of populations.

Another indirect indication of food problems in specific areas is the price of food in relation to income levels or the ability to purchase food. There is abundant evidence showing clear relationships between poverty and malnutrition. Below certain income levels, it may simply not be possible to obtain an adequate diet. This is generally the case in rural areas where formerly self-sufficient farmers with presumably adequate diets have been forced to replace traditional food crops with cash crops that do not generate enough income to allow them to purchase sufficient food (Gross and Underwood 1971). Urban populations must rely entirely on cash to provide their food. The President's Science Advisory Committee report presented data for India showing that in 1961-62, 20 percent of the population fell within income levels that allowed them to obtain on the average only about 80 percent of their caloric requirements and less then their needed protein. In 1958, in Maharashtra State, poor people at the lowest income levels were consuming only 58 percent of their caloric requirements and 64 percent of their protein needs, whereas those at the highest income levels received 131 percent and 148 percent, respectively. It is significant that estimates of malnutrition derived from income levels correspond quite closely to estimates based on total availability of nutrients in relation to total need, such as those proposed by the FAO *Third World Food Survey*.

Since 1974 the United Nations has operated a World Food Programme and a World Food Council to monitor the food crisis and help individual nations design specific programs to increase their food self-sufficiency. Within the UN Food and Agriculture Organization, the Freedom from Hunger/ Action for Development Programme is also aimed at the food problem. More recent attempts to calculate the extent of world hunger demonstrate that there has been no real improvement. Figures published by the World Bank for 1980 showed that the available food supplies of 42 countries would provide less than 100 percent of the caloric requirements of their populations (World Bank 1983:194–95). Furthermore, 52 countries were producing less food per capita in 1980 than they were in 1970 (World Bank 1983:158–59). What we are seeing might be somewhat less sudden and dramatic than expected, but a very real world food crisis is nevertheless taking place. For example, the trend in Africa is unmistakable. According to Brown and Wolf (1984:16), "Africa is slowly losing the capacity to feed itself." This is apparent in the fact that grain imports tripled in Africa between 1970 and 1983, while per capita grain production has steadily declined since 1970 and serious environmental deterioration is occurring. The outlook is not hopeful.

It is important to remember, however, that the food crisis is not simply a technological problem, or a population pressure problem; it is a problem inherent in state-level organization in which social inequality is a major factor. The following example from Bangladesh makes this clear.

Needless Hunger in Bangladesh

Bangladesh, the former East Pakistan, is often presented as one of the most extreme cases of hopeless population pressure and Malthusian famine and malnutrition. The human problem is certainly conspicuous. For example, in 1974, it was estimated that 100,000 people died of starvation. A nutrition survey conducted in 1975–76 found that over half of the families in the country were eating fewer calories than they needed and suffered from protein deficiencies. Not surprisingly, life expectancy stood at just 47 years (Hartmann and Boyce 1982:9).

With one of the largest and densest populations in the world, Bangladesh would certainly seem to be a prime example of a Malthusian "basket-case" country. However, when re-examined from a different perspective emphasizing cultural, rather than biological, constraints in the food system, the picture changes considerably. Such a perspective emerged dramatically in 1977 with the publication of *Food First: Beyond the Myth of Scarcity*, by Frances Moore Lappé and Joseph Collins for the Institute for Food and Development Policy, and *How the Other Half Dies: The Real Reasons for World Hunger*, by Susan George. These two books convincingly argue that the world potential for food production is not presently being strained by overpopulation. On the contrary, grain production is so abundant that wealthy countries can turn vast quantities into animal feed. People are hungry because they have been removed from the land by large landowners and multinational agribusiness interests and because they cannot earn enough to purchase the food they can no longer grow. The demand of poor people for food cannot even be expressed in the marketplace because their purchasing power is too weak.

Paradoxically, Bangladesh is potentially a very rich agricultural land with excellent climate, abundant water, and fine alluvial soils. Before the British arrived in 1757, the region (then called Bengal) supported a prosperous local cotton industry. The peasantry was well able to feed itself because land was not privately owned and was not part of the market economy. The British forcibly introduced cash cropping for export, first of indigo, and then of jute, and they made land a commodity to be individually owned. Through a variety of legal and extralegal means, the peasantry was steadily deprived of the land. A study published in 1977 (Jannuzi and Peach 1977: xxi, 30) showed that nearly two-thirds of the rural households held less than 10 percent of the land, whereas one-third were totally landless. In this system, not having access to land means being unable to eat adequately. Landless peasants were found to consume 22 percent less grain than small landholders, whereas they burned 40 percent more calories because of their increased work loads. Many of the landless worked as sharecroppers, providing labor, and often seeds and fertilizer, while the owner claimed at least half of the crop. Those who worked as wage laborers earned 20 to 30 cents per day. The local elites used their power to manipulate wages and prices to ensure that the peasantry were invariably underpaid, relative to official prices, for the crops they produced, while they were overcharged for the commodities they had to purchase. International development aid and even emergency food aid were invariably monopolized by the landed elite. The conclusions of researchers Hartmann and Boyce, after two years in the country from 1974 to 1976 and nine months in a representative village, clearly place the blame for hunger on the cultural system:

> Hunger in Bangladesh is neither natural nor inevitable. Its causes are deeply rooted, but they are man-made. The surplus siphoned from the peasants is squandered; land, labor and water are underutilized; and, at the national level, financial resources and skilled manpower are allocated for the benefit of a few rather than for the well-being of the majority (Hartmann and Boyce 1982:35).

It is significant that the food system of prerevolutionary China as described for 1938 (Fei and Chang 1945; Bodley 1981) was very similar to the situation in Bangladesh in 1975. In a sample village in Yunnan, 41 percent of the land was owned by 15 percent of the households, and more than one-third of the households were completely landless. Landed households were consuming the equivalent of five times the caloric intake of the landless households. Famine was a chronic problem for the impoverished majority. However, after the drastic social leveling of the revolutionary government, China was providing adequate nutrition to its entire population of 800 million, with even less agricultural land per person than Bangladesh (George 1977:36).

5
INDUSTRIAL FOOD SYSTEMS

If we insist on a high-energy food system, we should consider starting with coal, oil, garbage—or any other source of hydrocarbons— and producing in factories bacteria, fungi, and yeasts. These products could then be flavored and colored appropriately for cultural tastes.

John S. Steinhart and Carol E. Steinhart, "Energy Use in the U.S. Food System"

The food systems of industrial nations represent an enormous advance in evolutionary progress and a proportionate loss in long-run adaptive success. The primary distinguishing feature of these systems is their fossil fuel energy subsidy, which permits very high crop yields for very low inputs of human energy. Other critical aspects are the extreme complexity of the production-consumption chain, and the tendency to increase the per capita energy and resource cost of food consumption through expanded dependence on synthetic and highly processed foods and inefficiently produced animal protein. These systems are not only far more costly in terms of per capita demands for energy and resources, but they are unquestionably more frail than tribal systems, they demand much more intensive ecosystem management, and they have greater potential for environmental deterioration. Perhaps, most critically, they can clearly not be sustained at present rates of increase or even at present levels unless they are radically restructured. It is also very doubtful that, if such systems diffuse, they could be supported at all on a global basis, given present population levels. These are critical issues because the present strategy for solving the world food crisis not only ignores the fact that many of the problems are inherent features of state-level cultures based on intensive food production systems, but also makes the dangerous assumption that industrial food systems will feed the world if only they can be established everywhere.

Factory Food Production

If the nonhuman energy expended in the production, processing, distribution, storage, and preparation of food in America is ignored, the system may indeed appear to be very efficient. Anthropologist Marvin Harris (1971) gave the American food system highest ratings in "techno-environmental advantage"* in comparison with the energy efficiency of hunters, shifting cultivators, hoe farmers, and wet rice growers. His figures

---

*In his 1975 edition of *Culture, Man and Nature* (renamed *Culture, People and Nature*), Harris revises his efficiency rating for the United States food production system on the basis of the fossil fuel costs, following Steinhart and Steinhart (1974) and others.

T A B L E 5 - 1 Energy input-output efficiency in five food systems.

Culture	Technology	Calories produced per calorie expended
Bushmen	Hunting/gathering	9.6
Tsembaga (New Guinea)	Shifting cultivation	18.0
	Pig raising	2.1
	Total	9.8
Genieri (Gambia)	Hoe farming	11.2
China	Irrigated wet rice	53.5
United States	Factory farming	
	Human labor	210.0
	Nonhuman energy	0.13

Sources: Data from Harris 1971:203–17; Steinhart and Steinhart 1974:307–16.

were based on a simple estimate of the hours expended per farm worker, multiplied by a fixed rate of 150 calories expended per hour, and divided into the quantity of food calories produced in a given period of time. These calculations may be a reasonable approximation of energy input-output ratios for tribal farmers and hunters, but they are completely inadequate when they ignore the fossil fuel subsidy in the industrial food system. Table 5-1 presents the basic technoenvironmental efficiency rating of the five cultures evaluated by Harris, but adds a correction for the efficiency of the United States system by counting separately the non-human energy inputs from production to consumption. The surprising fact is that whereas American farm laborers may only expend 1 calorie of human energy for every 210 food calories they produce, approximately 8 calories of nonhuman energy, primarily in the form of fossil fuels, are also required for each calorie produced. It is apparent that the industrial food system is actually operating at an energy efficiency deficit.

Ecologist Howard T. Odum (1971) has brilliantly outlined the energy flow systems underlying subsistence patterns at different levels of cultural development using carefully designed cybernetic models. Odum uses a variety of symbols to represent the pathway of energy through an ecosystem, from the sun, through green plants and herbivores to the human consumers. The resulting diagram resembles a complex electrical schematic with switches, gates, and heat sinks, etc., all showing how energy is transformed, stored, and regulated. One need not understand all the complexities of this method of analysis to appreciate how it can illustrate the general design of different subsistence systems and their relationship to the ecosystem. These diagrams dramatically show how fossil fuels are used to replace energetic functions that are performed more efficiently and at lower cost by nature in solar-powered tribal subsistence systems. As hunters and gatherers, humans were dependent for their subsistence on highly complex and stable ecosystems that were largely self-regulating, closed cybernetic systems. In a tropical rain forest, for example (see Figure 5-1), the diverse species of the forest do all the work of concentrating energy and nutrients and regulating their flow. Nutrients are largely stored in the living plants and animals and are quickly and efficiently recycled after their death. Tribal shifting cultivators adjusted to the forest ecosystem by making use of the artificial energy pulse generated each time a forest plot was cut and burned (see Figure 5-2). This pulse temporarily eliminated competitor species and concentrated nutrients to briefly transfer the energy flow into food crops. Except for this minor intervention, the system continued to be basically self-regulating and immediately began to return to its starting point; that is, natural forest succession began at once. Thus, nature did most of the work, and as long as their power base remained restricted to local inputs of solar energy, tribal cultures were generally unable to harness enough power to seriously disrupt their supporting ecosystems.

When modern nations began to channel fossil fuel energy into their food systems, the picture was suddenly and radically changed. Odum describes the new fossil fuel food systems very neatly as follows:

> One of the results of industrialization based on the new concentrated energy sources was abundant food rolling out from huge fields which were sowed with machinery, tilled with tractors, and weeded and poisoned with chemicals. Epidemic diseases were kept in check by great teams of scientists in distant experiment stations developing new and changing varieties to stay ahead of the evolution of disease adaptation. Soon a few people were supporting many, and most of the rural population left the little farms to fill the new industrial cities. (Odum 1971:115)

The greater crop yields that followed industrialization must not be considered simply the result of brilliant inventions, education, deter-

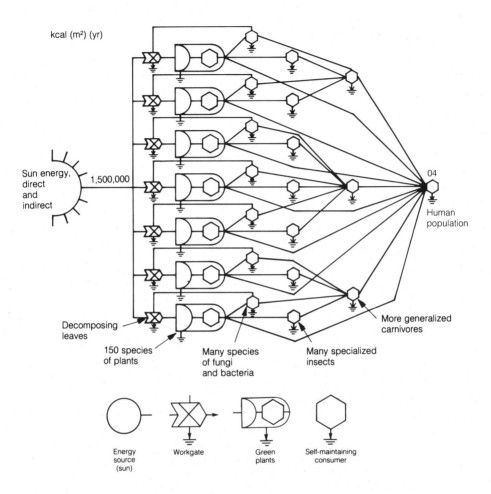

FIGURE 5-1 Hunting Systems. Network matrix supporting and stabilizing a tropical rain forest system. People are a minor component, but they have integrating and control functions because of the convergence of pathways.

Source: Howard T. Odum, *Environment, Power, and Society.* (New York: Wiley, Inter-Science, 1971), 87.

mination, and great technological know-how. An enormous energy subsidy was essential. Factory farms do not achieve more efficient rates of photosynthesis and energy conversion. Actually, even some of the most productive factory farms, such as industrialized rice farms, convert only about 0.25 percent of incoming solar radiation into useful energy, whereas

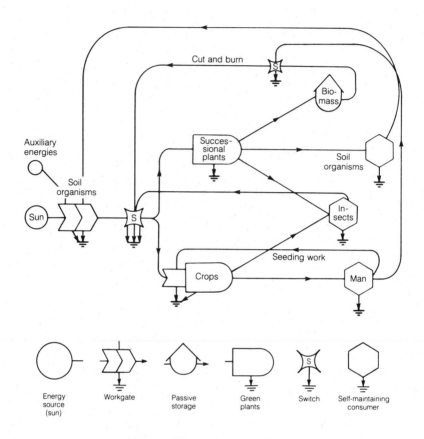

Cut and burn

Bio-
mass

Auxiliary
energies

Succes-
sional
plants

Soil
organisms

Soil
organisms

In-
sects

Sun

S

Seeding work

Crops

Man

| Energy source (sun) | Workgate | Passive storage | Green plants | Switch | Self-maintaining consumer |

F I G U R E 5 - 2 Shifting Cultivation. Energy diagram for shifting agriculture. Humans serve as switching timers, transferring the flow of energy into food crops made temporarily possible by the material and work accumulated during the long period of plant succession between short agricultural cycles.

Source: Howard T. Odum, *Environment, Power, and Society* (New York: Wiley, Inter-Science, 1971), 113.

a tropical rain forest operates at 3.5 percent efficiency (Odum 1971). Larger per acre yields are possible on factory farms because fossil fuels replace the energy loop the natural ecosystem reserved for its own mechanisms of self-regulation (see Figure 5-3). This system is simply a means of converting oil into food. In effect, as Odum phrases it, in a factory

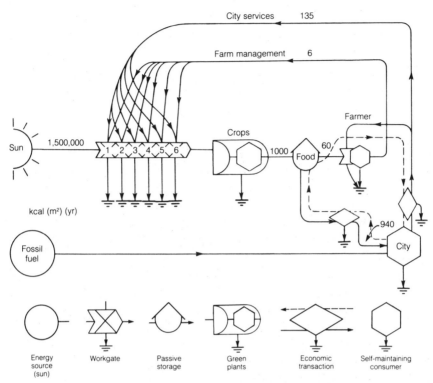

F I G U R E 5 ‑ 3 Factory Farming with Fossil Fuels. People in a system of industrialized, high‑yield agriculture. Energetic inputs include flows of fossil fuels that replace the work formerly done by people, their animals, and the network of animals and plants in which people were formerly nursed. Work flows include the following: (1) mechanized and commercial preparation of seeding and planting, replacing the natural dispersion system; (2) fertilizer excesses, replacing the mineral recycling system; (3) chemical and power weeding, replacing the woody maintenance of a shading system; (4) soil preparation and treatment, replacing the forest soil‑building processes; (5) insecticides, replacing the system of chemical diversity, and carnivores for preventing epidemic grazing and disease; and (6) development of varieties capable of passing on the savings in work to net food storages. New varieties are developed as diseases appear, thus providing the genetic selection formerly arranged by the forest evolution and selection system. In this system 170 persons per square mile support 32 times this number in cities. The level of grain production in the United States is about 1000 kcal/(m²)(yr). The fuel subsidy is calculated using 10^4 kcal/dollar. If production yields \$60/(acre)(yr) and if the costs are 90 percent of the gross, then \$54/acre is the measure to use of materials and services from the industrialized culture. This becomes 54×10^4 kcal/acre or 135 kcal/(m²) (yr).

Source: Howard T. Odum, *Environment, Power, and Society* (New York: Wiley, Inter‑Science, 1971), 119.

agricultural system, "fossil fuel supported works of man have eliminated the natural species and substituted industrial services for the services of those natural species, releasing the same basic production to yield" (Odum 1971:117).

A factory farm is actually an extremely costly, sloppy, and inefficient attempt to replace nature with a very simplified, artificially maintained and subsidized machine. Chemical fertilizers manufactured and transported with fossil fuels replace the tightly calibrated nutrient cycles of the natural ecosystem. More chemicals and machinery control the weeds that in a swidden system are merely part of the restart mechanism and are shaded out as the successional pattern they initiate proceeds. Plant geneticists working in laboratories replace the natural process of biological evolution based on natural selection and species diversity. The delicate natural balances that prevent consumer species from overgrazing are eliminated by heavy application of chemical poisons. Pollution and environmental deterioration are unintended direct by-products of industrial farming, because the exotic nutrients and insecticides do not fit into natural ecosystem cycles but instead merely pile up in unexpected places to block these cycles. The massive use of chemical pesticides also has serious direct implications for public health, and has stirred widespread public concern and controversy on many occasions.

Much of the energy and workforce needed to support an industrial food system is disguised by statistics that focus on farm labor and yields per acre. Harris (1971), in the estimate of the efficiency of United States food production cited earlier, used a figure of 5 million farm workers in 1964. Newer figures, presented in Table 5-2, prepared from data in the *Statistical Abstract of the U.S.*, suggest that in 1982 more than 11 million people were full-time workers in the food system, even with a reduction of over 2 million in the count of actual farm workers! The addition of some 200,000 support workers in the manufacturing and marketing of farm machinery and chemicals, agricultural sciences, and the federal Department of Agriculture brings the total number of workers in direct support of food production up to 3.1 million. Some writers have even estimated that as many as two support workers are needed for each farm worker (Pimentel 1973).

T A B L E 5 - 2 Labor in the United States food system, 1982 (in millions of workers)

Farm labor	2.9	million
Support sectors	0.136	
Farm machine manufacturing		
Agri-chemical manufacturing	0.065	
Total, primary production	3.1	million
Food processing industry	1.6	
Eating and drinking places	4.82	
Retail grocers	2.45	
Total, processors and distributors	8.87	million
Food system total	11.97	million

Source: United States Bureau of the Census, *Statistical Abstract of the United States: 1984*, 104th ed. (Washington, D.C.: U.S. Government Printing Office, 1983), tables 707, 1135, 1176.

Factory Potatoes Versus Swidden Sweet Potatoes

Profit is the only reason for growing potatoes. (Knudson 1972:76)

The extent to which fossil-fuel-subsidized farming systems have artificially replaced the functions of the natural ecosystem, and the incredible energy and environmental costs of this change, stand out with remarkable clarity when the production of Irish potatoes on a typical American farm* is compared with the methods of raising sweet potatoes in traditional New Guinea swidden gardens (Rappaport 1971). Potatoes (Irish or sweet) occupy roughly the same position in each culture, in that they are quantitatively the most important single vegetable consumed and are unquestionably basic staples in the diet. In American culture, meat and potatoes make a meal complete.

According to the account of the Tsembaga in highland New Guinea,

---

*Talburt and Smith (1967) and various of the *Proceedings of the Annual Washington Potato Conference and Trade Fair* (Washington Potato Commission).

provided by Rappaport (1968, 1971), sweet potatoes directly contributed 21 percent of the diet by weight for the local group of 204 people who were actively cultivating about 1000 acres in 1962. Much of the sweet potato crop was fed to domestic pigs, and thus indirectly contributed animal protein to the diet in the form of pork. The basic cultivation system was carried out entirely by hand. The forest was cleared and burned, fences were built to keep out the pigs, and crops were planted with a sharpened stick. Crops were harvested by hand and carried in net bags to the house for consumption. There is no elaborate processing; sweet potatoes are simply roasted whole in the fire or steamed in earth ovens. There is also no significant storage, except in the ground before harvest. Energetically, the system is quite efficient, with approximately 16 kilocalories of sweet potatoes produced for each kilocalorie of human labor. Only about 10 percent of the easily arable land was under active cultivation at a time, and there appeared to be no danger of resource depletion. The basic objective of the gardening activity was to meet human nutritional needs, and this was being done very well. No crops were grown for the market.

On a factory farm in the United States, potatoes can be grown as a successful monocrop only with the help of vast energy inputs to maintain correct soil conditions, moisture, and nutrients, and to control weeds, epidemic diseases, and insect infestations. On the swidden sweet potato farm, all of these functions are carried out by the natural ecosystem, and by the diversity of the garden plantings, which imitates that natural system. No irrigation or fertilizer is required on swidden plots, but factory potato farmers must apply chemical fertilizer constantly and in many areas must irrigate to maintain their high yields. In areas where overhead sprinklers are used, special chemicals may be applied to the soil to prevent compaction and lost filtration caused by the perpetual mechanical rain (Hagood 1972). Weeds, insects, and diseases may be variously controlled before planting by chemical treatment of the tubers, by application of chemical herbicides and insecticides to the soil, and sometimes even by soil fumigation, which kills virtually all soil organisms. There are specialized preemergence weed killers, and a wide variety of other herbicides and insecticides, that may be applied while the crop is growing. In some cases, special chemicals are sprayed on the crop to inhibit sprouting after harvest, or to intensify the red skin color of certain potatoes to increase their market value. It may be noted that part of this energy-expensive chemical program is carried out as a cosmetic treatment to prevent unsightly blemishes that may lower consumer acceptance but have little effect on increasing actual yields. Where potatoes are contracted to go into chips, the vines must be chemically killed weeks before harvesting to prevent starch buildup in the tubers, which causes an undesirable darkening in the finished potato chips.

The extent of some of this chemical maintenance may be seen in specific production statistics from Washington State, which was third in the nation for potato production in the late 1960s. In 1969, 60 percent of the potato acreage on farms devoted principally to that crop was chemically sprayed by airplane for insect control, and some farms required as many as five to nine separate treatments (United States, Department of Commerce 1969 a, b). Only slightly fewer acres were treated chemically for disease control, and 40 percent were treated for weeds. In addition to the tractors and trucks normally required on farms, there were hundreds of specialized machines on Washington farms in 1967 to cut potato seed, and for use as potato harvesters, windrowers, diggers, and planters. In 1969, more than 36,000 tons of liquid and dry fertilizer were applied to 62,500 acres of potatoes—more than a thousand pounds per acre—and virtually the entire crop required both fertilizing and irrigation.

With this kind of treatment, it is not surprising that yields increased from a national average of 65 hundredweight per acre in 1920 to 480 hundredweight in Washington in 1982. In caloric terms, this means that over 12 million calories were being produced per acre (United States, Bureau of the Census 1983: table 1204). In comparison, New Guinea sweet potato farmers were producing approximately 5 million calories per acre with more than a dozen major crops combined. In addition to the direct energy subsidy from fossil fuels, Washington potato farmers were passing on other hidden costs, which makes full assessment of the costs impossible in the short term. For example, extensive irrigation already seems to be causing minor microclimatic alterations in the region; there is the danger that irrigation will also lead to soil salinization; heavy use of fertilizers and other chemicals will in time increasingly leach into rivers and underground water sources, killing susceptible species and overnourishing others; in addition, intensively cultivated areas are more subject to wind erosion.

Energy Costs of the Distribution System

In a tribal culture, as we have seen, food is largely produced by the households that consume it. Only small quantities are normally distributed beyond individual households, and this distribution occurs within a framework of reciprocal sharing between close kinsmen. In stratified chiefdom-level societies, production and consumption still remain largely at the household level; but some foodstuffs may be concentrated by chiefs as tribute, to be partially redistributed at feasts or in times of crisis, and to support craft specialists for the production of sumptuary goods. With the evolution of the state and the appearance of urban centers, large quantities of food had to be transferred from the rural subsistence farmers or peasants to the cities to support the non-food producers. This transfer has been variously effected through the payment of taxes, through the operations of special trader classes, or through well-developed market exchanges. Reliance only on solar-energy-powered agriculture apparently placed severe limitations on the extent to which the population of a given culture could be concentrated in cities, not only because of the restrictions that were placed on food production, but also because of the energy costs of transportation. With the tapping of fossil fuels and the rise of industrialized urban centers, which concentrated up to 95 percent of the population, the energy costs of the food distribution system have suddenly come to over-shadow totally the costs of actual production.

Only a very rough estimate of the *total* energy costs of the present American food system are possible. John D. Steinhart and Carol E. Steinhart (1974) calculated that in 1970, 8 to 12 calories were expended in the production, distribution, and consumption of a single calorie of food. This figure includes such energy costs as the manufacturing and operation of farm machinery, fertilizer, irrigation, food processing, packaging, transportation, and manufacturing of trucks, and both industrial and domestic cooking and refrigeration (see Table 5-3). Higher estimates would include the energy cost of shipping food by rail, ship, and air, disposal of food-related wastes, maintenance of buildings and equipment, a percentage of highway construction costs, agricultural research, and domestic use of private automobiles to move food from supermarket to home. Other estimates have placed the figure as high as 20 calories in for 1 calorie out, and this may be far more realistic.

TABLE 5·3 Energy use in the United States food system in 10^{12} Kcal

Component	1940	1947	1950	1954	1958	1960	1964	1968	1970
On farm									
Fuel (direct use)	70.0	136.0	158.0	172.8	179.0	188.0	213.9	226.0	232.0
Electricity	0.7	32.0	32.9	40.0	44.0	46.1	50.0	57.3	63.8
Fertilizer	12.4	19.5	24.0	30.6	32.2	41.0	60.0	87.0	94.0
Agricultural steel	1.6	2.0	2.7	2.5	2.0	1.7	2.5	2.4	2.0
Farm machinery	9.0	34.7	30.0	29.5	50.2	52.0	60.0	75.0	80.0
Tractors	12.8	25.0	30.8	23.6	16.4	11.8	20.0	20.5	19.3
Irrigation	18.0	22.8	25.0	29.6	32.5	33.3	34.1	34.8	35.0
Subtotal	124.5	272.0	303.4	328.6	356.3	373.9	440.5	503.0	526.1
Processing industry									
Food processing industry	147.0	177.5	192.0	211.5	212.6	224.0	249.0	295.0	308.0
Food processing machinery	0.7	5.7	5.0	4.9	4.9	5.0	6.0	6.0	6.0
Paper packaging	8.5	14.8	17.0	20.0	26.0	28.0	31.0	35.7	38.0
Glass containers	14.0	25.7	26.0	27.0	30.2	31.0	34.0	41.9	47.0
Steel cans and aluminum	38.0	55.8	62.0	73.7	85.4	86.0	91.0	112.2	122.0
Transport (fuel)	49.6	86.1	102.0	122.3	140.2	153.3	184.0	226.6	246.9
Trucks and trailers (manufacture)	28.0	42.0	49.5	47.0	43.0	44.2	61.0	70.2	74.0
Subtotal	285.8	407.6	453.5	506.4	542.3	571.5	656.0	787.6	841.9
Commercial and home									
Commercial refrigeration and cooking	121.0	141.0	150.0	161.0	176.0	186.2	209.0	241.0	263.0
Refrigeration machinery (home and commercial)	10.0	24.0	25.0	27.5	29.4	32.0	40.0	56.0	61.0
Home refrigeration and cooking	144.2	184.0	202.3	228.0	257.0	276.6	345.0	433.9	480.0
Subtotal	275.2	349.0	377.3	416.5	462.4	494.8	594.0	730.9	804.0
Grand total	685.5	1028.6	1134.2	1251.5	1361.0	1440.2	1690.5	2021.5	2172.0

Source: John S. Steinhart and Carol E. Steinhart, "Energy Use in the U.S. Food System," *Science* 1984 (1974): 309.

According to Steinhart and Steinhart's conservative estimate, less than 25 percent of the total energy expended in the American food system actually went to support primary production on the farm; the other 75 percent plus went to processing, marketing, and domestic uses. Significantly, more work force was also engaged in the food distribution network than on the farm, even if labor costs in the transportation system are disregarded (see Table 5-2). Clearly, the distribution component of the industrial food system is responsible for much of the enormous energy cost of the total system and for this reason deserves special investigation.

Many of the increased energy costs of the United States food system appear to be related solely to the marketing process. There has been little change in the actual quantity of calories and protein consumed by Americans per capita in recent decades, and there are obvious limits to expansion of these rates; but even so, the per capita costs of American food consumption doubled between 1940 and 1970. During this period the per capita energy costs of packaging increased 119 percent; and the overall per capita energy costs of processing, packaging, and transportation from factory to marketplace increased by 95 percent (Steinhart and Steinhart 1974). Due to the rising costs of energy since 1973, there have been some reductions in energy inputs in the food system, but the scale of energy use is still enormous in comparison with smaller, more self-sufficient systems.

There has been a dramatic switch in recent years toward the consumption of more energy-intensive food. By 1970, America's food was more transported and more expensively processed and packaged than ever before. These changes can be seen in many areas. For example, since 1950, there has been an almost fivefold increase in the per capita production of frozen food in this country. The introduction of these foods raises overall energy requirements because their distribution requires preparation, packaging, and transportation and storage facilities. Certain new food products, such as potato chips, may be vastly more costly to transport and store because of their increased bulk and fragility compared with their less processed counterparts. Trends in packaging since 1950 that have raised energy costs include a general increase in the use of packaging solely to increase the consumer appeal of foodstuffs and also a switch to more energy-expensive materials. Wood, paper, and reusable glass bottles have been steadily replaced by plastic, nonreturnable bottles and aluminum cans. The latter require approximately twice as much energy to manufacture than the steel cans that they replace! Cultural changes in patterns of food consumption must also account for part of this increase. The most striking change since 1940 is the fact that consumption of beef has more than doubled. This is especially significant because cattle are relatively inefficient converters of vegetable protein, requiring approximately 20 pounds of protein to produce one pound for human consumption. This ratio would not be critical if cattle were grazed on rangeland that would not produce other food crops, but a high proportion of America's beef cattle are fed high-quality grains in feedlots before being slaughtered. It has been estimated that in 1968 as much as 78 percent of the American grain crop was used as animal feed.

Modern marketing practices in the American food system were investigated in detail in an important study carried out for the National Commission on Food Marketing at the request of President Lyndon B. Johnson and published in 1968 (Marple and Wissman 1968). This study was based on the work of 19 academicians and seven private researchers and considered the cost structure of food from farmer to consumer, product innovation and competition, and consumer "needs." The findings are of particular interest because they help pinpoint factors in the processing and distribution component of the food system that seem to promote increased energy costs.

It is striking that productivity in the food-marketing industry is not measured in terms of how efficiently human need-satisfying nutrients can be distributed to the population; rather, it is computed in terms of dollar output per hour of labor or return on investment. In this accounting, staple foods such as meat, flour, and sugar, which require little processing, are considered to be less productive because they have a relatively low "value added" in comparison with soft drinks and cold cereals or other highly processed food "products." If the population is growing very slowly and is already satisfying its basic food needs, then logically the only way for food companies to increase their domestic profits is through increased competition between companies or through the production of increasingly more expensive new food products. Food markets may also be increased through exports in a world market system. Limited increases have also been obtained by raising the nutritional standard for domestic pets. It is well known that Americans have recently begun purchasing more high-quality protein for their dogs and cats than families in poor countries can provide for themselves. New food products in general have become one of the most important means of conducting competition between giant food corporations struggling for a larger share of the relatively fixed market. The importance of new food products is underscored by the comments of a president of the Campbell Soup Company, cited in the National Commission study, to the effect that a company without new products would see a 50-percent drop in profits within a year and would be losing money within five years.

Thus the introduction of new food items and a corresponding continual upgrading of the energy intensity of subsistence seem to be a logical outgrowth of an expanding economy in a culture of consumption. However, it can be assumed that the food habits of any culture, including a culture of consumption, will be relatively conservative and will be changed only with difficulty, regardless of how necessary it may be for manufacturers continually to create and market new food products. The findings of the National Commission clearly bear out this generalization; manipulating American tastes in food—introducing totally new foods or even permutations on existing products—has not been easily accomplished. It is instructive that ideas for new products do not normally originate with the consumer. Only 3 percent of the suggestions for 127 new products in a sample examined by the National Commission study actually came from future consumers. Consumers simply are not clamoring for new products. New product development is in fact a very expensive, very lengthy, and uncertain process of trial and error, in which most ideas prove unmarketable. In the mid-1960s a typical new cold breakfast cereal product required 4½ years of development activity, and nearly $4 million invested in physical design, market research, and advertising before full distribution could be achieved. Only some 5 percent of new product ideas ever reached full distribution, and only about 10 percent of these ever became well established. Even of products that made it all the way to the test market stage, 22 percent were withdrawn short of full development. Beyond that point, another 17 percent were quickly withdrawn. Manufacturers assumed that a product "life cycle" existed, and that every new product would experience a very slow rise in sales or consumer acceptance until it reached a saturation point. A gradual decline would set in as customers dropped the product entirely or shifted to rival brands.

The amount of money that must be spent on advertising and promotion of new products totally dwarfs expenditures for research and development. Only the largest food corporations could afford to develop new products, but the heavy advertising expenses were made less burdensome because they were also tax deductions. Enormous advertising expenditures are an accepted part of the process, as the National Commission study explains, because of the "inertia" of consumers, "arising primarily from reluctance to change established behavior patterns which delays customer acceptance of the new product" (Marple and Wissman 1968:40). The entire process bears a disturbing resemblance to the work of cultural change experts attempting to convince reluctant self-sufficient villagers that they should adopt expensive factory farm techniques. It is happily concluded by the food manufacturers that those products that survive the risky promotion procedure do so because they satisfy a "real" consumer "need."

The nonrandom pattern of advertising expenditures clearly demonstrates that reluctance to change established food habits is strongest when such habits already adequately satisfy basic nutritional needs. Products that appear to be of little nutritional value, or that are at least not a clear nutritional gain over the foods they would replace, often require the most intensive advertising campaigns. The study found this to be true for cold cereals but considered it to be merely the reflection of "higher-than-average uncertainty as to consumer acceptance . . ." (Marple and Wissman 1968:185). In general, staple foods such as fresh fruit, vegetables, meat, and milk, with minimal processing and little added "value," which could form the basis of a nutritionally sound diet, were promoted very little. "Impulse" items such as soft drinks, candy, and other snack foods and new products generally, were heavily dependent on continual promotion. People must be persuaded to accept food products that are not necessarily good for them, just as peasant farmers must be urged to accept energy-intensive farming practices that in the long run may be highly detrimental.

The "need" for new food products has been supported in an important sociological study by Cyril Sofer (1965), which argues that food habits are not necessarily "rational" from a nutritional viewpoint, anyway, and that food may often serve critical nonfood cultural functions other than nutrition. This generalization is of course true; but it seems to be only in state-level cultures, and particularly in the culture of consumption, that nutritional needs become *secondary* to other cultural functions, such as maintaining food industry profits. This seems to be a very crucial difference between major cultural systems. As was noted in the discussion of potato production on the factory farm, profit was the only reason for growing potatoes; in food marketing the only reason for new food products may also be profit. As the National Commission study explains: "[The] risky and expensive venture of new product development and introduction is undertaken in hopes of finding a new product which yields a higher gross contribution to overhead and profit on invested assets" (Marple and Wissman 1968:7).

A further argument in the Sofer study is that people have a basic "need" for new products as an escape from food monotony. Variety is of course also an advantage nutritionally, and it may be that people have a basic need for a varied diet to the extent that it is nutritionally adequate. However, there is no reason to believe that new food products are any advantage in that sense, and there is abundant evidence to the contrary. Sofer indirectly acknowledged the nutritional shortcomings of new food products by stating that people often eat food that they recognize to be harmful, thereby further absolving the food industry from any criticism for actively promoting nutritionally inferior but profitable foods.

Potato Chips and Manioc Cakes

Food processing and varied and nutritious diets were not invented by industrial civilization; they have been with us since the beginnings of culture and our first use of fire. There is a clear difference, however, between food processing in tribal culture, which is unquestionably "consumer-oriented," and industrial food processing for a profit. Some of these differences have already been demonstrated, but a brief comparison between manioc cakes and potato chips will heighten the contrasts.

One of the finest examples of food processing in tribal cultures can be seen in the manioc complex of South America. Bitter manioc is the staple food crop for many Amazonian Indians (Dole 1978; Lancaster 1982). Before the starchy tuber can be eaten, it must be peeled, grated, and squeezed to remove the poisonous juice from the flour. This process is accomplished by means of a variety of specialized graters and squeezing devices (see Figure 5-4). The end products may then be further processed into a wide range of foods. The Waiwai of Guyana have developed at least 14 different kinds of bread and 13 beverages based on bitter manioc and its by-products (Yde 1965:28–51). The flour may be sifted in various ways, baked in bread, eaten toasted by itself, or used in soups and stews. The juice is used in soups, and the tapioca extracted from it finds a variety of food uses, sometimes in combination with the flour. All of these processes, of course, take place in the household. They involve no external energy inputs, and no extended shipping or storage. It is erroneous to consider tribal diets dull and monotonous because they do not benefit from supermarkets. There is also no question here of eating potentially harmful food to assure someone else's profit.

In the United States, in 1964, only about half of the potato crop was shipped to consumers as raw tubers to be processed in the household (Talburt and Smith 1967). Even these "unprocessed" potatoes had to be washed mechanically, chemically treated to inhibit sprouting, in some cases colored or waxed, and transported and stored under temperature-controlled conditions. Potatoes destined for chips—and in 1964, this involved about 20 percent of the crop—would go through the washing, sprout inhibition, and temperature control, and in addition might sit in storage for six to eight months. Further chemical treatments included gases or chemical solutions to prevent discoloration of peeled potatoes before cooking and again to avoid after-cooking darkening that occurs as a natural enzymatic process and has no effect on taste or nutritive qualities, but is thought to reduce consumer appeal. Oils, salt, preservatives, and sometimes special artificial flavorings are then added in the final processing, and the end product is packed and shipped in special containers. Then, of course, people must be convinced to eat the product. In 1974 the all-new, vitamin-enriched chip made an experimental appearance on the market to satisfy the "needs" of those who were worried about the nutritional value of the standard chip. The success of the potato chip as a food product is not of course attributable to its nutritional quality, but rather that it is many times more expensive per pound at the retail level than the ordinary raw potato. As an element in the diet, potato chips have been criticized for having too much fat and salt, and otherwise too little nutritional value.

136

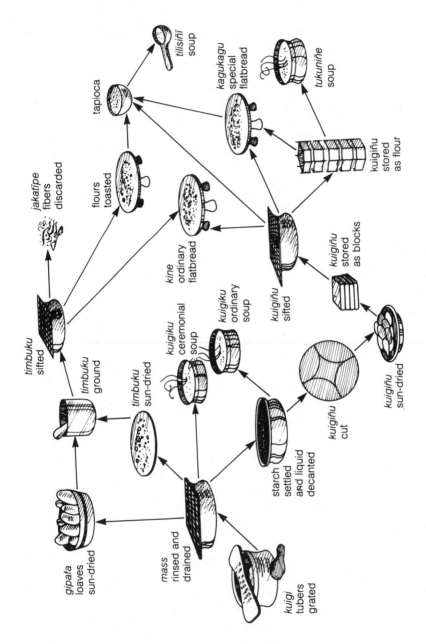

FIGURE 5-4 Steps in the preparation of manioc among the Kuikuru (Dole 1978).

Obviously, then, an important dimension of industrial food systems, which should not be overlooked, is that marketing requirements for food that looks attractive, ships well, and can be stored for extended periods in warehouses and on supermarket shelves mean that many new chemical ingredients are added for strictly economic, nonnutritional reasons. A bewildering array of food additives, estimated in 1972 at some 2,500 different substances, are now being added to food products as coloring agents, synthetic flavors, and preservatives; to prevent caking or separation; to provide body; and for a wide range of other specialized functions (Kermode 1972). Only a few of these additives are used for the purpose of replacing some of the nutrients destroyed in processing. As with pesticide residues, much controversy has arisen over the possible lack of safety of these additives, but few people have questioned the basic marketing system that makes them necessary. Since 1972 many new additives have appeared; others have been banned when they were discovered to be harmful. There is an ongoing struggle between health authorities and the food industry over how to control these nonnutritional additives (Freydberg and Gortner 1982; Hunter 1982).

Fishing, Trading, and "Ghost Acreage"

Some modern nations have so far managed to keep ahead of their food problems by supplementing their own limited food production capability through heavy reliance on fishing and world trade. Fish may be eaten directly or used as a substitute for feed crops for the production of meat, milk, eggs, and poultry. This seems to be a logical step ahead of the Malthusian controls on overpopulation. When the intensification of agriculture has reached the point where further increases can only be achieved if truly prohibitive energy deficits are incurred, then fishing fleets may be expanded and favorable trade agreements reached with nations producing food surpluses. In 1965, food scientist Georg Borgstrom introduced the concept *ghost acres*, referring to the fact that trade and fishing were ways of gaining extraterritorial acres. Ghost acres were calculated in terms of the amount of land a given country would need to put into production to gain an amount of animal protein equivalent to its net food imports and fishery production. According to this reckoning, many nations are shown to have far exceeded the carrying capacity of their farmlands, at least given their present culturally prescribed food patterns, and are now precariously dependent on uncertain international markets and frail marine resources. Japan's ghost acres, for example, exceed its agricultural acreage by more than six times, and the United Kingdom's effective acres are nearly tripled by ghost acres.

World trade is not presently operating as a means of allocating food to countries on the basis of critical nutritional requirements; rather, as with other facets of the industrial market economy, it supports and reflects the world ranking of nations in terms of economic wealth. Scarce protein resources in the form of meat, fish and fish products, nuts, and oilseed cakes move along with bananas, cocoa, coffee, and tea from protein-poor, hungry nations to rich, well-fed nations, propelled by the exigencies of the world cash economy.

Peru, for example, instead of satisfying the obvious needs of the substantial segments of its population that are protein-deficient, finds it more profitable to ship its rich fish meal resource to the United States, where it is fed to chickens to subsidize energy-intensive egg industries. Likewise, Indian oilseed cakes are fed to European cattle, while millions of Indians are starved for protein.

Borgstrom points out that the world's refrigerator ships are at present almost exclusively engaged in moving bananas and frozen meat from Central and South America, Australia, and New Zealand to Western Europe and North America, where they will bring the highest prices. The curious feature of this trade is that in many cases it does not fill a nutritional need in the rich countries that could not be satisfied by simply replacing the imported supplies with domestic equivalents. Brazilian meat and Peruvian fish meal in the United States might be considered an anomaly, but actually it is the logical outgrowth of a system of world market exchanges between nations that have institutionalized inequality.

This system in many cases quite literally plucks food from the hands of starving people, and it also indirectly deprives them of the ability to produce their own badly needed food. Millions of acres in Africa, Latin America, and Asia that are presently devoted to the satisfaction of the culturally prescribed "need" of the developed nations for chocolate, coffee, and tea might instead be converted to the production of food to satisfy local needs.

Anthropologists Daniel R. Gross and Barbara A. Underwood (1971) have shown how such trading patterns may be directly related to malnutrition in Brazil. Vast areas of the Brazilian northeast were converted from subsistence farms feeding peasants to large-scale sisal plantations on which the peasants became poorly paid laborers. The sisal plantations supplied twine to the United States, where it was used to tie bales of hay, which were in turn used to feed American cattle. Unfortunately, the former subsistence farmers whose lands were converted from food crops to an export crop found themselves unable to buy enough food on the market with their meager wages to satisfy the minimal nutritional needs of their families. Systematic malnutrition resulted as the peasants were forced to rely on cheap, high-calorie foods that were low in protein. Different permutations of the same situation have occurred throughout the world where the growing of cash crops for export, either to world or to national markets, has replaced food crops grown to satisfy the nutritional requirements of local peoples.

Such disparity between the nutritional needs of people and the distribution of food has no parallel in tribal culture. In fact, while food may circulate between local households according to need, it is very unusual for cultures not to be totally self-sufficient in their subsistence requirements. In a remarkably few cases, cultures are unable to satisfy their needs either because of periodic misfortunes or because of peculiarly limiting environmental factors. Food can then indeed be distributed through an "international" trade system that characteristically does *not* operate in terms of normal market principles that determine prices and profits (Sahlins 1972, chapter 6). The critical aspect of these systems is that exchange rates are socially prescribed and are not set by market competition. The obvious conclusion is that the market rationale is not a logical means of satisfying human nutritional needs.

In many cases, what can analytically be recognized as "international food aid" between nonstate societies is actually regulated by ideological aspects of the culture. For example, Australian aborigines can safely share unusually abundant resources with neighbors on ceremonial occasions, and can welcome temporary refugees from drought-stricken areas, because their elaborate system of clan totemism virtually guarantees that guests will return to their sacred home territories (Birdsell 1971). The rivalrous potlatch feasting characteristic of Northwest Coast chiefdoms may also indirectly help smooth out irregularities in resource availability, fish runs in this case, between groups (Suttles 1960). Tiny, isolated, coral atolls in Micronesia maintain long-distance contacts with other islands, including the large, high island of Yap, by means of an elaborately ritualized tribute hierarchy. In the event of drought or devastating typhoons, threatened islanders can always count on food aid or a temporary refuge (Alkire 1978).

In simple chiefdom societies, food consumption patterns may be related to rank. Certain foods may be consumed only by individuals occupying specific ranks as part of a system of sumptuary regulations, but this system is not strictly comparable to the present world food distribution system, which reflects the ranking of nations. In a simple chiefdom, individuals were not systematically deprived of their nutritional needs to support the inequity of the social system, but this is what now happens on a world scale. In 1965, Borgstrom computed agricultural self-sufficiency for various nations on the basis of their reliance on ghost acres and showed that poor Asian nations such as China and India were more than 90 percent self-sufficient, whereas the wealthy Western European nations such as England, the Netherlands, Belgium, and West Germany were only 37 to 60 percent self-sufficient. Clearly, these "developed" nations are being supported by a food system that could not long be sustained if world fisheries declined from overfishing and pollution, or if the world trade network were to collapse or be seriously modified.

There exists, in effect, an international series of trophic levels, in which the nations at the bottom are supported by high-calorie, low-protein diets and supply their high-protein resources to the nations at the upper levels. The upper nations are able to consume the highest quality animal protein and a wide array of very costly sumptuary foods imported from nations where these foods are economically inaccessible to the bulk of the population.

The continued expansion of the world trade and the proliferation of new food products in industrialized nations adds enormously to the energy costs of food, not only because of additional processing, but also because of the further requirements of storage and transportation. There are also diminishing energy returns due to increasing waste and losses. It is normally assumed that at least 10 percent of the food supplies of a given nation is lost annually to spoilage and pests before it even reaches consumers. This loss may be serious enough in a market system that moves food from one end of the country to the other through complex networks of intermediary wholesalers and retailers. It becomes critical in a system in which food may be shipped halfway around the world.

The Limits of Food Production

World leaders seem to be committed to increased food production as the perpetual solution to the Malthusian dilemma and have so far not given sufficient attention to the need to stabilize population growth and to restructure the food distribution system. More intensive subsistence technology has been one of the principal components of international proposals for dealing with the food problem for decades now. The famous "Point Four" program of technical assistance launched by the United States in 1949 made this a prime objective. Since then the United States has been heavily committed to speeding the diffusion of agricultural technology. Private foundations such as the Ford Foundation, Rockefeller Foundation, and the Kellogg Foundation have devoted millions of dollars since the 1950s to programs of agricultural extension and research designed to raise food production in underdeveloped countries. The United Nations Food and Agriculture Organization has been dedicated to increasing food production throughout the world since its inception. Agricultural development was a key element in UN proposals for the Second Development Decade (1970–80), and continues to be a central focus in the Fourth Development Decade (1980–1990). In 1969 the FAO unveiled its Indicative World Plan for agricultural development, which continues to form the basis for UN food strategy. The plan, as outlined in 1970 by Addeke H. Boerma, then FAO head, calls simply for "increasing productivity through more intensive use of physical resources and modern agricultural technology." Cereal production, because of its crucial dietary role, has been singled out for special attention. The plan also assumes continued economic growth to support the further development of technology and to help poor nations purchase the food imports they will still require even if agricultural development succeeds.

The strategy of intensifying production was pioneered by the Rockefeller foundation and Nobel Prize—winning plant scientist Norman Borlaug. It involves simply exporting the fossil-fuel-subsidized factory farm systems of the highly industrialized nations to the rest of the world. More specifically, it means applying biological engineering to the design of specialized plants that will respond with high yields to the application of large doses of chemical fertilizer, pesticides, and water, in the tropical setting where most of the hungry people are now located. "Miracle" plants have been designed through selective breeding that divert more of their energy into seed production and less into foliage, and that may permit multiple cropping. Such plants may give enormous yields, but in some cases the grain is of markedly reduced nutritional quality or possesses qualities that the target peoples find objectionable. These technical problems, however, are being solved.

This so-called Green Revolution was quickly hailed as an enormous success when per acre yields in many countries soared as these new techniques were applied in the late 1960s, and there were many optimistic statements about rapid doublings in food production and a final conquest over all of nature's limitations. Malthus, it seemed, had been refuted. Some of the most enthusiastic observers felt that the new problem of the disposal of crop *surpluses* would now replace famine as a worry for once-hungry nations:

> It is difficult to remember that only a few years ago there
> seemed to be a very serious prospect of starvation in Asia. Local
> agricultural yields seemed stationary while population was rapidly
> increasing. . . . Now only a decade later, the pendulum of
> anxiety has swung considerably. The apparent success of the
> Green Revolution, at least in cereal production, is beginning
> to raise doubts not about famine but about disposal of surpluses to
> national requirements. (Nulty 1972)

Many agricultural success stories have been cited as justification for renewed faith in the unlimited power of technology. Mexico, for example, was able to triple its wheat production and double its corn output within roughly 20 years after agricultural scientists financed by the Rockefeller Foundation began applying modern technology toward the development of miracle plants in 1944 (Fabun 1970).

Regardless of the outstanding successes, many problems have arisen in specific countries that have made implementation of the new technology difficult. Many agricultural extension workers have been frustrated by stubborn peasants who refused to believe that the new crops would really be an advantage for them because of their obvious vulnerability and the increased dependency on outsiders that they implied. There have also been serious problems in financing the new technology at both national and local levels. Small farmers cannot afford the investment in expensive seeds and chemicals, and neither can poor nations. As was noted earlier, this system ultimately depends on a vast fossil fuel subsidy that has seldom been readily available to poor countries. With recent price increases in petroleum on the world market, and energy crises even in the developed nations, these energy sources are now almost out of reach, and the Green Revolution may simply wither. Even if financing and the energy base were not a limiting factor, water availability and unfavorable weather conditions could be. Even unlimited energy would not solve all the problems involved in getting enough water to enough acres to support an unlimited Green Revolution. Some of the new technology may require so little labor that unemployment results and rural people are forced to move to the cities. It may also prove more successful if practiced on large land-holdings, and small farmers may be driven out. In some cases, transportation and storage facilities have not been adequate to handle either the increased crops or the needed fertilizer. High production may reduce prices below the profit margin, but the prices may still be higher than the poor can pay. Indeed, the social and economic barriers to intensification of food production may be so critical that the actual physical limits may never become a problem.

Many experts fear that the successes registered so far in the Green Revolution might be only temporary, and that serious reversals can occur as the biological liabilities of the new experimental crops begin to surface. It must be assumed that these plants will turn out to be highly susceptible to many new pests and blights or to minor fluctuations in weather. A further unknown is the extent of the ecological impact of industrial farming on a global scale. It is almost certain that further eutrophication will clog inland waters as fertilizer use increases and that pesticides will threaten marine food resources. With the full application of fossil-fuel-powered, factory-farm food production, humanity may be taking an irreversible step with implications fully as grave as when tribal hunters first turned to simple farming. Now, however, the price could be much higher.

Perhaps the most dramatic proof of the vulnerability of a strategy of subsistence intensification based on greater inputs of fossil fuel energy began with production disruptions and price increases initiated by the Organization of Petroleum Exporting Countries in 1973–74. Between 1972 and 1975 world oil prices increased approximately sixfold until they reached about $12 per barrel in 1975. This change set off price increases throughout the global economy and made it extremely difficult for developing countries to continue to intensify agricultural production by following the Green Revolution. By 1982 further oil price increases placed oil at $35 a barrel and created staggering problems for food production in poor countries. Military crises such as the Iran-Iraq war in the Persian Gulf region (through which much of the world's oil must flow) further increase the vulnerability of fossil fuel–based food production systems. Although there has been much talk of appropriate technology and striving for local self-sufficiency in food production as a development approach, dominant planning still calls for fossil fuel intensification.

6
THE POPULATION PROBLEM

The explosive growth of the human population is the most significant terrestrial event of the past million millennia. . . . No geological event in a billion years—not the emergence of mighty mountain ranges, nor the submergence of entire subcontinents, nor the occurrence of periodic glacial ages—has posed a threat to terrestrial life comparable to that of human overpopulation.

Paul Ehrlich and Anne Ehrlich, *Population, Resources, Environment*

It has been relatively easy for Americans and other members of the comfortably wealthy industrial nations to see overpopulation as the "root" of all the world's environmental problems, and of many of its other difficulties as well. Resource depletion, food shortages, and environmental deterioration, plus war and poverty, must all be caused by the presence of too many people in the world. Birth control and family planning programs are the obvious solutions. In 1968, biologist Paul Ehrlich presented this viewpoint dramatically in his book, *The Population Bomb*, which popularized the expression "population explosion," and focused wide attention on the problem and this particular cause. Ehrlich emphatically linked "too many people" together with "too little food" as the cause of hunger in underdeveloped countries and environmental troubles worldwide. On the latter issue, he declared: "The causal chain of the deterioration is easily followed to its source. Too many cars, too many factories, too much detergent, too much pesticide, multiplying contrails, inadequate sewage treatment plants, too little water, too much carbon dioxide—all can be traced easily to *too many people*" (Ehrlich 1968:67).

In 1972, Paul and Anne Ehrlich declared in "The Crisis," the first chapter of their human ecology textbook, that the population explosion was "the most significant terrestrial event of the past million millennia" and warned that it was suddenly bringing all life on earth to the edge of extinction (1972:1). Many other writers reject the notion that we are really in a *population* crisis and argue that if we simply achieve an equitable world distribution of wealth and full economic development, the earth can comfortably support many billions more people. Colin Clark even suggested that population growth itself will be the means of bringing further progress to underdeveloped peoples:

> It [population growth] brings economic hardship to communities
> living by traditional methods of agriculture; but it is the only force
> powerful enough to make such communities change their methods,
> and in the long run transforms them into much more advanced and
> productive societies. The world has immense physical resources for
> agricultural and mineral production still unused. In industrial
> communities, the beneficial economic effects of large and expanding
> markets are abundantly clear. (Clark 1968, preface)

Both of these extreme views are misleading. There can be little doubt that rapid population growth and the absolute level of population are important aspects of the environmental crisis, but the level of consumption is in many respects more critical. As we shall see, quality of life, or standard of living, must be considered in any attempt to assess carrying capacity for given environments. Population pressure is always relative to particular cultural conditions. Instead of treating population as *the* problem, we shall in this chapter examine it in broad cross-cultural and evolutionary perspective, and the present uncontrolled population growth will be seen as one symptom in a world dominated by the culture of consumption. Given present consumption patterns, it is equally misleading to deny the reality of the environmental crisis that accelerates with each increase in population or consumption. Global economic development may well be a false hope, both because it may be unattainable and because, if attained, it will only elevate consumption and cancel any environmental gains that may be achieved, even if world population can be stabilized before a collapse.

There is no disagreement on the basic fact that world population has grown enormously since the beginning of the industrial era, and that virtually uncontrolled growth continues in much of the world. It is also generally recognized that present growth patterns cannot continue indefinitely. Paul Ehrlich calculated in 1968 that, given a doubling time of 37 years, which was the estimated world rate at that time, there would be 60 million billion people, or 100 persons per square yard over the entire surface of the earth within just 900 years. Isaac Asimov estimated in 1971 that at growth rates prevailing at that time, the human population would equal the mass of the globe within 1,560 years; and within 4,856 years, it would equal the mass of the universe. The real question is obviously not whether growth will continue, but rather when and how it will stop. Estimates of the maximum feasible global population range from below to double the present level of approximately 4 billion, while some super-optimists feel that we might accommodate well over 100 billion. Predictions of global population based on conditions in the late sixties warned that there could be 8 billion people in the world by A.D. 2000. However, the actual rate of increase has been slightly lower. The *Global 2000* study (Barney 1980, vol. 2:10–11) relies on the "medium" population projections of the U.S. Census Bureau for a global population of 6.3 billion by the year 2000. This modest prediction assumes continuous social and economic progress throughout the world, following established patterns.

A major assumption concerning the origin of the population problem, which is at the base of much current policymaking, is that the rapid growth now experienced by the underdeveloped world is simply the result of the combination of traditionally high fertility rates with the sudden lowering of traditionally high mortality rates that has accompanied incomplete modernization. It is usually felt that a value lag relating to family size has somehow not caught up with the drop in mortality, and that futher economic development and education will correct the situation, as they have in the developed nations. This interpretation is based on a number of conclusions about tribal demographic conditions that have been shown to be untenable by recent anthropological research, as will be shown directly.

Population Pressure, Carrying Capacity, and Optimum Population

It makes little sense to speak of overpopulation and the need to halt growth if there is no discussion of carrying capacity, optimum population size, and what constitutes population pressure. Surprisingly, these topics are often completely ignored in population programs, even though they must be at least implicit in any attempt to regulate population or set demographic goals. This failure to deal adequately with these aspects of the population problem is perhaps understandable when it is realized that they are culturally and environmentally *relative* concepts and directly involve the most basic characteristics of any culture.

An optimum population would exist at what Hassan (1981:167) has called the optimum carrying capacity for its technology and environment—that is, the level of population that could safely maintain itself over several generations without drastic crashes as the resource base fluctuates. This is precisely where a population concerned with minimizing subsistence risk (Gould 1981; Hayden 1981a) would find itself. Tribal cultures are designed to satisfy basic human needs on a long-term basis, so they will always attempt to maintain themselves at optimum population levels.

Population pressure is a widely discussed component of the population problem and is frequently assumed to be some readily apparent, absolute quality: But on closer analysis, it proves, like carrying capacity, to be neither easily recognized nor absolute. As Cowgill (1975), Hassan (1981), and others point out, population pressure can not be profitably treated in isolation from other cultural, demographic, and environmental factors. The problem with the concept of population pressure is that it places undue emphasis on population, although the real issue is how to maintain a balance between the total human demand for resources in a given area and the sustainable supply, given a certain technology. In fact, population pressure is culturally defined and can only be relative to particular technological systems, environments, and per capita consumption levels. In traditional New Guinea cultures, population pressure has been found to occur only rarely in an absolute sense, but may be frequently manifest as a *local* imbalance between people and land experienced by particular local clans (Kelly 1968). Local imbalances may occur even when the total population is stable simply because random demographic processes, including variation in the sex ratio, birthrates, and mortality, may, under different cultural circumstances, have widely varying impacts on local groups of different size. As a result, certain clans may outgrow their land base while neighboring clans dwindle to extinction. Many cultural devices are employed to relieve this pressure of population on land resources, including transfers of land and people between clans through gifts, adoption, and warfare. Where population pressure is not compensated for by normal redistributive measures, it may be felt as a steady reduction in the culturally defined standard of living in which people are forced to work longer hours to increase food production. Eventually, there may be a switch to less desirable food sources (Bayless-Smith 1974), or a move to marginal ecological zones (Zubrow 1975). Thus, "absolute" population pressure might be relieved by simply redefining what the members of a culture consider an acceptable standard of living, by technological innovation, or by a reduction in population.

Population redistribution has sometimes been developed to a high degree, particularly in island cultures in which adoption is widely used, but it can be only a temporary solution. Resource distribution may help raise regional carrying capacity by evening out local surpluses or seasonal fluctuations; but in many cases, elaborate redistribution systems are dependent on formal political offices and thus can only occur at certain levels of social integration. Migration to relieve population pressure is probably a normal response that occurs automatically whenever ecologically similar territory is readily available for occupation.[*]

The final option, population control, has been followed by virtually all tribal cultures to some degree. Tribal hunting cultures have followed this course almost exclusively and achieved remarkably stable populations. Cultivators have often established equilibrium systems as well balanced as those of the hunters, but have far more often slipped into subsistence intensification and predatory expansion against their neighbors as their populations have gradually increased.

Population Control Among Tribal Hunters

Whereas many demographers believe that the human population has grown at a slow and steady rate from the very beginning to the origins of agriculture, recent anthropological research suggests that the thousands of years before domestication were characterized by population *equilibrium*, punctuated by only occasional and unusual growth phases. By the eve of the transition to settled farm life, the human population had grown to an estimated 8–9 million over a time span of perhaps 3 million years (Hassan 1981:199).[**] Much of this increase represented expansion into empty lands. Only very slight local increases in density occurred prior to the introduction of agriculture. As a general principle, it can be assumed that tribal cultures quickly established a culturally regulated equilibrium as soon as their populations had grown to a culturally defined carrying capacity within specific territories.

It is apparent that *cultural* factors, and not food shortages or high mortality rates, were the primary factors in setting limits to population

---

[*]See Dumond (1972) for discussion of responses to population growth.
[**]See Deevy (1960); Coale (1974); and Hassan (1981:193–208) for general discussion of global population history.

growth in tribal cultures. * This is a particularly significant point, because it is still widely believed that tribal or traditional cultures were characterized by uniform high fertility and high mortality rates and a precarious food supply, but such was decidedly not the case. Tribal cultures were generally stabilized at a level considerably below the maximum population densities that their technology and environment might potentially have sustained. Even Paleolithic hunters, if they had chosen to work harder and had adjusted their food preferences away from big game toward a concentration on small mammals, might have increased their population densities many times over. This is of course precisely what happened during the Mesolithic period. It is also likely that real famines were very rare during the Paleolithic period; and while the availability of game certainly did influence population densities, food shortages per se definitely appear not to have been the primary factor limiting population growth.

There is overwhelming evidence to suggest that mortality was also not a significant limiting factor for hunters. Deaths due to epidemic disease were apparently far lower before the establishment of permanent villages than at any time thereafter. Tribal hunting peoples were consistently well nourished, they led physically very active lives, and they apparently avoided most infectious epidemic diseases by maintaining their populations dispersed so that these diseases could not become established and spread. Hunters may also have developed high levels of natural immunity thanks to strong selective pressure enforced by relatively high infant mortality rates and constant exposure to endemic pathogens. Deaths due to warfare were probably very infrequent during the many thousands of years that humans lived as hunters, and homicide and suicide are both decidedly uncommon among undisturbed hunting peoples. The probable occurrence of accidental deaths is more difficult to evaluate, but it seems reasonable to assume that they were not a major factor. Demographic data based on age estimates of selected prehistoric skeletal populations and modern ethnographic data reveal that hunter-gatherers at age 15 could expect to live an average of 26 additional years. This is

*I have drawn heavily on the surveys of Polgar (1972) and Hassan (1981) for supportive data. It should be borne in mind that all estimates of prehistoric population levels are subject to considerable error.

of course about half the figure for peoples in industrialized nations today, but it is roughly the same as life expectancy at age 15 in 13th-century England and higher than has been described for some Neolithic populations (Hassan 1981:118).

Tribal cultures held in reserve an enormous potential for rapid population growth, which was activated only under special conditions. Even if mortality rates as high as 50 percent to age 15 are assumed to have been typical for hunting and gathering peoples (half of the population dying before reaching reproductive age)—and this is by no means easily demonstrated (Weiss 1973)—it still would have been easily possible for the population to have doubled each generation if high fertility was culturally encouraged. Such rapid growth probably did occur at times, but was only a regular pattern when previously unoccupied territory was first entered or when a population was recovering from some natural disaster. In the New World, for example, people were well established in North America by 10,000 B.C. and were settled in the far south of South America by 9,000 B.C. Such rapid spread could hardly have been achieved by cultures that were barely keeping ahead of extinction.

The full significance of this new picture of the demography of early hunters can perhaps best be appreciated if it is contrasted with the grim view presented by modern demographers in their attempts to describe the history of population growth and the origin of our present dilemma. Paul Ehrlich (1968:29), for example, in *The Population Bomb*, states that "our ancestors were fighting a continual battle to keep the birth rate ahead of the death rate." The distinguished demographer Donald T. Bogue summarizes this period in his major textbook, *Principles of Demography*, as follows:

> During the many thousands of years of man's existence on the earth before the beginning of civilization, the population problem facing most communities was that of survival—to offset successfully the terrible attrition of death on their numbers. . . . When population did manage to grow, there was always the threat of famine, war, and epidemics. Such a situation is the only conjecture that is consistent with the facts. . . . We are forced, therefore, to conclude that the human race has been required by circumstances of high mortality to reproduce at near-biological capacity and that a whole system of

fertility-promoting practices has evolved as an integral part of every culture. (Bogue 1969:53-54)

In fact, precisely the opposite situation now appears to have been the case, and the problem that remains is to outline precisely what fertility-*dampening* practices maintained tribal populations in equilibrium.

Among hunters, density limits seem to have been set by the availability of culturally recognized food sources and by the lack of formal political structures to deal with conflict. Small local bands of 20–30 people were apparently the most efficient hunting and gathering groups. Fewer people would have difficulty feeding themselves because of random accidents and runs of bad luck, whereas larger groups would experience diminishing returns as local resources were depleted too quickly. Expansion of subsistence through intensified collecting or domestication was apparently rejected as a solution far more often than not, and seems to have been a course that was only reluctantly followed in the face of environmental changes. Migration certainly occurred among hunters, but only rarely at the expense of other groups already firmly in possession of their territories. Perhaps most critical was the fact that there was no culturally encouraged reason for increasing population density beyond a certain level. Birth spacing by means of abortion and infanticide seem to have been the primary mechanisms of fertility regulation.

Infanticide has received much attention as the basic method of population control among hunter-gatherers, but this is a complex issue and many questions remain unanswered. Some writers argue that baby girls were killed so that boys could be raised to become warriors or hunters (Riches 1974; Divale and Harris 1976). However, computer simulations suggest that selective female infanticide could never have been very common, because it would easily cause an irreversible decline in a small population (Schrire and Steiger 1974). It has also been argued that detailed census data provides no real evidence for female infanticide (Yengoyan 1981). Furthermore, both the actual rates and individual motives for even general infanticide are not well recognized. Birdsell (1979) suggests that 15–30 percent of births in aboriginal Australia ended in infanticide, but convincing supporting evidence has not been provided and is unlikely ever to be obtained. Some authors offer antagonism between the sexes as an important motivation for infanticide (Freeman

1971; Cowlishaw 1978), but it seems more likely that it occurs primarily as a birth-spacing mechanism when a woman realizes that attempting to raise a new baby might threaten the welfare of her older child.

It has been assumed that women in nomadic hunting societies were forced to space their children approximately four years apart because of the difficulty of carrying two dependent children on daily foraging expeditions and on the frequent moves to new camps (Sussman 1972). This may be a critical consideration motivating, or at least rationalizing, the family planning decisions of individual women; but if it were an absolute necessity, it would be difficult to explain the rapid growth known to have occurred when virgin territories were occupied. Whatever the motivation for such spacing, and regardless of the methods employed, it will yield a stationary, no-growth population, assuming that an average woman attempts to raise four children and that half of them survive to reproduce.

Population Equilibrium in Aboriginal Australia

One of the most outstanding and best-documented examples of the maintenance of population balance by tribal hunting cultures is presented in J.B. Birdsell's analysis of Australian aborigines, based on 25 years of intensive research. According to Birdsell's (1953, 1971, 1979) findings, Australia supported a constant population of 300,000 aborigines, the maximum that could be supported by a hunting and gathering technology, for perhaps 30,000 years, with only minor fluctuations related to overall changes in the environment. They were not constantly tottering on the edge of disaster, with their numbers held in check by high mortality rates, and they did not continually outstrip their meager resources only to crash precipitously and later rebound. In contrast, the industrial culture now controlling Australia has grown to 13 million in barely 200 years, and shows no indication of being in equilibrium.

The forces that maintained constant population levels involved not only environmental factors, but also included culturally defined territorial spacing mechanisms. Australian cultures were organized into linguistically distinct tribal groups averaging 500 people, which were in turn divided into bands of 25 people composed of families of 5 persons. Tribal territories were large enough to provide a reliable subsistence base for the population roughly 98 percent of the time, while individual band territories might be somewhat less self-sufficient so that resources from neighboring bands might be needed in 10 or 15 out of every 100 years. Band territories were carefully laid out to ensure that they allowed access to all critical food resources in sufficient quantity for long-range survival. In some coastal regions where a tribal territory included several diverse ecological zones with different resource potentials, each band territory would include portions of each zone. Interband and intertribal ceremonies normally occurred in times of plenty and helped distribute seasonal or random concentrations of food and equalized resources, and thus helped bring population densities closer to the maximum carrying capacity. Bands in drought-stricken areas might be temporarily taken in by more comfortably situated neighbors. Individuals were so emotionally attached to the sacred sites within their traditional territories that represented their totemic origin points that there was no danger that they would ever choose to remain permanently in their refuge. Boundaries were also clearly defined by the wanderings of spirit beings, which were recorded in myths and commemorated in intergroup ceremonies. The religious and ceremonial system played a vital role in supporting population balances through boundary maintenance and resource redistribution.

The upper limit for tribal population was set by the density of the communication network that could be supported by hunters and gatherers restricted to foot travel. As tribes grew larger, it became more difficult for the bands within them to remain in contact. When more bands appeared, the frequency, intensity, and length of interactions such as joint ceremonies and intermarriage declined, and linguistic diversity increased, making further communication more difficult. Tribes that grew too small, that lost bands, until they numbered under 500, would automatically interact more with bands in neighboring tribes until they were absorbed into them. Bands needed to include at least 25 people to maximize the availability of food, given random variations in hunting success; to provide task groups of optimum size; to ensure demographic viability, given sex fluctuations in births; to defend themselves; and to ensure a large enough pool of marriageable individuals to meet the cultural requirements of band exogamy. Upper limits to band size were apparently set by the lack of strong political controls, which meant that the increased conflicts arising with denser population could only be adequately controlled by fissioning, and by the need to minimize the strain on local ecosystems. Random fluctuation in local band size was regulated through selective infanticide, adoption, and transfers of people in "violation" of normal residence and exogamic norms. Local boundaries were also adjusted by means of occasional duels and skirmishes.

Actual tribal densities varied from lows of perhaps 80 square miles per person in the interior deserts, where rainfall might drop to a mean of only 4 inches per year, to densities as high as 2 square miles per person in rich coastal or riverine environments. Optimum carrying capacity for tribal territories remained within 10 to 20 percent of the maximum density that could be supported in the best years, thanks to the cultural mechanisms that helped level out the long-range fluctuations in resources due to droughts and other unpredictable events.

It is uncertain what means of birth spacing were most common, but it is clear that infanticide was often practiced by Australians; abortion and contraception may also have been important spacing mechanisms. It is important to note in this context that the distinction between abortion and infanticide may not be culturally meaningful. Some tribes may induce labor in the third trimester of pregnancy and then kill the fetus if it survives. "Birth" itself, and "humanness," may be culturally defined at a quite different point than that normally recognized by state legal systems (Neel 1968).

It is apparent from the data that Birdsell presents that a system of density equilibrium was indeed operating among Australian tribes and bands. The primary density determinant seems to have been environmental, as reflected by a statistically significant inverse relationship between rainfall and size of tribal territory. Deviation from this relationship can be accounted for by the presence of extra water and consequently greater biological productivity in riverine or coastal regions, where carrying capacity is higher than would be expected otherwise. Further evidence can be seen in the fact that large tribes were in the process of splitting into smaller tribes of 500 members when they were first contacted by Europeans. It has also been shown that tribes that were initially fragmented by the acquisition of new initiation ceremonies quickly returned to their original size after the diffusion wave had passed.

The Neolithic Population Explosion

The relatively rapid growth in population that accompanied and perhaps contributed to the adoption of farming is one of the most significant demographic events in human history. It marked the end of the long period of successful population equilibrium that hunting peoples established and initiated a period of almost continuous population growth and a rapid series of interrelated changes that led successively to urbanization, the state, and industrial civilization. It has been estimated that world population suddenly jumped from approximately 8 million in 8000 B.C. to 86 million by 4000 B.C., a tenfold increase (Deevy 1960; Polgar 1972; Coale 1974; Hassan 1981). The fourfold increase related to industrialization between 1650 and 1950 seems relatively minor in comparison, although this later increase did of course occur over a much shorter time period. The scale of the Neolithic expansion is even more dramatic in specific countries. France, for example (Nougier 1954), experienced a hundredfold population increase by 3000 B.C. over densities obtaining during the Upper Paleolithic period, and only a tenfold increase between 3000 B.C. and the 20th century.

Explaining the breakdown of "Paleolithic" population equilibrium mechanisms must surely be one of the most critical theoretical problems in anthropology. Unfortunately, this question has only recently been posed. Some writers see it as a result of sedentary living, which reduced the need to space births; others see the increase in the food supply made possible by agriculture as a key factor. Both of these explanations have serious problems, however.

It is quite reasonable to assume that hunters spaced births to protect the health of mother and child as well as because of the mobility problem, and thus the practice might have been continued even after sedentarization. It is well known that many settled village peoples space births four years apart, or even longer, for precisely this reason. Particularly where protein is not widely available, prolonged nursing can be very important to the health of the infant; and where women are heavily involved in agricultural labor, continual pregnancies would be an increased burden.

Increases in food production in a given region, as discussed earlier, are perhaps more likely to be *results* rather than *causes* of imbalances in the resources/population equation. Randal A. Sengel (1973) has suggested a rather novel solution to this vexing problem. He argues that in the Near East an increased reliance on wild grains, ultimately caused by climatic changes that increased their prevalence, may well have resulted in a significant augmentation of the protein intake of the population, which in turn lowered the age of menarche and increased the reproductive span of the women. Empirical evidence from Europe indicates that nutritional improvement has apparently had that effect in modern times, and it is by no means certain that the age of menarche is a constant in all human populations. Some writers, however, suggest that the domestication process resulted in the displacement of wild plant foods, which were richer in protein, so the question is by no means settled (Flannery 1969).

It *is* clear that even a slight increase in the reproductive span could result in a gradual population growth even if the original pattern of birth spacing were retained. It might be assumed that such increased growth would quickly be recognized and the birth-spacing mechanism would be adjusted to restore equilibrium. However, it is not obvious that population control in tribal cultures was really carried out with long-range social goals in mind; rather, individual women made "family planning" decisions that were for their immediate self-interest, and in the aggregate these decisions proved to be highly adaptive for the entire culture.

Although these demographic changes, whatever their causes, were in the long run revolutionary in impact, they were so slow that, like the domestication process, they would have been imperceptible to the actors. In the Near East, for example, the population may have grown from 100,000 in 8000 B.C. to 2.5 to 12 million by 4000 B.C., with an annual growth rate of only 0.08-0.12 percent (Carneiro and Hilse 1966). At such gradual rates a tribe of 500 people would add only about 12 people in a generation.

Population Control Among Tribal Village Farmers

Population growth was a much more difficult force to contain for sedentary or semisedentary cultures based on domesticated, and thus inherently more elastic, food sources. Tribal farmers certainly have in many cases achieved remarkable population equilibrium, as will be shown in the following sections. But in general, domestication touched off a period of great cultural instability in the world. Suddenly, expanding cultures pushed hunters out of the most fertile lands only in turn to be themselves incorporated into expanding conquest states, and ultimately into an expanding industrial civilization. Hunters, newly transformed into farmers, found their resource bases increasingly inadequate for the support of their growing populations and were forced into more difficult environments or into cultural transformations that they might not otherwise have chosen. In some cases, growing populations simply expanded beyond the carrying capacity of their environments and collapsed without the development of complex political systems or "advanced" technology.

The American Southwest affords an example of this latter outcome. From approximately 7000 B.C. to A.D. 100, that area was occupied by hunters and seed collectors of the so-called "desert tradition," which must have constituted a relatively stable adaptation. Toward the end of that period, domesticated plants from Mesoamerica were gradually adopted; and by A.D. 400, farming villages were becoming established.

Through intensive analysis of the archaeological record in one small valley in Arizona, Ezra B. Zubrow (1975) has reconstructed 1,400 years of population history from the beginnings of domestication up to A.D. 1400. His study shows a steady increase in population within the valley and a continual expansion into more marginal environments as the carrying capacity in the most favorable zones was reached. The population peaked shortly after irrigation was introduced in approximately A.D. 1000, and then began to decline as pressure on the resource base and a change in the rainfall pattern beginning in A.D. 1150 drastically lowered the carrying capacity of the valley. Population densities plunged rapidly between A.D. 1100 and A.D. 1200 to a small fraction of the peak, and by A.D. 1400 the valley was abandoned completely. Thus a culture of village farmers that was unable to establish a population equilibrium expanded for perhaps 700 years and then totally collapsed. This record stands in striking contrast to the 7,000 years of success that hunters and gatherers enjoyed in the same general environment.

There are many other examples in the archaeological and ethnographic record of village farmers who were able to support their population growth by pushing out their neighbors. Neolithic farmers moved steadily out of the Middle East and spread throughout Europe from 8000 B.C. to 5000 B.C. The fate of the prior hunting peoples is uncertain. Although some may have adopted farming or been incorporated into the invading culture, it seems more reasonable to guess that they resisted the change and simply moved into marginal environments and gradually declined. In East and South Africa, Bantu farmers and herders were still expanding into territory occupied by the Bushmen and other hunters when the Dutch began to settle South Africa in the 17th century. Their growth was not halted until the militaristic Zulu empire was finally overwhelmed by the British army in the late 19th century. Marshall Sahlins (1961) has shown how growing African tribal cultures such as the Nuer and Tiv have utilized their segmentary lineage systems as a means of mobilizing on their boundaries, in the absence of formal political leadership, to expand their territory against weak neighbors.

In South America, it is assumed by some investigators that village farmers were well established in the central Amazon Basin, utilizing manioc as their primary staple, by 3000 B.C. (Lathrap 1970). Almost from that point on, the evidence indicates that a continuous period of population growth, migration, displacement, and differentiation of cultures began that continued into modern times. Equilibrium cultures, or those with relatively small, slow-growing populations, were simply pushed up the smaller tributaries, and finally into the interfluvial hinterlands, by successive migration waves from the expanding centers. Among the best known historically of these expanding Amazonian village farmers were the Tupi. They, like the Zulus in Africa, were still spreading south and east up the Amazon and even down the Brazilian coast, pushing aside prior hunters and more stable farmers, when the Spanish and Portuguese arrived in the 16th century.

Chronic warfare and head-hunting recorded for shifting cultivators in many other parts of the world, including New Zealand and Southeast Asia, may also be viewed as responses to a failure to maintain population equilibrium. The Ibans in Borneo were actively expanding against their neighbors, some of whom were hunters, in the late 19th and well into the 20th century. Traditionally oriented hill tribes in northwestern Thailand in the 1960s were growing rapidly, but maintained their cultures intact without warfare by crowding out neighbors and through high rates of migration into lowland areas, where excess population was absorbed into other ethnic groups (Kunstadter 1971).

In spite of these examples of population growth among village farmers, considering the time periods involved, it is apparent that very few such cultures reproduced at the maximum rate for more than a very brief time. Cultural regulation of population growth certainly continued to be a very significant factor even after domestication began. As with hunters, fertility control was probably the most important regulating mechanism for village farmers, although increased mortality through warfare was sometimes an additional control. Abortion, infanticide, contraception, and birth spacing remained the primary means of limiting fertility, although many specific cultural practices that limited the frequency of coitus, or shortened the fertile period by delaying marriage, also became important.

One of the most common birth-spacing practices is the long postpartum taboo on sexual intercourse that occurs widely among shifting cultivators in tropical climates. The taboo often extends for more than a year after the birth of each child and has been shown to be related to reduced fertility rates in cultures that practice it. The taboo correlates with a number of other cultural practices, and elaborate causal explanations for its occurrence have been proposed (Saucier 1972). It is quite possible that this is not always practiced as an intentional means of birth spacing; but whatever its "cause," it does serve as a critical check on fertility.

The Tsembaga Equilibrium Model

The Tsembaga of New Guinea offer a well-researched example of a horticultural tribe with a complex system of cultural regulation that prevents population pressure on the land from increasing to the point at which famine, technological innovation, or migration would become necessary. The Tsembaga system has been described in detail by anthropologist Roy Rappaport (1968) in his monograph *Pigs for the Ancestors,* and his data have been reduced to a computer simulation model by systems researchers Steven B. Shantzis and William W. Behrens III (1973) of the Massachusetts Institute of Technology. The critical component of the system is the growth of the pig herd to a point that triggers a ritual cycle involving warfare and pig slaughters, which balance both human and animal populations.

A growing pig herd is highly desirable, because pigs are important as status symbols and as sources of high-quality animal protein; but a pig consumes as much of the cultivated crops as an average adult, and the herd quickly becomes more bother than it is worth. A growing pig herd means that people must devote a larger and larger proportion of the cultivated land to raising pig feed, and greater labor efforts must be expended per capita to tending pigs and gardens. Increases in both the human and the pig populations cause a sharp rise in internal conflicts, not only as competition for resources increases, but also because the pigs themselves are a perpetual source of disputes. When these disturbances become intolerable, a ceremonial pig slaughter is held.

In a pig feast, which Rappaport (1968) observed in 1963, the Tsembaga pig herd was reduced from 169 animals to 60, and new garden plots were reduced by more than a third below what had been required earlier to support the full herd.

In the simulation model constructed by Shantzis and Behrens (1973), the human population maintains itself indefinitely, fluctuating in 11-year cycles between approximately 220 and 230 persons, while the pig herd fluctuates between 60 and 145 (see Figure 6-1). Both populations remain in dynamic balance well below the point at which destructive shortening of the fallow cycle would become necessary. The slight increase in normal human fertility rates that might result from the intervention of modern medicine would, if not compensated for by other cultural controls, reduce the ritual cycle to 10 years and shift population levels much closer to the critical carrying capacity. If new health programs were to raise the annual population growth rate from 1.3 to 2.0 percent a year, the control mechanisms would quickly break down, and the human population would peak at over 400 within 120 years and would then quickly plunge to nearly zero. A permanent peace would have a very similar catastrophic impact. It seems clear that as government control is extended over the area, bringing both peace and new medical technology, the Tsembaga will sacrifice long-run stability for short-run gains and will face very serious problems in only two or three generations.

If we assume that the Tsembaga kept no pig herds, held no festivals or wars, practiced no population control through infanticide or contra-

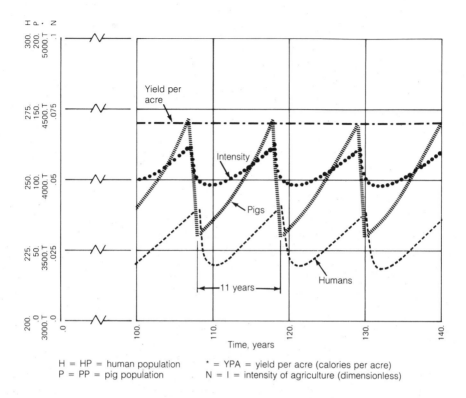

H = HP = human population   * = YPA = yield per acre (calories per acre)
P = PP = pig population   N = I = intensity of agriculture (dimensionless)

F I G U R E 6 - 1 The Tsembaga Model.

Source: Steven B. Shantzis and William W. Behrens III, "Population Control Mechanisms in a Primitive Agricultural Society," in *Toward Global Equilibrium*, edited by D. H. Meadows and D. L. Meadows (Cambridge, Mass.: Wright-Allen Press, 1973) 275.

ception, and experienced no migration, the dynamics of their population might be expected to be far different from that described above. Shantzis and Behrens have constructed a computer simulation of just such a case that dramatically illustrates the inherent imbalances that would arise. Under such conditions, population growth would be constrained only by the availability of land and productivity per acre. Given a slow rate of uncontrolled population growth based on average fertility and life expectancy rates drawn from United Nations estimates for similar peoples, and starting with only 196 people and 972 acres of potentially arable land, it quickly becomes necessary to shorten the 15-year fallow period to put more land into production to feed the growing population. Within less than 60 years, this intensification of food production surpasses the carrying capacity and initiates a continuous decline in yields per acre, reflecting a progressive degradation of the land. Within approximately 80 years, the population would peak and then suddenly plunge to near zero as a result of famines and an almost total decline in soil fertility. This, of course, assumes no technological innovation to increase per acre yields. It seems obvious that under these conditions the Tsembaga would recognize the declining yields within 2 or 3 years and would be confronted with the choice of either reducing population growth or technological innovation to prevent the collapse that would be barely three generations away.

Rappaport's original account of the Tsembaga equilibrium model has touched off a lively debate among anthropologists. Some critics argue that the model is based on simple functionalism and cannot explain how the system came about—that is, Rappaport describes how the system works, or could work, but does not account for how it got that way (Rappaport 1979). Others argue that environmental limits are not really operating; rather, political factors overshadow ritual regulation (Friedman 1974). Some writers also suggest that the pig-feasting system originated and persisted as a means of rewarding military allies (Peoples 1982). More detailed computer simulations indicate that the demographic impact of intergroup conflict was probably overemphasized (Samuels 1982). The Tsembaga model is of course highly idealized, and no empirical data exist to suggest that it has operated as described for any length of time in the past. What is important, however, is how the system could operate. It certainly illustrates the complexities of the interconnecting cultural variables that relate human populations to their resource bases.

The Havasupai Indians

Well-documented cases demonstrating population equilibrium in tribal populations and the mechanisms involved are not common because normally historical depth is absent from the anthropological record. However, the Havasupai Indians of Arizona have been shown historically to have maintained a relative population equilibrium for at least 200 years (Alvarado 1970). Since the first census of this small tribe of farmers and hunters in their Grand Canyon home in 1776 up to the present, their population has fluctuated between a low of 166 (due to a measles epidemic) to a high of 300. The present rise to 350 has only occurred as outside intervention has increased over the past 40 years.

Such stability, in spite of abundant food resources, led anthropologist Anita L. Alvarado to investigate possible explanations, and it was determined that cultural factors limiting fertility have been largely responsible. Among these cultural factors are an imbalanced sex ratio with a preponderance of males, probably due to selective female infanticide, and a significant delay in first marriages. Women traditionally did not marry until age 25–30, and men not until 35–40. The combined effect of these customs is to reduce fertility by not only reducing the number of years when a given woman would be a pregnancy risk, but also by structuring it so that men would be married during their least fertile adult years. The Havasupai also tolerated a rather high proportion of unmarried, widowed, and divorced individuals, who would otherwise have been marriageable. Furthermore, they made use of herbal contraceptives and abortion, and nursed their babies for approximately two years, thereby undoubtedly delaying the resumption of ovulation. Extensive use of the steam bath by the males, followed by a dip in very cold water, might well have been an important spermicide. It is known that the testes produce viable sperm only within a very narrow temperature range, and that extremes can produce temporary sterility. Mortality rates do not appear to have been significantly high aboriginally. Warfare was virtually unknown, and the people were apparently exceptionally healthy.

Island Population Problems

Perhaps the severest test of their ability to regulate population growth that tribal cultures have faced has been the problem of maintaining equilibrium on the small islands and coral atolls of the Pacific. Certainly, cultures with such restricted land bases would run up against physical limits to population expansion much more quickly than would cultures in continental areas.

The general adjustment process to island environments has been outlined in a theoretical model by Tim Bayliss-Smith (1974) that recognizes three phases of population growth and cultural response. Following the initial settling of an island, there may be rapid expansion and an extensive—i.e., low labor input—subsistence system, which continues until the available land base is filled. Intensification of the food production system may then follow, with greater labor inputs and new technology, or "lower" dietary standards may be introduced. Finally, emigration and direct cultural controls on population growth become necessary. Many of these islands have been settled for a very long time; much of Micronesia, for example, may have been occupied for a thousand years, and the maximum practical limits of technological intensification in food production must have been reached very early, so that this solution would have been quickly exhausted. Actually, many of the coral atolls required an extremely high degree of technological development before *any* kind of gardening could have been established because of the absence of soil and the shortage of fresh water.

In practice, various cultural controls helped maintain population well below any theoretical maximum carrying capacity based on the ultimate limits of food production. In the Polynesian outlier atolls, the critical population ceiling seems to have been set by the environmental limits to taro production. Taro was a daily element in the diet and a prime measure of the overall adequacy of the food supply. If cultural preferences were not a factor, then presumably these cultures might have simply switched to crops that provided more calories per acre or per unit of labor, such as coconuts, and supported even denser populations. However, it appears that the ideal was for taro to supply approximately 50 percent of the caloric intake, and it was culturally intolerable for it to drop below 25 percent. Coconuts were not expected to constitute more than 25 percent of the diet. Population pressure was clearly present to the extent that the proportions of these critical foods deviated from the cultural ideals. A further form of cultural control of carrying capacity was the planting of nonsubsistence crops, such as ritually important turmeric, which displaced food crops, and the social and ceremonial stress placed on certain marine resources.

Various social and political adjustments helped maximize available resources while minimizing possible ecological stresses to the food systems from overuse. For example, higher levels of social stratification, in which political leaders were given authority to regulate production and distribution of food, seem to have arisen in both Micronesia and Polynesia wherever resources were sufficient to support such developments. Shortages of food and "overpopulation" here, as in the New Guinea example, were in effect treated as problems of allocation; but in this case, they were critical enough that political authority was needed to solve them. Other social mechanisms for allocating people to land, and vice versa, were also widely employed. For example, cognatic descent systems, which were common in the Pacific, were easily manipulated to relieve local pressures. Adoption was also widely practiced; in some Micronesian islands, as many as half of all children were actually adopted (Knudson 1970).

At the interisland level, various cultural practices helped relieve local problems and permitted larger densities than might have otherwise been possible, in much the same manner as intertribal relations in aboriginal Australia. For example, if typhoons temporarily destroyed the food resources of a particular atoll, the residents might be temporarily taken in by the residents of unaffected high islands, or they might be sent emergency food. Likewise, if a critical imbalance in the sex ratio developed, individuals might be exported or imported as needed.

Virtually the entire range of fertility control mechanisms were practiced by Pacific island cultures. In Micronesia a woman was often restricted to no more than three children; and abortion, infanticide, coitus interruptus, and frequent periods of ritual celibacy all occurred. In Tikopia (Firth 1957), in addition to these controls, complete celibacy was sometimes required of the younger males in a family if productive land was not available. These unmarried men often set out on overseas voyages and never returned, although if they remained, extramarital access to women was not denied them. When population pressures became intolerable on Tikopia, an entire clan or other social segment was simply driven away, although that was a very rare event. Raymond Firth's conclusion for Tikopia is probably generally applicable for the Pacific as a whole before European intervention: "It can be safely said that until recent years the population of Tikopia was normally in a state of equilibrium with its food supply" (Firth 1957:414).

The State Intervenes

When tribal populations came under the influence of industrial states, three things drastically modified the demographic picture. In the first place, the traditional population control mechanisms invariably dropped out. The disappearance of these control measures may be due to deliberate pressures aimed at eliminating them, as when missionaries halt abortion and infanticide, or when the government forbids warfare, or many important regulating practices may simply be abandoned as other practices that support them are modified. For example, the traditional religious system provides essential support for the postpartum taboo and a variety of other ceremonial regulations. If the Tsembaga were converted to Christianity, they might voluntarily abandon pig sacrifices, and many of their control mechanisms would collapse. Even if no other modifications in the culture occurred, the elimination of traditional population controls would be certain to lead to rapid population growth.

The state has also provided positive incentives for population growth with its policies designed to extract as many resources from former tribal areas as possible for the smallest capital investment. Labor-intensive agricultural systems, which provide cash crops for export or to pay taxes, generally created a situation in which a large family was more advantageous for a peasant farmer than a small one. Extra children would contribute more to the labor force than their maintenance cost, at least until the limits of labor intensification were exceeded. Clifford Geertz (1963) provides a well-documented case example of such a situation from Java.

The third effect of state intervention—the modification of traditional mortality rates—has received the most attention as the principal cause of the population explosion, but it is unlikely to be the most important factor. During the early phase of state intervention with tribal cultures, mortality rates are typically elevated because of violence and the disruption of cultural change. In many cases, tribes have been simply exterminated at this point. Extinction has sometimes actually been accelerated by the retention of traditional fertility checks even in the face of severe depopulation. Good examples of this process can be drawn from South America (Wagley 1951) and the Pacific (Schneider 1955).* When it

---

*Underwood (1973) argues that Schneider (1955) mistakenly identified the continuation of traditional abortion practices as a factor in the depopulation of Yap in Micronesia, but other traditional controls could certainly have come into play.

has been advantageous to retain a native labor force, however, the cultural-change process has usually been regulated to minimize undue increases in mortality; and new health measures reducing infant mortality and controlling endemic diseases such as malaria have in the long run succeeded in lowering overall mortality rates. It is quite possible that if the traditional culture remained intact, and if no new incentives for population growth were introduced, a reduction in mortality rates might be easily countered with an adjustment in fertility control mechanisms and no dramatic population explosion would need to occur. Unfortunately, a real test of this hypothesis might never be possible, because modern medical technology has invariably been accompanied by both a loss in traditional fertility controls and the appearance of new incentives for growth. The main point is clear, however—traditional cultures are not in themselves the primary cause of the present population explosion.

Policy Implications

In view of this evidence, many present policies aimed at reducing population growth in the underdeveloped world are based on faulty premises and thus have doubtful chances of success. Mass education as a solution means assuming that "ignorance" is the problem, when actually people may be making very rational individual decisions under the circumstances and they may be very much aware of the long-range consequences of population growth. Policies aimed at instilling new values on family size may actually be quite irrelevant because many traditional population-limiting practices were not directly related to family planning at all. Even the concept of an ideal family size may not be meaningful cross-culturally. Instead, birth spacing, age at marriage, and cessation of childbearing may be the critical factors. Traditional lineage and extended family systems have often been singled out by demographers as specific incentives for high fertility, but this assumption cannot be supported by ethnographic data. Perhaps most importantly, the belief that economic development will be the key to reduced population growth may be erroneous. This belief is the fundamental assumption shared by many planners in underdeveloped countries today, who continue to see overpopulation as the result of "backward" cultures. It may be true that as economic prosperity has spread through industrial societies, population growth rates have declined; unfortunately, however, there can be no guarantee that this will occur in the underdeveloped world. An even more serious difficulty is the probability that the present rapid rates of growth, combined with the environmental limitations that are already being met, will preclude the attainment of a sufficient level of industrial prosperity to achieve population stability.

Arguing from what we know about the population policies of tribal cultures, it might make as much sense to recommend *de*development or *de*modernization, and a restoration of tribal equilibrium, as to call for further development, which has so far only increased the misery of millions of people. At another level, world planners might pursue the kinds of solutions that tribal cultures have followed when population pressures have arisen. In this light, it would be reasonable to attempt technological intensification; but failing that, a global political system might be in order. Such a system would attempt to redistribute people and resources to obtain some equitable, world-maximum living standard, after the fashion of island cultures. This would be a logical advance in a general evolutionary sense, but would probably be very undesirable in an adaptive sense because a one-world culture would be highly unstable. In the end, demodernization might be the only viable solution, whether it is deliberately chosen or not.

7
INTERNAL ORDER

*Violence is dangerous to our society. It is disfiguring
our society—making fortresses of portions of our
cities and dividing our people into armed camps. It is
jeopardizing some of our most precious institutions—
poisoning the spirit of trust and cooperation that is
essential to their proper functioning. It is corroding the
central political processes of our democratic society—
substituting force and fear for argument and
accommodation.*

Justice: To Establish Justice, to Ensure Domestic Tranquility

In addition to establishing a successful adaptation to the natural environment, every human society must maintain a certain minimal level of internal order if it is to survive. Conflict and violence must be carefully regulated. Individuals, households, and other social units must have access to basic resources and sufficient involvement with decision-making processes to protect their self-interests. During the thousands of years before the first states appeared, tribal societies successfully minimized this universal problem because they remained basically egalitarian. Differential access to wealth and power did not occur and was therefore not a potential source of conflict. In small, face-to-face communities, in which everyone participated in all basic cultural activities, individuals easily found personal satisfaction and fulfillment. Poverty and alienation simply did not exist. Conflicts did of course arise, but they usually took the form of interpersonal antagonisms and domestic quarrels, and seldom represented serious challenges to the established social order.

With the rise of social stratification and the economic specialization that accompanied the appearance of the first states a mere 6,000 years ago, social order suddenly became a far more difficult and dangerous problem. For the first time in human experience, whole segments of a society were denied direct access to and control over their basic subsistence requirements, and real political power rested with a favored few. Poverty and powerlessness became intrinsic aspects of the new social system, and new institutions with internal police powers were needed to maintain a precarious social order. Since their beginning, states have been subject to frequent collapses of social order, civil wars, peasant revolts, and popular uprisings, which, in combination with foreign invasions, have destroyed many individual states. Indeed, seldom have any states survived more than a few hundred years. In view of their obvious instabilities, and considering the relatively recent appearance of state organization, we might be justified in viewing it as a cultural experiment that might yet prove maladaptive.

The modern industrial state, if we consider any of its major variants, is quite clearly not immune to the threat of social disorder in spite of all our efforts at creating stability. This is true even though high levels of productivity have made more material wealth available to more people,

and democratic political processes have distributed decision-making powers more equitably. Relative and absolute poverty and powerlessness, and
many other problems seemingly inherent in any complex political system,
continue to threaten the internal security and domestic tranquility of
virtually all states.

The collapse of democratic political systems and their replacement
by overwhelmingly powerful and oppressive totalitarian forces represent
the ultimate domestic political crisis. Such an event would mean the
curtailment of many of the individual freedoms now enjoyed in most
industrial nations and might be followed by a period of intensifying civil
strife that could effectively destroy civilization as we know it. Such an
outcome might occur quite independently of international conflict. Disastrous internal disorders could be precipitated by a major downturn or
collapse of our precarious consumption-based economic system; by un-
resolved urban, ethnic, or racial stresses; and by unresponsive political
processes. Terrorist acts and civil disturbances on the part of dissident
political groups, racial conflict, spontaneous urban riots and looting,
labor strife, organized crime, corruption among high political officials
and illegal use of power, rising rates of violent crime and juvenile delin-
quency, drug abuse—all are symptoms of serious underlying conflicts and
contradictions within industrial states.

Anthropologists have traditionally been concerned with a variety of
problems relating to social order that are directly relevant to a better
understanding of our present crisis. However, before considering the
anthropological perspective in detail, a brief review of the social order
crisis in America will be presented to clarify both the nature of the crisis
and current attempts at its solution. The United States provides an
excellent starting point for any treatment of this topic because it is among
the most "advanced" of the industrial nations; yet its violent crime rate
is far higher than that of any other modern nation. Perhaps even more
importantly, in recent years the American government has supported
several massive studies of the problem in an attempt to pinpoint its causes
and to work toward the prevention or at least the reduction of violence
and disorder.

Violence in America

Violent crime, political terrorism, assassinations, riots, and various other forms of social disorder have always been part of the American scene. It was not until the assassination of President John F. Kennedy in 1963 and the outbreak of widespread urban rioting in 1967, followed in 1968 by violent political demonstrations, campus disturbances, and the assassination of Martin Luther King and Senator Robert F. Kennedy, that the government began to ask serious questions. Several national commissions were called together in the late 1960s to examine various aspects of the crisis. Perhaps the most comprehensive of these commissions was the National Commission on the Causes and Prevention of Violence, established in June of 1968 by President Lyndon B. Johnson. He directed it to "go as far as man's knowledge" could take it in the search for the causes and prevention of violence.

The 13-person commission, headed by Milton S. Eisenhower, worked for a year and a half with a research staff that numbered 100 persons at its peak and was divided into eight major task groups. A total of more than 200 leading scholars assisted the commission with the preparation of 150 separate papers and projects. The latter were published in 13 volumes of task force reports, 5 investigative reports, and a commission final report. Thirty days of public hearings, in which 150 witnesses testified, were also held. This massive project surely represents the single most ambitious attempt to understand the problem of violence and social disorder undertaken in any modern industrial nation, and its conclusions merit careful consideration.

The final report of the National Commission (United States, National Commission on the Causes and Prevention of Violence 1969) concluded that whereas the United States has always been a relatively violent nation, during the 1960s the occurrence of virtually all types of violence increased dramatically over the levels of recent decades. This increase was not a mere reflection of population growth, changes in the demographic structure, or changes in detection and reporting procedures. Between 1958 and 1968 the rate of reported violent crimes (homicide, forcible rape, robbery, and aggravated assault) per 100,000 people doubled. Between mid-1963 and mid-1968, nearly 2 million people were involved in group protests, urban riots, and demonstrations of various sorts that resulted in an estimated 9,000 casualties, including nearly 200 deaths. This relatively sudden increase in *group* disorders caused widespread alarm and spawned several special commission studies, but such group disorders were not unique in American history. For example, during labor violence between 1902 and 1904, 200 persons were killed and 2,000 injured.

In view of this undisputed general increase in overall violence in America, the commissioners felt that the basic foundations of our society were clearly being threatened and urged that immediate action be taken to control the problem. The dangers of internal disorder were considered to be fully as serious as any external threats, and a reassessment of national priorities, along with a scaling-down of military expenditures for national defense, was called for. As the commissioners stated: "We solemnly declare our conviction that this nation is entering a period in which our people need to be as concerned by the internal dangers to our free society as by any probable combination of external threats."

They called for a doubling of expenditures on the criminal justice process, and greater coordination and efficiency in law enforcement activities in general. They also felt that firearms should be regulated and the availability of handguns restricted. If drastic action was not taken quickly, they foresaw a bleak future for Americans. There would be isolated "safe" areas occupied by upper-income families protected by armed guards and electronic surveillance equipment in central city areas, where crime and terror would prevail for the poor at night, when there would be no possible security. Public facilities such as schools, libraries, and playgrounds would also require armed guards. Commuters from safe suburban compounds would travel carefully patroled and "sanitized" corriders in armored cars, while guards would "ride shotgun" on public transportation. All of these defensive measures would lead to further intensification of terror and violence.

The commissioners recognized that merely increasing the efficiency of law enforcement was not sufficient if the underlying causes of violence were not corrected. In their view, violence was a *sickness*, a social pathology: "Necessary as measures of control are, they are only a part of the answer. They do not cure the basic causes of violence. Violence is like a fever in the body politic: it is but the symptom of some more basic pathology which must be cured before the fever will disappear" (United

States, National Commission on the Causes and Prevention of Violence 1969:xix).

To discover the underlying causes of violence, the report attempted first of all to pinpoint where crimes occurred most often and who committed them. It was confirmed that violent crimes were most prevalent in cities of over 50,000 people, where crime rates were 11 times greater than in rural areas. Crimes were most often committed by young, low-income males living under urban slum conditions. An earlier National Commission (United States, National Advisory Commission on Civil Disorders 1968) had declared that this association between crime and slum living conditions was "one of the most fully documented facts about crime." The present report agreed with this assessment and specifically listed poverty, poor housing, and unemployment among the most important factors in an interrelated combination of "powerful criminogenic forces" present in urban slums. The general conclusion was that the urban poor were trapped in a situation from which they could not easily escape because of their inability to earn adequate income. This situation generated frustration and violence because the dominant culture measured success in terms of material wealth, which, in the popular ideology, was considered to be equally available to all who put forth the individual effort to achieve it. The final commission report summarized some of these criminogenic forces as follows:

> To be a young, poor male; to be undereducated and without means
> of escape from an oppressive urban environment; to want what the
> society claims is available (but mostly to others); to see around
> oneself illegitimate and often violent methods being used to achieve
> material success; and to observe others using these means with
> impunity—all this is to be burdened with an enormous set of
> influences that pull many toward crime and delinquency.
> (United States National Commission on the Causes and
> Prevention of Violence 1969:xxi)

The basic causes of violence were listed as follows:

1. Revolution of rising expectations
2. Inadequate law enforcement
3. Loss of institutional legitimacy

The commission argued that economic progress brought rapid social change and greatly increased wealth for some persons while denying it to others. At the same time, it weakened traditional mechanisms of social control and led to frustrations due to inequities in wealth distribution. Inadequate law enforcement and reduced respect for elected authority and established institutions were thought to encourage further crime. All of these causes were seen to be concentrated in urban centers.

Considering all of these "criminogenic" forces, the commissioners felt that it was almost remarkable that more crime did not occur. Since 1968 however, crime rates have of course increased. Within four years, by 1972, the rate had risen a further 30 percent over the already high 1968 level. In 1974, as the unemployment rate and prices began to rise generally, the crime rate reached new heights, rising 17 percent over 1973 levels. Further dramatic increases have occurred since then, reflecting the downturn in economic growth during the late 1970s and early 1980s. By 1982, violent crime rates had risen to 555 per 100,000 persons, one-third higher than in 1973 (United States, Bureau of the Census 1983: Table 655). These increases corresponded with an increase in unemployment to 9.4 percent of the labor force in 1982, which was nearly double the average rate during the previous two decades.

Other studies on violence and disorder in America have often emphasized the "deviant" aspect of this behavior, and have explained it as—at least in part—a problem of faulty socialization or inappropriate values fostered by a subculture of poverty. From this viewpoint, causes are seen to lie largely with the poor people themselves, and the recommended solution becomes "education" in the broadest sense. This view represents a misunderstanding of the adaptive value of deviant behavior under poverty conditions and seriously overemphasizes the role of values in initiating such behavior. It also mistakenly equates such behavior with criminality. Cross-cultural research reveals a common pattern of behavioral coping responses to material deprivation throughout the underdeveloped world and in urban slums in developed nations that is strikingly similar to patterns followed by the urban poor in early industrial England (Eames and Goode 1973). Deviant marriage arrangements, the "matrifocal" family, various forms of petty marketing practices, and many other patterns are simply ways of making the best of a difficult situation. Poverty behavior, indeed, presents a consistent picture, but it is because people are adapting to the same problems and not because they are locked in their own self-replicating culture of poverty.

In order to eradicate the basic causes of violence and disorder, the National Commission recommended a major restructuring of urban life, greater expenditures on welfare and improved housing, and so on. Unfortunately, as promising as these recommendations sound, they still leave unchallenged the fundamental problem of stratification itself, which may be the real cause of the social order crisis.

Social Order in Egalitarian Societies

Solving our social order crisis is indeed a formidable task, particularly when it is realized that humanity's most basic social patterns are perhaps best suited to conditions far different from the highly stratified urban societies to which we are now attempting to adjust. It may be that our most critical social problems can only be treated symptomatically. A certain uncomfortable level of crime and violence and periodic social upheaval may simply be the price that must be paid for the apparent advantages of life in a densely populated, intensely hierarchical society based on differential access to wealth and power. It is certain that most of the criminogenic factors identified by the National Commission are absent in tribal egalitarian societies. With low population densities, with no emphasis on material wealth as a source of status, and with free access to basic resources guaranteed to all, tribal societies face a very different problem of social order, and it is solved in very different, but highly effective ways.

Data on the actual frequency of violence in tribal societies that could be compared with data from our own society are not readily available, but anthropologists who have observed the most traditional hunting and gathering egalitarian societies have generally been impressed with their relatively low levels of internal violence. Some societies, such as the Bushmen of southern Africa and the Semai of Malaysia, * have been

---

* This emphasis is illustrated by the title of Dentan's (1968) book: *The Semai: A Nonviolent People of Malaya.*

characterized as almost totally nonviolent, and it would be easy to assume that all tribal peoples led perpetually harmonious social lives. Such, however, is not the case. Some tribal societies, such as the Yanomamo of the Orinoco rain forests, have been described as highly violent (Chagnon 1968). Whatever the actual levels of violence, it is important to note that they generally managed to keep such problems within safe limits. The basic survival of society as a whole was seldom threatened by internal conflict. It could hardly have been otherwise, considering the thousands of years tribal societies endured. There was no "war of all against all" that Thomas Hobbes envisioned, nor was there total harmony. It is of special importance for our purposes that these societies maintained internal order without formal legal codes and specialized law enforcement institutions, and even without formal political offices invested with coercive authority. Tribal societies are dramatic proof that the expensive law and order machinery that we now require is not the only route to social order.

Any superiority of tribal cultures in the maintenance of social order is unlikely to result from an innate moral superiority of the "noble savage"; rather, it must be due to differences in cultural conditions. Crime and disorder simply could not flourish in a tribal culture. Perhaps one of the most important overall characteristics of tribal cultures likely to predispose them to lower crime rates was the fact that individual self-interest seldom conflicted with the long-range interests of society. Excessive conflict, theft, use of force, or hoarding of resources for exclusive use would all be self-defeating in a tribal society in which everyone's survival ultimately depended on mutual trust and cooperation. As was noted in earlier chapters, this same correspondence of interests has also contributed to the ecological success of tribal societies and to the maintenance of population equilibrium.

In low-density tribal societies, conflict is unquestionably further minimized by extreme flexibility in group membership and by the small size of the local, face-to-face residential group. A typical hunting band averaged only approximately 25 people, including children; thus, relatively few adults were ever forced into close interaction. Camps shifted location every few days or weeks, and such moves were often used as an excuse for changing band personnel. Careful studies of modern hunting bands such as the Bushmen have revealed that individuals and families constantly shuffled between bands and that many of these shifts were simply a means of resolving interpersonal conflict without violence (Turnbull 1968:132-37; Woodburn 1968b:103–10).

The Importance of Equality

The concept *equality* is critical for an understanding of the differences between tribal societies and states on the question of social order. No one is of course ever totally equal with anyone else in any society; but in tribal societies the differences that separate people are age, sex, and unique personal qualities exclusively. Positions of prestige and influence are open to all persons qualified to occupy them. For example, anyone with sufficient skill may become a respected hunter or a band leader. Morton Fried has defined an egalitarian society very neatly as follows:

> An egalitarian society is one in which there are as many positions of prestige in any given age-sex grade as there are persons capable of filling them. Let it be put even more strongly. An egalitarian society does not have any means of fixing or limiting the number of persons capable of exerting power. As many persons as can wield power— whether through personal strength, influence, authority, or whatever means—can do so, and there is no necessity to draw them together to establish an order of dominance and paramountcy.
> (Fried 1967:33)

Of equal importance is the situation with regard to basic physical necessities. No one in an egalitarian society is denied access to the means of production. Fried is emphatic on this point: "In no simple society known to ethnography is there any restriction on access to the raw materials necessary to make tools and weapons. This statement can be made flatly about resources in the habitation area of a given unit. . . ." (Fried 1967:58)

Land, water, and game are always open for use. This is the "irreducible minimum" we referred to earlier. Although boundaries may be recognized for tribal, band, and occasionally family territories, trespass regulations usually mean that permission to use an area must be requested but cannot reasonably be denied (Myers 1982), and actual group membership fluctuates widely. The trespass rules themselves often serve the important function of helping people monitor who is using resources to better manage their availability. Among tribal horticulturalists, access to land may be regulated by corporate descent groups, but these are not rigid organizations, and membership changes may commonly occur if land shortages arise. Individual ownership of property certainly does occur, but it is normally restricted to personal weapons and artifacts, game killed, herd animals, and crops—things in which personal labor has been invested. With use-access to basic resources open to all, and particularly when residential shifts are part of the subsistence round, there are no real advantages to be gained by asserting individual title to land. In regard to movable property, one can only make practical use of so many goods; and given both the need for mobility and the cultural emphasis on generosity, there is no incentive either to hoard or to steal property. Furthermore, in a small society a thief would be unable to hide. All these factors are almost certain to minimize the occasion for interpersonal conflict.

Many anthropologists describe differences in age and sex status in tribal societies as "inequality," and these differences are occasionally described as oppressive and exploitative. For example, Bern (1979) uses such language to describe the dominance of the old men in traditional Australian society. Many observers recognize the differences that exist between the sexes and between individuals of different ages in tribal societies. However, any inequities that exist do not deny anyone the opportunity to marry, raise a family, and make a living. We can say that, in spite of age and sex differences, everyone is guaranteed the "irreducible minimum." Age differences are of course only temporary, and tribals themselves usually do not consider different sex roles to be oppressive. Two women anthropologists, Kaberry (1939) and Bell (1982), investigated the position of aboriginal women in Australia in the field and specifically rejected the charge that women were exploited by the traditional system. In virtually all tribal societies, women do tend to work closer to the home and care for children more than do men, and their work is often more routine. Men often do heavier work and their work can carry them far from home. However, where detailed time-expenditure studies have been carried out (Johnson 1975; Lee 1979; Modjeska 1982), they indicate that the total work load appears to be relatively equitable between the sexes.

Thus, there exist in tribal societies cultural conditions that reduce the basic causes of violence and disorder, and specific mechanisms to reduce the frequency of otherwise unavoidable problems. There are also direct and effective means of handling any trouble that does arise, and there are specific mechanisms to channel conflicts. Serious breaches of norms could result in expulsion from the society—which would mean the loss of all physical and emotional support for the recalcitrant individual. Survival without kinspeople is virtually impossible, and an exiled troublemaker would have difficulty being accepted by other societies in which there is no anonymity. Such a drastic sanction rarely needs to be applied, but the threat is always in the background. In many societies the threat of witchcraft accusation may be an effective means of compelling conformity. Chronic troublemakers might find themselves accused of witchcraft, and they may be blamed for causing a variety of sicknesses and community misfortunes. In extreme cases, accused witches are publicly executed.

Conflict Resolution
In addition to simply moving away, egalitarian tribal societies often employ highly ritualized methods of conflict resolution. Ingroup interpersonal violence may even be encouraged by some cultures, but it is usually very carefully regulated. The Yanomamo Indians (Chagnon 1968), for example, recognize several distinct levels of violence in a carefully graded series of increasing intensity. Their disputes might be settled by ritual duels, which range in extremes from chest pounding (in which two men exchange bare-fist blows to the chest) to spear-throwing duels. Intermediate duels involve blows to the side and club fighting. Minor injuries and prominent scars may result from these actions, but deaths are uncommon. More pacific ritual forms of conflict resolution in egalitarian societies include Eskimo song duels, in which the disputants publicly insult each other until the loser is laughed down by the audience. Generally, in these cultures, when disputes are not settled by the individuals most directly involved, they are resolved by community consensus. The objective is merely to restore order, not to punish. Abstract notions of "justice" are quite irrelevant in this situation.

Leadership
Tribal societies are essentially "anarchistic" (Barclay 1982), because they lack a formal government, but this does not mean that they lack order.

Although there is no concentration of coercive power in political offices in egalitarian societies, this does not mean that there is no leadership or political organization. Headmen have been described for some of the most simple hunting bands, but their authority is severely limited. For example, among the Nambikuara Indians of Brazil, described by Claude Levi-Strauss (1944), the band headman is delegated primary decision-making responsibility for band subsistence activities, selection of routes and campsites, and interband relations. He is only a leader as long as his followers consent to his leadership, and he must not recommend actions that band members would not agree to. A chief's success is measured by his ability to see that the band is well fed. He is also expected to excel in generosity, and constant demands are made on him for food and small articles.

Thus a Nambikuara headman must be an especially skillful, dedicated, and hardworking individual. He bears a heavy responsibility for band well-being and security, but his position is always tenuous. If his leadership qualities falter, the band may simply disintegrate as disgruntled individuals and households seek out other band leaders with whom to align themselves. A headman was generally allowed a young second wife to ease the burdens of leadership. The only other rewards appear to have been highly personal, and few persons desired the position. Band headmanship in tribal society, therefore, is not the kind of political office that occurs at higher levels of sociopolitical integration. In fact, Levi-Strauss had a difficult time explaining why anyone would even aspire to such a position in Nambikuara society and concluded that "there are chiefs because there are, in any human group, men who, unlike most of their companions, enjoy prestige for its own sake, feel a strong appeal to responsibility, and to whom the burden of public affairs brings its own reward" (Levi-Strauss 1944).

Richard Lee's (1981) description of leadership among the !Kung Bushmen presents a similar picture. He found that the !Kung went to such lengths to prevent the accumulation of power in a leader and were so fiercely egalitarian that it was not always obvious that "headmen" even existed. In fact, when he asked a Bushman whether the !Kung had headmen, the man replied, "Of course we have headmen! . . . Each one of us is headman over himself" (Lee 1981:93–94). Lee concluded that leadership existed, but it was very diffuse, totally noncoercive, and represented a form of "political reciprocity" much like the reciprocity characteristic of tribal economics.

Social Order in Nonegalitarian Societies

The simplest nonegalitarian societies are often called chiefdoms (Service 1962, chapter 5), and many ethnographic examples are known from the Pacific, Africa, and Northwest Coast of North America. Chiefdom societies restrict the number of individuals who can occupy important positions within the society, but still permit relatively free access to basic natural resources. Social control remains largely a matter of kinship, but true political offices exist. Ranking within a chiefdom may be highly elaborated, with a hereditary chief at the top, and each corporate descent group may be ranked both relative to each other and internally. The authority of the chief is defined by the position he occupies, and his personality and special skills are a relatively minor aspect of his qualifications. The office of chief is ritually set apart and reinforced by a variety of sumptuary regulations or taboos, such as the right to eat special foods or to own certain articles. Conflicts may become intense as individuals vie for status, and rebellions may occur when particular chiefs overstep the customary bounds of their office; but in general, the social order problem is qualitatively much simpler, even given ranking, than when full stratification exists.

Stratified societies, most fully represented by states, begin with all the potential social order problems implied by ranking in chiefdoms, but they add the critical element of restricted access to strategic resources. According to Morton Fried's (1967:186) concise definition, "[a] stratified society is one in which members of the same sex and equivalent age status do not have equal access to the basic resources that sustain life." This involves the arrangement of people into classes according to their degree of access to power and resources. There is also a pervasive division of labor by economic specialization, such that no one except certain rural peasants can directly provide for more than a very small proportion of their basic needs. The ruling elite at the top of the hierarchy can effectively regulate access to and use of both critical natural resources and the technological means of production. Control over water, soil, and air may in this way be denied to large segments of society.

With the development of stratification, for the first time in human history, cultural conditions arose in which internal exploitation of one subgroup by another could exist. Exploitation is an emotional and value-laden concept that many social scientists prefer not to deal with, but in discussing problems of social order, it cannot be avoided. Webster's Dictionary defines exploitation as "unfair utilization." The catch here is in the meaning of "unfair," because no one would dispute that "utilization" of one class by another exists in a stratified society. Certainly, the ruling class is totally dependent for its well-being on the lower classes because it draws its labor force and all its food, goods, and services from them. The "fairness" of this arrangement may be judged from both an inside and an outside view. From the inside, if the members of the lower class do not feel they are being treated unfairly, exploitation would not exist. From the outside, the system might be labeled exploitative when the lower class is clearly deprived of basic physical necessities, while the upper class basks in costly luxury. This kind of material deprivation can be objectively measured and clearly defined in terms of health status, food supply, clothing, housing, and other indicators, and may relate to both a minimal *survival level* and a culturally defined minimum *comfort level*. Material deprivation of either sort is absolute deprivation and is encompassed by the popular concept *poverty*. Relative deprivation, or the feeling that one is not as "well off" as one would like to be in comparison to the next higher class, may exist whenever there is an inequitable distribution of wealth and power, and can occur above the absolute level. Deprivation of some kind seems to be a universal feature of all stratified societies. Some socialist countries may be more successful in easing the absolute deprivation of different classes, but classes exist in these countries nonetheless, and so does the potential for alienation and disorder. Classical Marxian theory, of course, calls for the ultimate end of social stratification and the state after the dictatorship of the proletariat crushes any counterrevolution, but this utopia has not yet arrived.

It is difficult for anyone viewing a particular stratified society from the outside to understand why the impoverished lower classes so often seem to accept their lot without a struggle; but in fact, such systems could not exist without the threat of physical coercion and the use of powerful forms of thought control (Harris 1971). The use of police force, brutality, and imprisonment in support of the political power, wealth, and property rights of the ruling class is certainly a familiar element in the history of all states. However, in many of the ancient agrarian states, such as those in Egypt, Mesopotamia, Mexico, and Peru, the need for such force was apparently minimized by the force of the great state religions, which encouraged the lower classes to accept their position as part of a divinely established order. An elaborate esoteric priesthood, awesome pyramids, and complex, dramatic ritual would have been highly intimidating for people who doubted their place in the divine scheme. In fact, many impoverished peasants may never have considered them-selves to have been exploited. In modern industrial societies such as the United States, the recommendation of the National Commission that police forces be strengthened is clear indication of the continuing im-portance of physical coercion. The mass media and the institutions of formal education may also be interpreted as forms of thought control that perhaps replace the role of a state religion and fully support the established order. Anthropologist Marvin Harris (1971) suggests that television may be a very important new means of minimizing social disorder in highly stratified societies by occupying peoples' minds and providing at least vicarious involvement with all levels of the society. A further stabilizing factor, as was noted earlier, has been continuous economic growth, which has helped convince the people in the lowest strata that they are moving up even though their relative position has remained constant.

Population Density, Stratification, and Conflict

Many of the social order problems in modern society seem to a consid-erable extent to be density-related phenomena. As we noted, a hunting band is a very successful, egalitarian, and low-friction group, but it in-cludes only about 25 people. Tribal village farmers require more formal means of conflict resolution, but they may still avoid any political cen-tralization. It has been suggested that a truly egalitarian society can only be maintained within a continuously interacting, face-to-face population of no more than approximately 250-500 persons that have common goals to pull it together. As population densities increase, not only do people have a more difficult time keeping track of their relationships simply because there are now too many to sort out, but the probability of conflict over everyday irritations becomes much more likely. Invariably, population densities greater than 500 in a single social unit either break up into antagonistic factions, and/or they become hierarchically ordered (Reynolds 1972). Either of these developments can increase the per capita violence level over that of lower density societies, but still hold it within bounds.

Modern urban centers are thus heavily and perhaps unavoidably predisposed toward conflict. Relative and absolute deprivation usually exist because of stratification; and because of economic specialization, there are numerous mutually competing factions, many of which are not directly represented in the hierarchy of political power. A further problem is that young males in the lowest classes often have little hope of gaining full adult status in the society because they are systematically excluded from culturally approved forms of self-assertion and competition.

The Origin of States and Inequality

> How did vast segments of humanity get cut off from access to the earth's natural resources? Why was control of the soil, water, and even the air yielded up into the hands of a relatively small group of people? (Harris 1971:393)

State organization thus seems to be at the root of many of our social order problems, and if we are to understand the origin of these problems, we must consider the origin of the state itself. In view of the disproportionate cost that the majority paid to support the ruling classes, particularly in the earliest states, the origin of such a system has long presented social science theorists with a very knotty problem (Cohen and Service 1978; Haas 1982). The factors leading to the evolution of states are—like the causes of food production—varied, complex, and interrelated.

It seems clear that population growth, increasing control of food production by political authorities, economic specialization, regulation of regional trade and water control systems, and warfare over access to resources in restricted environments have all played a part, but no single theory offers a completely adequate explanation. There does seem to be a distinction between the development of *pristine* states, which would apparently only occur under very special cultural-ecological conditions, and the development of *secondary* states, which result from conquest or the threat of conquest by other states. It was noted earlier that population growth may itself be both encouraged by and result from political development; but whatever its cause, as population density increases, political hierarchies become almost inevitable.

The Disintegration of Social Order

> In a disintegrating society one would tend to find subcultures
> developing along all of these different lines in varying degrees: there
> will be an increase in delinquency violence, and all the various
> forms of retreatism, such as drugs, drink, strange religious cults, and
> mental disease. Such a society will be characterized by a general
> feeling of aimlessness, a frantic, almost pathetic search for
> originality, overpreoccupation with anything capable of providing
> short-term entertainment, and beneath it all a feeling of
> hopelessness of the futility of all effort. (Goldsmith et al. 1972:127)

There are strong reasons for suspecting that many of our most serious social problems afflicting individuals and families at a very personal level—such as alcoholism and other forms of drug abuse, child abuse, mental disorders, alienation, suicide, and the breakdown of families—all have a common cultural etiology. These can best be considered social pathologies symptomatic of industrial civilization's inability to provide adequately for the emotional needs of individuals. In some respects, they may indeed represent the disintegration or at least the failure of social order, but this does not mean that they foreshadow the imminent collapse of society. Social pathologies may be highly adaptive under certain cultural conditions, and like poverty-coping mechanisms, they may allow people to survive what would otherwise be an intolerable environment.

All of these problems have much in common. Like crime, they are often more prevalent in urban centers; and although statistics may be misleading, many of these pathologies seem to be on the increase. Although supportive data are not always available, anthropologists would generally agree that in undisturbed tribal cultures such conditions are either totally absent or very infrequent. There is also striking and undisputed evidence that as tribal cultures are absorbed by industrial states, they quickly begin to suffer from a wide range of social disintegration pathologies, among which alcoholism is perhaps the most conspicuous.

As in the case of crime, enormous attention has been focused on all these problems, and vast funds have been spent on discovering their causes and working toward their prevention. Entire "industries" are devoted to the treatment of specific problems, but significant results never seem to be achieved. Perhaps the only way to find the real causes of such problems will be to examine healthy cultures and determine what characteristics they possess that are lacking where psychopathologies are common. Anthropologist Stanley Diamond (1974, chapter 7) has carried out such an analysis for schizophrenia, a mental disorder that may afflict 60 million Americans. He concludes that schizophrenia is basically a way for individuals to deal with the inadequacies of their culture, and that it is culturally irrelevant among tribal peoples, who consistently satisfy their own basic human needs.

8
WAR AND
INTERNATIONAL ORDER

[The] one crisis that must be ranked at the top in total
danger and imminence is, of course, the danger of
large-scale or total annihilation by nuclear escalation
or by radiological-chemical-biological warfare
(RCBW).

John Platt, "What We Must Do"

The threat of nuclear war is the most critical world crisis in many peoples's minds, and certainly it is the crisis to which the United States government has devoted its largest share of national resources. John Platt (1969), in his crisis survey, cited in Chapter 1, ranked nuclear and what he called RCBW (radiological-chemical-biological war) as the most urgent and dangerous crisis now faced by humanity. He argued that because such a war could occur at any moment and might mean total annihilation, it deserved the top spot on his crisis intensity chart. In his view, however, this crisis will be short-lived; but he felt that this was no cause for optimism because if the crisis is not solved within the next 20 to 50 years, we may all be dead.

Anthropologists have rarely focused their attention on the specific threat of nuclear war, but they have devoted considerable research effort toward understanding intergroup relations at all levels of culture, the evolution of war, the cultural functions of war, and the nature of human aggression. This work has obvious relevance to the present international crisis and will be examined directly; but first the nature of the nuclear threat, and the current thinking of defense strategists and other specialists on the topic, must be considered.

The Doomsday Machine

> In a recent University of Chicago Round Table broadcast, Leo Szilard made some remarks which have caused something of an uproar. These comments, reprinted in the April *Bulletin* along with a few paragraphs amplifying the technical argument, relate to the possibility of using the hydrogen bomb to destroy the human race. The matter is obviously of some importance, and it seems worthwhile to check the technical side of the argument. (Arnold 1950)

A significant phase in the evolution of high-energy culture was entered in 1945 when atomic energy was directed toward military applications. The first atomic bombs released the destructive power of 20,000 tons of TNT (20 kilotons), a thousand times more energy than the largest bombs previously used in war. Subsequent advances in nuclear weaponry have made even these devastating bombs seem puny in comparison. The first hydrogen bomb, exploded just nine years after Hiroshima, was 750 times more powerful again and released energy equivalent to 15 million tons of TNT (15 megatons). It is estimated that this represents more than the total of all explosives used in all previous wars; but even these bombs are dwarfed by the 50- and 100-megaton superbombs that could be employed in future wars. The diminishing returns in military gains from use of the superbombs suggests that those with relatively low-megaton yields spread over a wider area would be more effective. This is particularly true given the increased precision with which bombs can be delivered to targets today, in comparison with the relatively crude bomber aircraft in use at the beginning of the nuclear era. This de-emphasis on the really large superbombs, of course, does not reduce nuclear terror. Fortunately, only the relatively lightweight 20-kiloton atomic bomb has seen direct combat use, when two bombs destroyed the Japanese cities of Nagasaki and Hiroshima in 1945, killing nearly 100,000 persons and causing more than 200,000 total casualties.

Although they have not been used in war, the superbombs have been extensively tested, and many of their effects can be quite precisely predicted. [*] It is known, for example, that a single 20-megaton ground burst on New York City would leave a crater 640 feet deep and half a mile across (Stonier 1964). The fireball would instantly consume everything within a circle 4.5 miles wide, or an area of more than 15 square miles. During the first 30 seconds the blast shock would generate 160-mile-an-hour winds and would demolish most buildings within a circle 15 miles across. The shock, together with the cratering effect, would destroy the underground subway systems. An air burst would cause heavy structural damage within a 20-mile circle, and would rip out windows and tear off doors within a 40-mile circle. Windows as far as 100 miles away might be broken. The intense heat would ignite secondary fires on combustible material within a circle 50 miles across. It is almost certain that these fires would create gigantic firestorms that would quickly incinerate all of New York City and its environs, burning perhaps 1,000 square miles. Six million people would probably die.

---

[*] See, for example, Glasstone (1962) for basic primary data; also Martin and Latham (1963); Stonier (1964); Wiesner and York (1964); York (1972).

If a single nuclear weapon can obliterate one of the world's largest cities, what about entire nations? Or all of humanity? Defense planners may publicly deal with the fate of nations and cities, but the larger question is left for science fiction writers, and most people prefer not to trouble their conscious minds with any of these matters. The ultimate survival of the human race is, of course, the principal topic of this book, and it would be absurd not to deal seriously with what must be the ultimate threat, regardless of how unthinkable or unpleasant it might be. The possibility of the extinction of humanity through its own actions was of course mentioned earlier in relation to ecocatastrophes touched off by the day-to-day pursuit of economic progress, but what we consider here is the destruction of humanity as a direct or indirect outcome of war.

Apart from science fiction, *the* basic question was asked of physicists as early as 1950, even before the hydrogen bomb was successfully exploded. In the radio discussion referred to in the opening quotation of this section (Arnold 1950), nuclear physicist Leo Szilard commented that it would probably be possible to construct a hydrogen-cobalt bomb that would generate enough radioactive global fallout to expose everyone on earth to 10,000 rems, many times over the 500 rems required for a fatal dose, and enough to kill most people protected by standard fallout shelters. He speculated that, although this exposure would kill virtually all of mankind, a handful of people might survive, because accidents of local weather patterns and topography might create safe pockets. Such intense radioactivity would of course also wipe out most other life forms, and would so disturb global ecosystems that even isolated pockets would have difficulty surviving very long.

The cobalt bomb is the factual basis for the so-called "doomsday machines" of science fiction writers, but there has been remarkably little discussion of the implications of such devices. Surely, it would be significant if humanity actually does now possess the technological capacity to construct an instrument of war that will exterminate the entire human race.

The technical side of Szilard's theory has of course been examined by other physicists, and there seems little doubt that such bombs are indeed possible. Szilard himself felt that the only technical uncertainty concerned the success of the hydrogen bomb itself, and that problem was quickly overcome. The only real barrier to the construction of such a doomsday weapon is simply that of time and money, and this could easily be overcome by a "dedicated" nation. In 1950, Szilard estimated that collecting the necessary ingredients and assembling the bomb would require $40 billion and 5-10 years of work, and he concluded that humanity was in no immediate danger. That cost might have seemed prohibitively expensive in 1950; but today, $40 billion represents just 12 percent of the $313.4 billion defense budget requested by President Reagan for 1985. Even more alarming than the technological feasibility of a doomsday device is the ease with which it could be fitted into the "arms culture" of a modern industrial nation. In view of current military logic, a doomsday machine could easily become the ultimate cornerstone of the policy of "nuclear deterrence," and it could be further justified as a certain employment boost for the economy. It represents an obvious evolutionary progression in both military technology and strategic concepts.

Anthropologist Leslie A. White, writing in 1949 as the full implications of the possible military use of nuclear energy were just beginning to be assessed, clearly foresaw the threat to both humanity and civilization posed by this new technology. He felt that total nuclear destruction was possible but not inevitable, and speculated that a world order might eventually emerge from the radioactive ruins. In any event, he was philosophically prepared to accept the worst:

> The belief and faith that civilization, won at such great cost in pain and labor, simply cannot go down in destruction because such an end would be too monstrous and senseless, is but a naïve and anthropocentric whimper. The cosmos does little know nor will it long remember what man has done here on this tiny planet. The eventual extinction of the human race—for come it will sometime— will not be the first time that a species has died out. Nor will it be an event of very great terrestrial significance. (White 1949:391)

MAD: Mutual Assured Destruction

> [We] must be able to absorb the total weight of nuclear attack on our country—on our strike-back forces; on our command and control

apparatus; on our industrial capacity; on our cities; and on our population—and still, be fully capable of destroying the aggressor to the point that his society is simply no longer viable in any meaningful twentieth-century sense. (Secretary of Defense Robert S. McNamara, public address, September 18, 1967)

The fundamental basis of military strategy between the nuclear super-powers has been their mutual ability to "deter" aggression by threatening the total destruction of a would-be aggressor. Critics have dubbed this concept of nuclear deterrence MAD—an acronym for *mutual assured destruction* (Carter 1974). This has been the basic strategic concept that has propelled the arms race and has resulted in the concentration by the Soviet Union and the United States of far more weapons than would ever be needed to execute their own mutual destruction. Since 1949, when the Soviet Union exploded its own atomic bomb, the world has witnessed a staggering increase in the destructive power of weapons, and a parallel increase in the speed and efficiency with which these weapons can be delivered to their targets. The Hiroshima bomb was delivered by a propeller-driven B-29 bomber flying at a speed of 300 miles per hour. Such a plane required 20 hours to reach a target on the other side of the globe. Today, missiles can do the job very precisely within minutes. An incredible redundancy and overkill characterize the arsenals of both super-powers. For example, in 1968, it was estimated that the United States required a mere 400 warheads to destroy the Soviet Union, but it then possessed 2,000 (Garwin and Bethe 1968); and now, with the deployment of multiple warheads, the figure has jumped to 10,000, while there has been no appreciable change in the defense capability of the Soviet Union. Each side possesses at least three independent weapons systems, consisting of bombers, ICBMs (intercontinental ballistic missiles), and SLBMs (submarine-launched ballistic missiles), and any of these could destroy the other side even after taking major losses. These systems have rapidly diversified as the arms race has progressed, but most experts now feel that no dramatically new surprises are in store, unless, of course, the arms race is moved to outer space with laser weapons and killer satellites. ICBMs have perhaps reached their effective practical size limits, and there seems little point in building larger bombs, but pinpoint accuracy can still be perfected. The MIRV (multiple independently targeted re-entry vehicle) concept has vastly increased the destructive capability of an individual missile but has not really altered the ability of either side to destroy the other. New arms developments, such as ULMs (undersea long-range missile systems), air-mobile cruise missiles, or the MX missile, represent only minor refinements of existing technology. The only serious challenge to nuclear deterrence would be the development of an effective "counterforce" program that would allow one side to destroy the retaliatory force of the other, but this is an unlikely possibility. Counterforce may be avoided by the simple expedient of launching the retaliation before the attacker's weapons hit, and serious attempts to develop a counterforce strike merely increase the likelihood of an accidental nuclear exchange.

The defense side of the arms race has always been at a disadvantage because it must be geared to a particular type of attack, and given the lead time required for the development and deployment of any military system, even the most elaborate defense system may be obsolete before it is in place. The most critical problem for defense against nuclear attack is that the defense system must be virtually 100 percent effective or the nation would still be destroyed, because even a handful of warheads penetrating the defense would be enormously destructive. In the United States, defense systems have expanded from the radar networks, jet interceptors, and fallout shelters of the 1950s, to the ABMS (antiballistic missiles), ASWs (antisubmarine warfare systems), AWACs (airborne warning and control systems), underground command centers, soft and hard missile silos, and satellite observation systems of the 1960s and 1970s (Garwin 1972; Scoville 1972; English and Bolef 1973; Greenwood 1973). An attack can now be detected at the instant it is launched, and some of the attacking missiles can be destroyed, but the employment of simple decoys and electronic countermeasures virtually guarantees that some warheads will penetrate even the most sophisticated defense systems. Thus the MAD doctrine seems assured indeed. The final irony of the entire arms race is that as military capabilities have increased, there has been a proportionate *decrease* in national security. Hence the generalization that evolutionary progress can be maladaptive is again confirmed.

Postattack Society:
Will the Survivors Envy the Dead?

> The combined assault of radiation, insects, disease, and fire could temporarily strip off the plant cover of vast areas. If the attack is sufficiently widespread, it is conceivable that a few years later almost all the forests would have been destroyed, and most of the countryside would have become converted into marginal grasslands, if not actually stripped, leaving a naked earth to be ravaged by the ever-present forces of erosion. (Stonier 1964:135)

> The recovery of nature is by no means a foregone conclusion. There is a very real possibility that if the United States were hit hard enough by a nuclear attack most of the country would be converted into a barren desert. (Stonier 1964:141)

It might seem that the mere existence of overwhelmingly destructive nuclear weapons would make the entire concept of war both obsolete and unthinkable, but this is unfortunately not the case. As a logical extension of the policy of nuclear deterrence, government planners and their research contractors have for more than two decades been busily exploring the feasibility of nuclear war. Their work describes "postattack society" in intricate detail, on the optimistic assumption that the country will indeed survive a nuclear war intact, and will then quickly proceed to restore itself to its prior condition. The theme underlying all of these studies, and perhaps best exemplified in the title of Herman Kahn's (1962) book, *Thinking About the Unthinkable,* is that nuclear war is not madness at all; rather, it is something that we had better go ahead and prepare for. This conclusion is based on research methods and value judgments that most anthropologists would find incredibly narrow and short-sighted—and even dangerous, considering that such work merely increases the probability of nuclear war by making it seem "feasible." It is also an ironic twist that demonstrating the feasibility of nuclear war of course actually undermines the mutual suicide basis of the deterrence policy, but few experts acknowledge this paradox.

Numerous computer simulations have been run as a basis for estimating total casualties, property damage, and projected rates of economic recovery for a wide variety of nuclear attacks on the country. For example, the so-called "Holifield Attack," run in 1959 for a congressional committee, assumed that 1,466 megatons would be ground-burst on military bases and on all major population and industrial centers. The "Spadefork Attack," run in 1962 for the U.S. Office of Emergency Planning, aimed 1,779 megatons primarily at military targets, and air-burst half of the weapons. The "UNCLEX Attack," simulated for the Office of Emergency Planning in 1964, assumed that 1,600 weapons were launched against the United States, and half reached their targets with a yield of 3,583 megatons. In this attack, half of the weapons were deployed against military installations, and the remainder were divided between industry and population. It should be obvious that data-skewing imponderables are numerous even at this point (not only the number of weapons employed and the targets selected, but the time of year and precise hour of attack are among the critical variables that must be specified), but the planners still present distressingly precise profiles of "postattack society."

On the basis of such simulations (Heer 1965), estimates have been made of the exact age and sex composition of "survivors," along with their maritial status, political affiliation, religion, ethnic identity, occupation, educational background, and even their attitudes on welfare and tolerance for nonconformists. One such study concluded that a nuclear attack would slightly increase the proportions of Republicans, Protestants, and conservatives in the total population—as if such considerations would even be relevant after the bomb!

Casualties vary tremendously according to which simulation is used; but of course, none even approach total destruction, because that would mean that there would be no "postattack society" to write about. The Spadefork Attack claims only 18 percent of the population, the Holifield Attack accounts for 30 percent killed, and the UNCLEX Attack for 50 percent killed (approximately 100 million people) and an additional 15 percent injured but surviving. After these attacks the surviving members of the work force immediately go back to their jobs. After UNCLEX, the planners project that 20 percent of our production capacity will be restored within ten days, 30 percent within a year; and the factories will be up to 60 percent of their preattack output after longer repairs. Optimists will be happy to know that, given the enormous population reduction, there will actually be a net increase in the per capita dollar value added in manufacturing. Kahn (1961) predicts that after a moderate nuclear war, if everything goes well, we shall have our gross national product and overall consumption levels back to normal within ten years or less.

Of course, none of these studies attempt to make nuclear war seem desirable, but they are very concerned with improving its bad public image and deemphasizing the horror it would bring. At the Third Interdisciplinary Conference on Selected Aspects of a General War held at Princeton in 1968, biophysicist Stafford Warren stressed the importance of making people believe that they would personally survive a nuclear attack: "[When] we talk about shocking conditions we've got to emphasize too the escape elements in this picture, since we can protect an awful lot of people. Each one must have the hope that he will escape unhurt or unirradiated. While the situation is admittedly grim we've got to do something better in order to break down this log jam of apathy" (DASA 1971:315).

Herman Kahn, in his major study *On Thermonuclear War*, minimizes the social cost of the genetic damage and other injuries that fallout might cause by stressing that these are problems that will be spread thinly and far into the future. For example, he estimates that even though the results of nuclear war are "long-lasting and somewhat incalculable," they *might* add only one percentage point to our present rate of serious birth defects, and he concludes optimistically that "most people will be able to live with such increased risks" (1961:47). He cautions that "we should not magnify our view of the costs of the war inordinately because such postwar risks are added to the wartime casualties" (1961:42). With incredibly shallow regard for the future, he affirms that "if you spread the genetic damage over tens of thousands of years you have done something very useful" (1961:48).

In fact, in spite of all the thousands of pages of special studies on the feasibility of nuclear war, no single definitive sociocultural and environmental impact statement has yet been written on the subject—or, indeed, ever could be written because, properly speaking, the impact of such a war is incalculable. The specialized studies undertaken so far serve only to give planners a false sense of security. By focusing on fragments of the total picture, researchers can very easily reach comfortable conclusions. A study of food availability in postattack society conducted by the Stanford Research Institute, for example, concluded that while

Thelma Lu's Candies would be a total loss when the bomb falls on Albuquerque, Pepsi-Cola and 7-Up bottlers would be back in business within a few weeks, and there would be plenty of potato chips to go around (Rapoport 1971:95–105). At the Third Interdisciplinary Conference, cited earlier, it was pointed out that in general the food problem wouldn't be as bad as some might imagine because "you'll have fewer people to feed . . ." (DASA 1971:311).

Surprisingly, the basic question of whether or not American society as a whole would survive is not usually even faced by most of the planners in their feasibility studies. This point became glaringly obvious at the Third Interdisciplinary Conference, and is well illustrated by the following comment by one of the participants: "[There] is a big difference between laying out the physical possibilities that you've got to work with and trying to answer the question of the extent to which you will have a viable functioning social system in the post-attack period. They're not trying to answer that question; they haven't yet" (DASA 1971:410).

These studies focus on isolated, short-term effects, and lack a real overview. They share the critical weakness of their failure to consider adequately the frailty of the highly specialized and interdependent industrial economic system and the total dependence of this system, in turn, on equally fragile and interdependent ecological systems. Not only will the energy systems be destroyed, but so will the transportation systems that must move the energy that fuels the transportation system. The factories will be destroyed, and so will the machines that make other machines. One study noted as an aside that all the conifers in the entire Northeast would be killed (DASA 1971:303). This would in itself be an ecological disaster that would dwarf any catastrophe in recent experience, and would set off a chain reaction of other totally unpredictable events. There would be staggering problems of social disorder, disease, insect infestations, and radiation contamination.

The Nuclear Winter

> Subfreezing temperatures, low light levels, and high doses of ionizing and ultraviolet radiation extending for many months after a large-

scale nuclear war could destroy the biological support systems of civilization. . . . Productivity in natural and agricultural systems could be severely restricted for a year or more. Postwar survivors would face starvation as well as freezing conditions in the dark and be exposed to near-lethal doses of radiation . . . global disruption of the biosphere could ensue . . . the extinction of the human species itself cannot be excluded. (Ehrlich et al. 1983:1293)

More careful studies of the global, long-term effects of nuclear war (National Academy of Sciences 1975; Ehrlich et al. 1983; Peterson 1983; Turco et al. 1983) have been published since these limited, and often outrageously optimistic, studies appeared during the sixties and early seventies. This new work presents an extremely frightening picture of the effects of even a limited war. It now appears that the most devastating results of nuclear war may be caused by the dust cloud that would be injected into the atmosphere. R. P. Turco and his associates (Turco et al. 1983) used a series of computer models based on previous studies of the climatic effects of atmospheric volcanic ash to show that explosions from even a relatively small portion of the global nuclear arsenal would put enough dust and smoke into the atmosphere to instantly produce a "nuclear winter." According to this research, a "baseline" nuclear war using less than one-third of the estimated 1982 global arsenal of 2,000 megatons would cause land temperatures to plunge within three weeks to lower than −70°F or −23°C. Temperatures would remain below freezing for two months. Similar or even more dramatic cooling effects could be produced by a mere 100 megatons targeted on cities because of the firestorms that would be generated. This study has been given the appropriate acronym of TTAPS after the authors, R. P. Turco, O. B. Toon, T. Ackerman, J. B. Pollack, and C. Sagan, and to emphasize the sobering implications for humanity of any nuclear exchange. Ehrlich et al. (1983), in reviewing some of the biological and ecosystem implications of the TTAPS study, emphasize that many ecosystems would be drastically altered by the nuclear winter. Photosynthesis would be reduced throughout the northern hemisphere, and many animal species would be exterminated. Food production systems would be drastically reduced, and it would be difficult to maintain human social systems. Within a decade, ecosystem recovery would be under way in spite of many irreversible changes, but great instability in natural systems would persist. The inescapable conclusion is that any nuclear war would be suicidal for industrial civilization.

The basic findings of the TTAPS study and their wider implications were reviewed by a distinguished panel of 40 scientists at a conference in Cambridge, Massachusetts, in April 1983. Remarkably, there was complete consensus on the conclusions. No serious faults could be found in any part of the work.

Cross-Cultural Perspectives on War

> A knowledge of how and why primitive peoples made war may shed light on the prospect for war or peace in our own time.
> (Naroll 1966:14)

Perhaps the single most important perspective that anthropologists can bring to the study of war is the contrast between tribal and nation-state war. In fact, depending on the definition of war, it may be said to be totally nonexistent among many of the simplest cultures; and even where it does occur in tribal cultures, there are significant qualitative differences that make tribal war profoundly different from its nation-state counterpart. These points are critical because they bear directly on the central question of whether modern war can be prevented. The evidence strongly suggests that war might be an inherent feature of civilization to such an extent that we cannot have one without the other.

The most widely accepted definitions of war would automatically exclude much of the intergroup conflict that typically occurs between tribal communities. War is generally considered to be an organized armed conflict between political units in pursuit of a group goal. To the extent that *organization* and *group objectives* are emphasized, this kind of war is absent at the lowest levels of culture. Bronislaw Malinowski was emphatic on this point: "[We] do not find among these lowest primitives any organized clash of armed forces aiming at the enforcement of tribal policy. War does not exist among them" (1944:277).

Many writers would further restrict the definition of war to armed conflict between nation-states carried out for national objectives. Quincy Wright, unquestionably the world's leading authority on war, used the term in its widest meaning to include violent intergroup conflict or armed aggression in any form; but in his monumental work *A Study of War*, he strongly emphasized the qualitative differences between tribal and civilized war: "War in the sense of a legal situation equally permitting groups to expand wealth and power by violence began with civilization. . . . Only among civilized people has war been an institution serving political and economic interests of the community, defined by a body of law which states the circumstances justifying its use, the procedures whereby it is begun and ended, and the methods by which it is conducted" (1942:39).

Certainly, the major conclusion of any evolutionary study of intergroup conflict, whatever we choose to call it, is that its form is strongly related to the form of political organization of a given culture. As an empirical generalization, it can be stated that as a culture's political system becomes more centralized, its military organization becomes more complex, its weapons and tactics become more effective, and individual engagements become more costly in terms of casualties (Otterbein 1970). There is also a predictable shift in the immediate goals for fighting and in the supporting ideology. The nature of the interrelationship between political centralization and war cannot yet be precisely explained, but they have evolved together. The state makes war, and war helped to create states.

If the immediate objectives that commonly motivated political communities to fight with their neighbors are analyzed, they can be grouped into four major categories, following the work of several researchers (Wright 1942:278–83; Naroll 1966; Otterbein 1970). These categories are *defense, plunder, prestige,* and *political control*; and it is assumed that they reflect considerations that both military decision makers and the combatants have in mind when they go to war. Anthropologists also recognize many other "functions" of war; these four categories do not pretend to include all the psychological factors that may motivate particular individuals to fight. What is significant about these categories is that they do not occur in different cultures in a random, unpredictable manner; rather, they tend to be distributed in an orderly arrangement that reveals a great deal about the nature of war and its relationship to political organization. There are cultures in which no organized fighting

T A B L E 8 - 1 Political organization and war motives

	Defense	Plunder	Prestige	Control
Uncentralized:				
Bands				
Copper Eskimo	0	0	0	0
Tiwi	+	0	0	0
Tribes				
Somali	+	+	0	0
Wondi	+	+	+	0
Centralized:				
Chiefdoms				
Sema	+	+	+	0
Mutair	+	+	+	0
States				
Thai	+	+	+	+
Aztec	+	+	+	+

Source: Data from a worldwide sample of 46 cultures in Otterbein 1970:148–49.

occurs for any of these reasons, and such societies may justifiably be said to lack war. In general, the motives for war tend to be cumulative, so that, for example, if a culture goes to war in order to extend political control over a neighbor, it will probably also fight for defense, plunder, and prestige. However, if a culture fights for plunder, it may not fight for political control, and those cultures that do not fight for defense do not fight at all. This property of related variables is called *scalability* and is demonstrated for a few selected cultures in Table 8-1. It will be noted that those cultures showing the most motives for war are politically centralized and usually states, whereas those with the fewest motives are politically uncentralized. Figure 8-1 illustrates this relationship more accurately, drawing on data from a worldwide sample of 46 cultures examined by Keith Otterbein (1970) in his cross-cultural study of the evolution of war. It is significant that none of the politically decentralized cultures in his sample used war for purposes of political control, and whereas all centralized cultures fought for defense and economic advantage, many uncentralized cultures did not.

Otterbein also worked with a composite scale of military sophistication that reflected the general military effectiveness of cultures. For

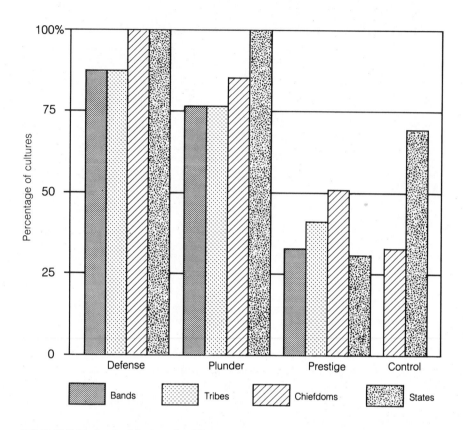

F I G U R E 8 - 1 Motives for War.

Source: Data from a worldwide sample of 46 cultures examined in Otterbein 1970: 66–67.

example, cultures with standing armies or age-grade warrior societies were considered to be militarily more effective than those lacking such organization. Likewise, more flexible tactics, more deadly weapons, the presence of fortifications, negotiations, and war for political domination were all treated as indicative of greater military sophistication. Here again, the split between decentralized tribal cultures and centralized chiefdom and state cultures was striking. Table 8-2 presents the data from the cross-cultural sample that confirms the generalization that more politically centralized societies tend to be more sophisticated militarily.

Attempts to estimate and compare casualty rates are difficult and often misleading, but some trends are obvious (see Table 8-3). Otterbein

TABLE 8-2 Political organization and
military sophistication

Political organization	Military sophistication		
	low	high	total
Centralized	3	13	16
Uncentralized	24	6	30
Total	27	19	46

Source: Data from a worldwide sample of 46 cultures in Otterbein 1970:74.

rated casualty rates as high if a third or more of the forces engaged in given battles are killed, and was able to show that, as military sophistication increases, so do battle casualties. Thus, to the extent that military sophistication is related to political centralization, more politically centralized cultures will tend to have higher casualties. However, it must be noted that in many tribal cultures, virtually all able-bodied males may engage in a particular battle, and thus relatively low casualty rates could be devastating or at least very significant demographically. High casualty rates for battles between states might have a relatively minor demographic impact when a relatively small proportion of the male population is engaged. It is of course true that there is a staggering increase in *absolute* casualties as political systems evolve, but this is only partly due to increased military effectiveness because the forces fielded are also larger in an absolute sense. Surely, however, a qualitative distinction must be recognized when hundreds of millions may be killed within minutes in a single engagement. This level of destruction is, of course, the highest expression of military sophistication.

Cross-cultural comparisons rating the frequency of war have also been used to test the validity of the argument that a high degree of military sophistication acts as a deterrent to war. The evidence suggests that this generalization does not hold true for tribal cultures and preindustrial states. Actually, quite the opposite situation is more likely. * The more sophisticated a community is militarily, the more frequently it engages in aggressive war and is itself attacked in turn. Thus, we may cautiously

---

*Both Otterbein (1970) and Naroll (1966) make this point.

T A B L E 8 - 3 Military sophistication and casualty rates

Military sophistication	Casualty rates		
	low	high	total
High	7	8	15
Low	13	5	18
Total	20	13	33

Source: Data from a worldwide sample of 46 cultures in Otterbein 1970. Data were not available to evaluate all 46 cultures on these variables.

generalize that as cultures become more politically centralized, they become more militaristic, fight more often, and have higher casualty rates.

Otterbein also noted a strong positive correlation between a high degree of military sophistication and military "success" measured in terms of expanding territorial boundaries. Approximately half of the militarily sophisticated societies in his sample were expanding their territories, while only 15 percent of the "unsophisticated" cultures were expanding. Thus, it would be easy to conclude that a more effective military capability is a selective advantage for a culture in competition with its neighbors. However, nuclear weapons, even though they may represent the highest degree of sophistication, would appear to be a distinct disadvantage. Cultures engaging in nuclear war are very unlikely to emerge victorious.

War can also be viewed in terms of the technological systems that support it. W. W. Newcomb, Jr. (1960) presents a four-part typology placing the simplest hunter-gatherers in Type 1, and arguing that their technology simply could not support large armies on extended campaigns and gave them nothing special to fight for, anyway. Type 2 war includes what is usually considered "tribal war." Here again, there is little economic incentive for prolonged fighting, but technological productivity is high enough to support more elaborate campaigns than previously. Type 3 war includes "civilized war" based on a developed agriculture and a complex division of labor. Type 4 includes modern war based on fossil fuels, and is vastly larger in scope and more destructive than any previous wars. A fifth type, "nuclear war," might obviously be added. This typology does not of course explain the existence of war, but it does help to specify some of the limitations and possiblilities inherent in particular technological systems.

War and Human Nature

> [It] is meaningless to say that war is inevitable because of the pugnacity of man as an animal. While man has original drives that make war possible, that possibility has only been realized in appropriate social and political conditions. (Wright 1942:5)

The issue of the relationship between war and human nature has been argued and reargued for many years. Quincy Wright's above-quoted response to the debate represents the careful conclusion of a scholar who directed the University of Chicago's Social Science Research Committee project on the causes of war from 1926 to 1941. Prominent anthropologists such as Bronislaw Malinowski (1941) and Margaret Mead (1940), who joined the debate during World War II, took much the same position; and this view remains the general consensus among anthropologists today. Humans may indeed possess an innate capacity for aggression, but this capacity must be culturally shaped.

Unfortunately, the basic question has apparently not been settled to everyone's satisfaction. The issue was revived in the 1960s by popular writers such as Robert Ardrey (1966) and Konrad Lorenz (1966), and the whole question continues to have important implications for the current debate on alternatives to war. Ardrey, for example, argues that man's innate agressiveness and territoriality are a basic foundation for war. This has practical implications because those who emphasize the instinctive argument would have us study our biological background to learn the causes of war and, presumably, methods of preventing it. This approach diverts attention from the critical *cultural* factors that are the real causes of war, and leads to the conclusion that war either is inevitable or can be prevented if humanity's innate aggression is channeled from war into harmless sporting events. Meanwhile, the fundamental cultural basis for war goes unchallenged.

Much of this debate has not been very fruitful and is certainly misleading. Aggression must be clearly distinguished from war; whereas agresssion per se might be understandable to some extent in biological terms, warfare is a *cultural* phenomenon carried on between cultural groups. From the foregoing discussion of the evolution of war, it should be clear that during most of humanity's existence, war, as usually defined, simply did not exist until the evolution of centralized political organization, even though humanity's biological inheritance must have remained constant. War very often does have an obvious boundary-maintaining aspect, but if "territoriality" is instinctive, this instinct, like the "instinct" for violence, is almost infinitely variable because many human groups do not fight over territory. It certainly does not seem very illuminating to view the present arms race as either a result of instinctive territoriality or aggression between the United States and the Soviet Union.

Another side of the human nature approach that is equally misleading is the view that we must understand individual psychology if we are to explain war. It is of course true that individuals must be psychologically prepared for war, and that soldiers may be motivated to fight by factors originating within their own personalities; but the fact remains that these "causes" of war are overshadowed by more basic cultural variables. The dynamics of individual psychology, like humanity's capacity for violence, can be culturally expressed in a variety of ways, which may or may not include war.

The Causes of War

> From an anthropological perspective any kind of war is generally a symptom of the absence, inadequacy, or breakdown of other procedures for resolving conflicts. (Koch 1970:43)

Anthropological research supports the conclusion that war is caused by many interacting variables, and it seems doubtful that any fully adequate single explanation for its existence will ever be found. However, the general factors predisposing a given culture to war, and some of war's probable effects or functions, can be outlined. At the broadest level, as the above quotation suggests, war is simply one way of dealing with conflict, but it must be stressed that the sources of conflict are largely culturally determined, as is the form the conflict will actually take.

Perhaps more anthropological attention has been devoted to developing functional analyses of war than to any other aspect of the problem.[*] Functionalist research merely attempts to answer the question: "What does war do in a given society?" It does not provide a complete explanation of why war exists or how it came to be. The assumption is simply being made that it must have had survival value for certain cultures under certain adaptive conditions. This stance should not, however, be construed as a defense of the status quo or a rationalization for war. When an anthropologist states that war in a particular society performs some critical adaptive function, that is not to say that something else might not do the job as well or even better. Critics (Hallpike 1973) correctly point out that war may be beneficial for certain groups at certain levels of analysis, whereas it may be very disadvantageous in other respects. It should also be stressed that funtionalists do not assume that individuals waging war are necessarily aware of the "functions" they are serving.

Many of the most convincing and interesting functional explanations of war deal with its role in maintaining ecological balances. Warfare serves the obvious function of helping to adjust local imbalances that may develop between land or other resources and people. There is ample evidence that even in tribal cultures, local groups may sometimes be wiped out and their territory confiscated by their neighbors, but such events are relatively infrequent. Chronic warfare may also have a significant demographic impact. Raiding for the express purpose of acquiring wives, and thereby redistributing women, is also not uncommon. It has been suggested that at least one effect of stock raiding in herding societies is to help maintain herd size at optimum levels (Sweet 1965). Groups with especially large herds might logically be more vulnerable to raiding parties than those with very small, easily defended herds. Empirical evidence to support this hypothesis is scanty, but it is an interesting possibility. War is certainly one possible outcome of "pressure" on resources; but, as was noted in a previous chapter, this kind of pressure is not easily defined, and there are many other cultural solutions to the problem. In view of the extraordinary resource consumption rates that have come to characterize industrial civilization, however, resource competition may well be one of the most important causes of modern war. Furthermore, the incredible global imbalances that now exist in consumption may become the basis for "wars of redistribution."

---

[*]See, for example, Vayda (1968).

War has many not so obvious side effects that merit consideration. For example, in the Tsembaga example cited in Chapter 6, war was apparently a critical element in a delicately balanced equilibrium system. An intriguing side effect of the warfare between the Chippewa and Sioux Indians from 1780 to 1850 was the conversion of their vast battleground into a de facto game preserve for their most important game animal—the Virginia deer (Hickerson 1965). Perpetual hostility between the two groups made hunting a very risky affair over a large area of prime deer habitat in western Wisconsin and central Minnesota. It is assumed that this buffer zone provided a steady stock to replenish the more heavily hunted areas and served as a strategic reserve in times of unusual scarcity when hunters might disregard the dangers of ambush and hunt within the contested zone itself. Similar buffer zones seem to be a common characteristic along the frontiers separating many tribal cultures, and in many of these cases a resource conservation effect may also be important.

At the lowest levels of sociopolitical organization, conflict arising from interpersonal relations involving individuals from different sovereign groups often resulted in chronic intergroup feuding and perpetual hostility. In many societies that lacked centralized political authority strong enough to punish offenders, personal revenge seeking through armed retaliation was the only way for dealing with intergroup crimes such as murder, theft, rape, and trespass. As political organization and economic productivity become more developed, intergroup competition for important resources replaces personal revenge as the most obvious cause of conflict. In fact, some authorities argue convincingly that conflict over restricted prime agricultural land between expanding societies was a principal cause of war and the evolution of the state itself (Carneiro 1970). This "environmental circumscription" theory does seem to explain neatly why most of the first states developed where they did and why states never evolved independently in many areas where basic resources were unbounded. It does not, however, explain the conflict-generating growth itself; but as was discussed in earlier chapters, this is one of the key problems for anthropology, and the "circumscription" theory cannot be faulted for not answering it. There are undoubtedly other intervening variables involved in state formation, but it is clear that war does become a basic factor in the continued growth and maintenance of states once they appear.

Perhaps the most important point to consider is that states possess unique features, absent in tribal cultures, that must increase the likelihood of war, and that industrialization makes these features even more pronounced. The intensification of economic production and consumption is an obvious feature of state systems that places great additional stress on natural resources and must make competition over resources much more likely. Social stratification by wealth must further intensify this major disequilibrium factor. Another critical aspect of the class system is that it creates politically powerful groups with vested interests in promoting wars for their own advantage and places them in a position to manipulate the lower classes to this end.

With industrialization, the development of world markets has added a new dimension to the potential for conflict, and global wars have made their appearance. Although many authorities may debate the role that resource competition played in the two world wars recorded in our history books, there can be little doubt that it was the principal cause for the long war between civilization and tribal cultures. During the final phase of this war, between approximately 1780 and 1930, as many as 50 million tribal people may have died and approximately half of the globe was wrested from their control (Bodley 1975:38-41). The terminal skirmishes of this conflict for resources are still taking place, but remarkably little note has been made of these events, even though in scale and importance they must dwarf our own world wars.

There is really no reason to separate war from the total world crisis because wars, like urban violence, overpopulation, and environmental deterioration, are merely symptoms of the underlying adaptive shortcomings of industrial civilization. The present sources of intergroup conflict may be sought in the imbalances of wealth and power that exist at both national and international levels, and in the rising stresses of population and increasing resource consumption. These destabilizing factors, together with the absence of effective alternatives to war as a means of conflict resolution, are at the root of our present crisis.

Preventing War

The most popular and obvious means of preventing war call for the establishment of some form of world political structure. Indeed, cultural evolutionist Leslie A. White argued more than 20 years ago that such a step would be a logical evolutionary development and the *only* way to bring world peace: "World peace will come, if it ever does, not because we shall have bred out the pugnacious instinct, or sublimated it in mass athletic contests, but because cultural development, social evolution, will have reached the ultimate conclusion of the age-old process of merging smaller social groups into larger ones, eventually forming a single political organization that will embrace the entire planet and the whole human race" (1949:134).

The United Nations is of course a step in that direction, and many other ingenious world political mechanisms have been proposed, but it seems unlikely that these efforts will be really successful unless the more basic causes of conflict and the deeper problems of industrial civilization are also dealt with. There is a clear need to increase research efforts toward understanding the causes and the extent of our present ecological imbalances, as well as the nature of stratification and the cultural foundation of the military system. We may also gain many useful ideas for the establishment of a viable world order by examining conflict-reducing mechanisms built into many tribal cultures. It could even be argued, as we point out in the following chapter, that the single, world political organization is the answer only if it is combined with a world organized along a tribal model of small, autonomous, "tribal" nations.

9
THE FUTURE

Obviously, we stand on the threshold of postcivilization.
When we reach solutions to today's problems, the
society and culture that we will have built for the
purpose will be of a sort the world has never seen
before. It may be more, or less, civilized than what we
have, but it will not be civilization as we know it.

Paul Bohannan, "Beyond Civilization"

The future cannot of course be precisely predicted, but no view of the future will be satisfactory if it does not consider the pervasive nature of the present crisis and the many separate risks it poses. The future will almost certainly be a "solution," either planned or unplanned, to the diverse problems created by industrial civilization. In this final chapter, we argue that all the crises discussed so far are manifestations of what is in fact a single world crisis that will only be solved by a complete cultural transformation. This is perhaps the most important conclusion to be drawn from the present work, and provides a basis both for assessing the effectiveness of the many planning programs now being developed to shape the future and for evaluating the many alternative futures that futurist researchers are exploring.

The Diagnosis: "Terminal Civilization"·

Our problems are all extremely complex, interrelated, and in a general sense multicausal, but many of the most critical are obvious correlates of evolutionary progress. Over and over in the preceding chapters, it has been shown that a specific crisis was either totally absent or at least not a serious problem before the evolution of civilization. Many crises have not arisen or not become critical until the appearance of industrial civilization. However, it would be misleading to state that civilization has itself been the direct cause of our most serious problems, because many of the conditions that we are here calling problems enjoy a peculiar cause-and-effect relationship with cultural progress. For example, war, population growth, and technological advance are all causes of and results of general evolutionary progress. Any attempt to single out causes is further complicated by the fact that individual crises are themselves interrelated in similar feedback mechanisms—population growth may lead to war, which accelerates technological advances, which promote population growth, and so forth.

This multicausality and complex interrelationship between problems has important implications for any attempt to identify causes and find

---

·This phrase was used in a cartoon by Ron Cobb published in 1970.

solutions. In many cases, it is apparent that current problem-solving efforts are inadequate because they treat isolated symptoms and avoid basic underlying factors. An example from the medical field may illustrate this point. In 1956, T. L. Cleave (1974), surgeon-captain of the British Royal Navy, linked together a list of seemingly diverse diseases, including dental decay, peptic ulcers, obesity, diabetes, constipation, and varicose veins, into a single category that he called the "saccharine disease." Using historical data and research on tribal peoples, he argued that all these conditions are caused at least in part by the extensive use of concentrated carbohydrates such as sugar and white flour by modern industrialized populations. This radical change in diet over the patterns that humans had evolved during many thousands of years altered body chemistry and greatly slowed transit times in the digestive tract by reducing dietary bulk, thereby creating many pathogenic conditions. Other researchers had simply not seen the problems as related, perhaps because they did not examine populations in which these pathologies were absent, and they did not seek basic cultural causes. At higher levels of analysis, it may be that virtually all of the easily recognized crises—including war, pollution, poverty, overpopulation, overconsumption, hunger, and alcoholism—are, like the saccharine disease, really different manifestations of a single interrelated cultural "disease" that might be labeled "civilization." Industrialization may be simply the terminal phase that has developed after a 5,000-year incubation period.

To be convincing, this "cultural pathology" approach must identify tribal cultures as the major cultural type that does not suffer from the disease, and it must also sort out the specific cultural conditions that seem to be most directly responsible for the symptoms. In a general sense, it appears that the closely interrelated variables, *social stratification* and extreme *specialization of labor*, are perhaps the most fundamental characteristics of civilization, from which other critical problem-causing features are ultimately derived. Stratification and specialization are the foundation of the market economy, wealth and concentration, political centralization, and the frequent conflict between individual and subgroup self-interest, on the one hand, and societal interest, on the other. All of these cultural arrangements, although they are not in themselves crises, do tend to promote overpopulation, overconsumption, and other symptoms of the environmental crisis, and are clearly linked to poverty, war, crime, and many personal crises.

At this phase of the disease, continued specialization may be a fatal flaw. Specialists are now busily treating symptoms as causes; and in many cases, certain groups even have a special stake in—and indeed may profit by treating—specific symptoms. The defense establishment, for example, "treats" war, the police and legal professions treat crime, and various health and social work professions handle personal crises. The very specialization of these fields makes it unlikely that researchers will perceive connections between deliberately isolated and apparently unrelated symptoms. In many cases, even if a definitive solution were discovered, it would almost certainly be resisted by specialist groups because it might be a clear threat to their job security. Real peace would cause enormous dislocation for the military, and numerous studies indicate that even disarmament would have far-reaching economic repercussions within the military-industrial complex and throughout the entire economy. It should be no surprise that the discovery of the saccharine disease and its simple cure has had relatively little impact on either the health or the food industries. In this case the investigation has not been carried far enough. The concentrated carbohydrates that seem to be the immediate cause of so many of our current health problems are produced and distributed by a massive food industry, which in turn is merely one expression of extreme stratification and specialization.

If this analysis is correct, radical surgery may be the only certain way to save the patient. Extreme forms of social stratification and economic specialization may simply be maladaptive. The kind of drastic cultural transformation that eliminating, or at least detoxicating, stratification and specialization would involve is so profound that it might seem sheer madness even to propose it. However, such a transformation and its full implications should be explored. It may be some comfort to realize that the kinds of cultural changes that might be required to effect a cure are no more sweeping than the kinds of changes that have been thrust upon much of the so-called "developing world" in recent decades. In fact, economist Robert L. Heilbroner's prescription for development may describe precisely the scope of the change that will be needed to solve the world crisis: "Nothing short of a pervasive social transformation will suffice: a wholesale metamorphosis of habits, a wrenching reorientation of values concerning time, status, money, work; an unweaving and reweaving of the fabric of daily existence itself" (1963:53).

Impact Assessment and Regional Planning

Large-scale regional planning projects and environmental impact studies are new efforts to identify and alleviate at least some of the adverse side effects of progress before they occur. Although this work does represent a very promising attempt to shape the future along more desirable lines, and even though it is wide in scope and interdisciplinary in nature, it still lacks the anthropological perspectives that would provide a broad sense of the problem and a clear definition of future goals.

In the United States the National Environmental Policy Act of 1969 (United States, Environmental Protection Agency 1973) provides the legal charter for a sweeping evaluation of the immediate and long-run impact of industrial expansion on humanity and on the environment. The broad purpose of the act is to make it official policy to encourage harmony between humans and nature, to prevent damage to the biosphere, and to stimulate human health and welfare. This purpose is to be accomplished without sacrificing a "high standard of living"; but it is clear that "progress," as it has been measured in the past, will not continue to be the sole standard of national welfare. There is explicit recognition of the fact that unchecked population growth, industrialization, urbanization, and resource exploitation represent serious threats to the well-being of the nation. The act specifically declares that "all practical means" be used to carry out the policy, and requires that all federal agencies use a "systematic, interdisciplinary approach," including the social sciences, in environmental decision making. Most importantly, the act requires that for every federal action "significantly affecting the quality of the human environment" an environmental impact statement must be prepared, detailing:

1. The environmental impact of the proposed action
2. Any adverse environmental effects that cannot be avoided should the proposal be implemented
3. Alternatives to the proposed action
4. The relationship between local short-term uses of the environment and the maintenance and enhancement of long-term productivity
5. Any irreversible and irretrievable commitments of resources that

would be involved in the proposed action should it be implemented

If these questions were raised for all major cultural activites in modern industrial states and were then systematically investigated, the underlying causes of the world crisis would almost certainly be uncovered, and basic remedial action might be possible. This is clearly an area of research in which anthropologists can make a profound contribution toward guiding our future cultural development. Assessing the impact of cultural practices on people, nature, and culture has long been a concern of anthropology; but in the past, this activity has not been directed toward specific goals, such as providing solutions to the world crisis.

Impact assessment is still in an experimental stage, but a number of weaknesses in the present procedure are already apparent. In the first place, future "needs" that proposed actions are designed to satisfy are characteristically identified on the basis of current cultural conditions and past trends. Thus an inherently conservative element is built in, and projections for future growth in population and consumption become self-fulfilling prophesies. There has also been a tendency to deemphasize the cultural implications of proposed actions in favor of detailed treatment of the immediate impact on nature, and a concomitant failure to explore fully the "no-action" or "no-growth" alternative.

In many cases, impact statements also suffer from the limitations of specialization. Problems are seen in isolation, and even though they may be explored individually in great detail, their aggregate consequences and implications may be overlooked. The construction of an electric transmission line in a particular county, the Alaska oil pipeline, and coal stripping in the West are treated in separate statements, while more fundamental questions of energy use in the culture may be either completely avoided or else handled by other specialists. Radically different solutions to the problems posed are simply not being adequately explored. Basic questions regarding human needs, the long-range viability of our system of cultural adaptation, and the assessment of human costs and benefits in a highly stratified society are still not being adequately addressed. These are anthropological questions; unfortunately, however, not even anthropologists have yet shown sufficient interest in them. Perhaps anthropologists should prepare an environmental impact statement for civilization as a whole and seriously attempt to detail the full consequences of this profound cultural transformation.

Planning Progress for the Pacific Northwest

The shortcomings of present planning processes and the possibilities for anthropological input may be explored further by a brief consideration of a concrete example. Among the most ambitious attempts at regional planning have been the massive studies of future land and water development in the United States that were authorized by the Water Resources Planning Act of 1965. Here, we shall examine the Columbia-North Pacific Region Comprehensive Framework Study (Pacific Northwest River Basins Commission 1971–1973) that was conducted over a five-year period by 20 federal agencies in cooperation with seven western state governments. The main report covering the entire region consists of a summary volume and an 18-volume appendix that runs into thousands of pages covering such topics as energy, flood control, wildlife, the economic base, and so on. In addition, there are subregional studies that are equally impressive. The overall purpose of the project was outlined as follows: "to provide a broad guide to the best use, or combination of uses, of water and related land resources of a region to meet foreseeable short- and long-term needs. This involves broad scaled analyses of the region's water and related land resource problems, both present and future, and general appraisals of the probable nature, extent, and timing of measures for their solution."

By A.D. 2020, the planners project that the population of the region will more than double its 1970 base population of 6.3 million, per capita incomes will triple or quadruple, requirements for electrical energy will increase tenfold, water requirements will triple, the potential for flood damage will quadruple, and there will be enormous unsatisfied demands for recreation, fish, and game. A vast, multibillion-dollar proposal was made for the development of new reservoirs, thermal power plants, and numerous special projects and programs, all designed to meet future "demands" and still preserve environmental "quality" and retain "flexibility" for future contingencies.

Some of the limitations of this immense planning project are immediately apparent when it is realized that economic efficiency and regional economic development are ranked among the primary objectives and that future needs are only projected for 50 years. There is no systematic treatment of the basic fossil fuel energy base and the implications of shortages. Likewise, there is no detailed consideration of radical alternatives to the need for electric energy such as the reduction of demand or the development of decentralized low-output domestic generators. Also overlooked is the basic question of what kind of regional culture might be developed if the billions of dollars slated for further expansion along the lines already laid down were to be diverted to the development of an essentially low-energy means of satisfying basic human needs. The anthropological record provides countless other solutions to the problem of developing land and water resources that simply have not been considered. By 1984 it became apparent that the planners had not anticipated the actual decline in energy demand that occurred following the dramatic global increases in energy costs beginning in 1973–74. People in the Pacific Northwest, as elsewhere in the industrial world, responded to the "energy crisis" by using less energy and by using it more efficiently. There have also been significant developments in the use of solar energy. Furthermore, the planners failed to anticipate the enormous cost of nuclear power plant construction and the widespread public opposition to this energy form. By 1984 several partly constructed nuclear plants were abandoned in the Northwest because they were no longer economically feasible.

Views of the Future

In recent decades, there has been an enormous outpouring of future-oriented literature. Although no attempt at a full survey of this work will be undertaken here, it is possible to examine some of the alternatives that futurists envision in terms of the anthropological perspectives on the world crisis developed in preceding chapters. For convenience, futurist writers may be grouped into three categories:

1. Biological evolutionists and consciousness transformationists
2. Scientific technocrats
3. Paraprimitivists

Biological evolutionists and consciousness transformationists such as Teilhard de Chardin are concerned with drastic transformations of humanity's present biological and/or psychic makeup. Possibilities here are almost endless, but if any should materialize, humanity's basic nature might totally change. However, such changes must either lie in the remote future or will be unaffected by deliberate planning, and need not concern us here.

Scientific technocrats such as Buckminster Fuller and Herman Kahn seem to have captured most of the attention of government planners. These futurists emphasize continual technological changes as the solution for all problems. Kahn and Anthony J. Wiener, perhaps the most influential of the futurists, present a detailed projection for the next few decades in their major work *The Year 2000*, published in 1967. This work grew out of attempts to explore alternative futures supported by the Commission on the Year 2000 of the American Academy of Arts and Sciences and the Hudson Institute, a private research organization. Much of the book is built around the basic assumption that there will be a continuation at least to A.D. 2000 of what the authors call the *basic, long-term multifold trend* of industrialization, modernization, urbanization, population growth, and technological advance. Whereas it is recognized that "surprising" deviations (such as war and natural disasters) from this "standard world" are possible, no serious internal problems are expected to prevent the arrival of a "postindustrial society" of mass leisure and affluence. There is no sense of an obvious world crisis in this projection. Five years later, in *Things to Come* (Kahn and Bruce-Briggs 1972), the "unlikely" possibility of a technological collapse, economic crises, and disillusionment with progress is given somewhat more credence, but the basic multifold trends still seem assured.

The Best of Both Worlds: A Paraprimitive Solution

[If] we are aware of our own best interests, we should try to restore to some extent to our own technological society the structured character of a pre-industrial society. Can we not combine the advantages of the former with those of the latter? Or, if we cannot have the best of both worlds, should we not find some compromise solution? (Taylor 1972:154)

For our purposes, the most important and promising group of futurist writers and planners are those who demonstrate a clear appreciation of the gravity and complexity of the world crisis and explore truly radical alternatives designed to solve the basic problems. One of the most thorough outlines for a national-level cultural transformation was published in 1972 by the editors of the British science journal *The Ecologist*, under the title *Blueprint for Survival* (Goldsmith et al. 1972). This work begins with the assumption that the continuation of present trends—or in Kahn's terms, the "long-term multiform trend"—will mean certain collapse for industrial civilization within the lifetime of many persons living today. The authors feel that radical change of some type is inevitable, and rest their argument primarily on the environmental crisis and related social system disruptions. The goal set for their planning is the creation of a truly stable and sustainable society that will "give the fullest possible satisfaction to its members" (Goldsmith 1972:21-23). Such a society would display the following characteristics (Goldsmith et al. 1972:23):

1. Minimum disruption of ecological processes
2. Maximum conservation of materials and energy
3. A population in which recruitment equals loss
4. A social system in which the individual can enjoy, rather than feel restricted by, the first three conditions

The specific means by which this goal may be achieved do indeed represent a sweeping transformation of industrial culture and are so clearly spelled out that they deserve to be presented in full (Goldsmith et al. 1972:23–24):

1. A control operation whereby environmental disruption is reduced as much as possible by technical means
2. A freeze operation, in which present trends are halted
3. A systematic substitution, by which the most dangerous com-

ponents of these trends are replaced by technological substitutes whose effect is less deleterious in the short term and whose use over the long term will be increasingly ineffective

4. Systematic substitution, by which these technological substitutes are replaced by "natural" or self-regulating ones
5. The invention, promotion, and application of alternative technologies that are energy- and materials-conservative
6. Decentralization of polity and economy at all levels, and the formation of communities small enough to be reasonably self-regulating and self-supporting
7. Education for such communities

At the heart of the proposals to reduce ecological disruption is basically a reestablishment of natural as opposed to technological regulation of ecological processes. In agriculture, for example, the *Blueprint* envisions heavy reliance on biological control of insect pests and on organic fertilizers. Resource management would be accomplished by a tax system that would punish wasteful use of energy and raw materials, and reward long-lived, labor-intensive products. Pressure on the natural environment would also be reduced by the establishment of a stationary population. In Britian, where population already exceeds the carrying capacity in terms of local food production, the plan calls for a reduction in population by 50 percent over the next 150 to 200 years.

Significantly, the key to the entire transformation lies in the social system, which of course should be no surprise to anthropologists. The *Blueprint* points out that within a small, relatively face-to-face and highly self-sufficient community, individuals would be much more likely to organize and accept the cultural restraints that would be needed to maintain long-term stability. Borrowing freely on anthropological views of tribal communities, the authors emphasize that such small-scale societies would also provide abundant personal satisfactions and stimulation that would more than compensate for the reduction in consumption that stability would require. Decentralization, self-sufficiency, and self-regulation would greatly reduce the need for transportation—and many obvious costs of urbanization and massive centralized political systems. What they recommend is not a total abandonment of the nation-state concept, but rather the establishment of a new political system based on neighborhoods of 500 people as minimal units organized into communities of 5,000 and regions of 500,000 with national representation. The selection of 500 as the size of the minimal unit is surely no accident because, as has been indicated earlier, this is the mean size for many tribal societies and may represent the operation of some fundamentally human characteristics. Their plans call for well-integrated, carefully timed implementation stretching over many years.

Biologist Paul Ehrlich has developed an alternative future along similar lines (Ehrlich and Harriman 1971; Ehrlich and Ehrlich 1974). He argues that the most developed nations (*overdeveloped* in his terms) must undergo dedevelopment, and he proposes a new constitution and complete political reorganization for the United States to help achieve such a goal. The presently underdeveloped areas must settle for semidevelopment emphasizing agrarian self-sufficiency, and a total restructuring of the world trade system will be required.

These proposals are drastic, of course, and they will be criticized as totally unreasonable and politically impossible to implement. The authors of the *Blueprint* have a very direct response to such criticisms: "If we plan remedial action with our eyes on political rather than ecological reality, then very reasonably, very practicably, and very surely we shall muddle our way to extinction" (Goldsmith et al. 1972:18).

What Ehrlich and the *Blueprint* propose is basically what Taylor calls the *paraprimitive solution.* It is an attempt to combine the best elements of industrial civilization with the obviously superior components of tribal cultures to establish a stable utopian society. The notion of such a synthesis has very strong appeal, as a brief glance at the strength of the so-called counterculture indicates. It was estimated by Conover in 1973 that there were then some 2,000 communes, 200 underground newspapers, 50 journals, and 500 free schools actively exploring alternatives to the dominant consumption culture in the United States. Although this "counter culture" attracts much less attention today than it did in the seventies, it is still very active in both the United States and Europe. There is, of course, great diversity in the degree to which these groups reject industrial technology, but their pervasive disenchantment with progress and their frequent use of tribal models is striking. Very few, if any, of these experimental communities are totally self-sufficient, or really tribal in the strict sense. They are still dependent on the larger culture for many of their basic needs and can exist only with its sufferance. Furthermore, as Gordon Rattray Taylor (1972) points out, for a paraprimitive community to prove really successful, it must involve a larger number of people than most present communes are working with. A model paraprimitive society would theoretically include several local communities of 500 people and would need to sustain a minimum level of "soft" industrial technology, presumably including medicine, engineering, electronics, and assorted other specialties. We do not know what the minimum size of such a society would be, but this is a question that could certainly be investigated. There could be wide differences in the technological mix, population density, and other cultural features that individual societies might opt for, depending on local environmental conditions and other considerations.

The most critical question, however, is whether industrial technology could be supported by a society that rejected stratification and extreme specialization. As long as these two fundamental elements of civilization are retained, it seems unlikely that the very real advantages of tribal culture can be secured. In a sense, the experiment has already failed. There have been countless well-intended efforts to guide the "acculturation" of tribal societies coming into contact with the industrial world to allow them to enjoy "the best of both worlds"; but invariably these tribal societies have been destroyed in the process. Elsewhere, I have argued that tribal cultures and industrial civilization are simply incompatible—no fruitful merging can ever be achieved. However, the concept of deliberately planned synthetic cultures may well be a different matter, and until such cultures have been seriously experimented with from an anthropologically solid base, the possibility of a truly successful paraprimitive solution should not be completely rejected.

The Small-Nation Alternative

> Thus we see that a small-state world would not only solve the problems of social brutality and war: it would solve the equally terrible problems of oppression and tyranny. It would solve all problems arising from power. (Leopold Kohr 1978:79)

In 1957, in an obscure book entitled *The Breakdown of Nations,* the economist Leopold Kohr modestly proposed a "new and unified political philosophy" based on a "theory of size"(Kohr 1978:xviii). This new theory contained the solution to all the world's problems, Kohr argued. According to Kohr, the basic problem underlying all forms of "social misery" was "bigness"—nations had become too large. Large nations simply could not prevent their power from becoming internally oppressive, and they could not prevent devastating wars. He identified precisely the problems in state organization that emerge when states are contrasted with tribal societies, even though he did not have a clear picture of what tribal societies were like. Kohr argued very persuasively that a world divided into small nations of relatively equal power would be safer and more humane. His conclusions were so profound, and were applied to so many diverse world problems, that he was virtually ignored. The original edition of the book was published in England, and only 500 copies reached the United States. The book was soon out of print, and it has now virtually disappeared. The work did inspire fellow economist E. F. Schumacher (1973) to write *Small is Beautiful,* stressing the advantages of small-scale solutions and "appropriate technology" for economic problems. The popularity of *Small is Beautiful* prompted the republication of Kohr's work, but it is again out of print and few people appear to have appreciated its significance.

However, it appears that Kohr has proposed the most comprehensive and perhaps the best solution to global problems. I find his solution particularly persuasive because, after finishing the first edition of *Anthropology and Contemporary Human Problems,* I had independently concluded that small nations—that is, autonomous states of a million people or less—could perhaps be designed to satisfy basic human needs on a sustained basis. They might in effect be "tribal states" that could implement the "paraprimitive solution." Kohr has made the argument for me, and carries it further by proposing a global system of small states. In 1977 anthropologist Sol Tax, also independently, made a strikingly similar proposal for the solution of global problems. Tax suggested that the world be divided into 10,000 relatively self-sufficient, politically autonomous "localities" averaging 500,000 people each (Tax 1977:229). These local territories would be connected by an egalitarian global communication network.

A world of small nations would of course still contain nations, and each nation would presumably still be stratified and hierarchical, but they could in theory be more responsive to the needs of their people. Furthermore, like tribes, they would be dependent on their own resources, and would have an immediate interest in taking care of them. There would be room for great diversity in the kinds of solutions that might be developed to solve problems relating local cultures to local environments. It is not assumed that a small-nation world would be a utopia or totally free from war. There would still be internal conflict and local wars, but both would be easier to contain and much less destructive. Nuclear weapons, however, would certainly present a special problem.

Kohr points out that the kind of small states that he envisions already exist, as represented by local cultural and linguistic groupings. These "nations" simply must be given political autonomy. He suggests that the large nations can break themselves down into appropriately sized small nations by providing local "nationalities" with equal voting power within a federal system, which can then dissolve itself. Kohr feels that this would be a perfectly feasible way to create a small-nation world, but he is not optimistic about this ever coming about. The shortest chapter in his book is entitled "The Elimination of Great Powers: Can It Be Done?" The chapter contains one word: "No!" (Kohr 1978:197).

BIBLIOGRAPHY

Alkire, William H. *Coral Islanders*. Arlington Heights, Ill.: AHM, 1978.

Alvarado, Anita L. "Determinants of Population Stability in the Havasupai Indians." *American Journal of Physical Anthropology* 33, no. 1(1970): 9–14.

Anderson, E. N., Jr. "The Life and Culture of Ecotopia." In *Reinventing Anthropology*, edited by Dell Hymes, 264–83. New York: Pantheon, 1969.

Anthropology Resource Center. *Native Americans and Energy Development*. Cambridge, Mass.: ARC, 1978.

Ardrey, Robert. *The Territorial Imperative*. New York: Atheneum, 1966.

Arnold, James R. "The Hydrogen-Cobalt Bomb." *Bulletin of the Atomic Scientists* 6, no. 10(1950): 290–92.

Asimov, Isaac. "The End." *Penthouse*, January 1971.

Barclay, Harold. *People Without Government*. London: Kahn & Averill & Cienfuegos, 1982.

Barnett, Harold, and Chandler Morse. *Scarcity and Growth: The Economics of Natural Resource Availability*. Baltimore: Johns Hopkins University Press, 1963.

Barney, Gerald O., ed. *The Global 2000 Report to the President of the U.S.* 3 vols. New York: Pergamon, 1977–1980.

Bartlett, H. H. "Fire, Primitive Agriculture, and Grazing in the Tropics." In *Man's Role in Changing the Face of the Earth*, edited by William L. Thomas, Jr., 692–720. Chicago: University of Chicago Press, 1956.

Basso, Keith. "Ice and Travel Among the Fort Norman Slaves: Folk Taxonomies and Cultural Rules." *Language in Society* 1(1972): 31–49.

232

Bayliss-Smith, Tim. "Constraints on Population Growth: The Case of the Polynesian Outlier Atolls in the Precontact Period." *Human Ecology* 2, no. 4(1974): 259–95.

Beckerman, Stephen. "Does the Swidden Ape the Jungle?" *Human Ecology* 11, no. 1(1983): 1–12.

Bell, Diane. *Aboriginal Women and the Religious Experience*. Young Australian Scholar Lecture Series, no. 3. Bedford Park, South Australia: Australian Association for the Study of Religions, South Australian College of Advanced Education, 1982.

Benedict, Ruth. *Patterns of Culture*. New York: Mentor, 1959. (Originally published in 1934.)

Bergman, R. *Shipibo Subsistence in the Upper Amazon Rainforest*. Ann Arbor, Michigan: University Microfilms, 1974.

Bern, John. "Ideology and Domination: Toward a Reconstruction of Australian Aboriginal Social Formation." *Oceania* 50, no. 2(1979): 118–32.

Berndt, Catherine H. "Interpretations and 'Facts' in Aboriginal Australia." In *Woman the Gatherer*, edited by Frances Dahlberg, 153–203. New Haven: Yale University Press, 1981.

Berreman, Gerald D. "Social Inequality: A Cross-Cultural Analysis." In *Social Inequality: Comparative and Developmental Approaches*, edited by Gerald D. Berreman, 3–40. New York: Academic, 1981.

Birdsell, J. B. "Some Environmental and Cultural Factors Influencing the Structure of Australian Aboriginal Populations." *American Naturalist* 87, no. 834(1953): 171–207.

———. "Ecology, Spacing Mechanisms, and Adaptive Behavior in Aboriginal Land Tenure." In *Land Tenure in the Pacific*, edited by Ron Crocombe, 334–61. Melbourne: Oxford University Press, 1971.

———. "Ecological Influences on Australian Aboriginal Social Organization." In *Primate Ecology and Human Origins: Ecological Influences on Social Organization*, edited by Irwin S. Bernstein and Euclid O. Smith, 117–51. New York: Garland STPM, 1979.

Boas, Franz. *Anthropology and Modern Life*. New York: Norton, 1928.

Bodley, John H. *Victims of Progress*. Menlo Park, Calif.: Cummings, 1975.

———. "Inequality: An Energetics Approach." In *Social Inequality: Comparative and Developmental Approaches*, edited by Gerald D. Berreman, 183–97. New York: Academic, 1981.

Boerma, Addeke H. "A World Agricultural Plan." *Scientific American* 223, no. 2(1970): 54–69.

Bogue, Donald T. *Principles of Demography*. New York: Wiley, 1969.

Bohannan, Paul. "Beyond Civilization." *Natural History* 80, no. 2(1971): 50–67.

Borgstrom, Georg. *The Hungry Planet*, 1st and 2nd eds. New York: Macmillan, 1965, 1967.

Boserup, Ester. *The Conditions of Economic Growth*. Chicago: Aldine, 1965.

Boulding, Kenneth. "The Economics of the Coming Spaceship Earth." In *Environmental Quality in a Growing Economy: Essays from the Sixth Resources for the Future Forum*, edited by Henry Jarrett, 3–14. Baltimore: Johns Hopkins University Press, 1966.

Brown, Harrison. *The Challenge of Man's Future*. New York: Viking, 1954.

———. "Technological Denudation." In *Man's Role in Changing the Face of the Earth*, edited by William L. Thomas, Jr., 1023–32. Chicago: University of Chicago Press, 1956.

Brown, Lester R. *Man, Land and Food*. U.S. Department of Agriculture FAE Report No. 11. Washington, D.C.: U.S. Government Printing Office, 1963.

Brown, Lester R. and Edward Wolf. "Food Crisis in Africa." *Natural History* 93, no. 6(1984): 16–20.

Brown, Paula, and H. C. Brookfield. *Struggle for Land*. Melbourne: Oxford University Press, 1963.

Campbell, Alastair H. "Elementary Food Production by the Australian Aborigines." *Mankind* 6, no. 5(1965): 206–11.

Carneiro, Robert L. "Slash-and-Burn Agriculture: A Closer Look at Its Implications for Settlement Patterns." In *Men and Cultures*, edited by A. F. C. Wallace, 229–34. Philadelphia: University of Pennyslvania Press, 1960.

———. "The Transition from Hunting to Horticulture in the Amazon Basin." *Proceedings of the Eighth International Congress of Anthropological and Ethnological Sciences*, 244–48. Tokyo: ICAES, 1968.

———. A Theory of the Origin of the State." *Science* 169, no. 3947(1970): 733–38.

———. "The Knowledge and Use of Rain Forest Trees by the Kuikuru Indians of Central Brazil." *Anthropological Papers* (University of Michigan Museum of Anthropology), no. 67(1978): 201–16.

Carneiro, Robert L., and D. F. Hilse. "On Determining the Probable Rate of Population Growth During the Neolithic." *American Anthropologist* 68, no. 1(1966): 177–81.

Carter, Barry. "Nuclear Strategy and Nuclear Weapons." *Scientific American* 230, no. 5(1974): 20–31.

Casimir, Michael J., R. P. Winter, and Bernt Glatzer. "Nomadism and Remote Sensing: Animal Husbandry and the Sagebrush Community in a Nomad Winter Area in Western Afghanistan." *Journal of Arid Environments* 3(1980): 231–54.

Caulfield, Mina Davis. "Equality, Sex, and Mode of Production." In *Social Inequality: Comparative and Developmental Approaches*, edited by Gerald D. Berreman, 201–19. New York: Academic, 1981.

Chagnon, Napoleon. *Yanomamo: The Fierce People*. New York: Holt, Rinehart & Winston, 1968.

Charbonnier, G. *Conversations with Claude Levi-Strauss*. London: Cape, 1969.

Chayanov, A. V. *The Theory of Peasant Economy*. Homewood, Ill.: Richard D. Irwin, for the American Economic Association, 1966.

234

Clark, Colin. *Population Growth and Land Use.* London: Macmillan, 1968.

Clark J. G. D. *Prehistoric Europe: The Economic Base.* New York: Philosophical Library, 1952.

Cleave, T. L. *The Saccharine Disease.* Bristol: Wright, 1974.

Coale, Ansley J. "The History of the Human Population." *Scientific American* 231, no. 3(1974): 40–51.

Cobb, Ron. *Raw Sewage.* Los Angeles: Sawyer Press, 1970.

Cohen, Ronald, and Elman R. Service, eds. *Origins of the State: The Anthropology of Political Evolution.* Philadelphia: ISHI, 1978.

Cohen, Yehudi, ed. *Man in Adaptation.* 2nd ed. Chicago: Aldine, 1974.

Cole, H. S. D., ed. *Models of Doom.* New York: Universe, 1973.

Colson, Elizabeth. "In Good Years and in Bad: Food Strategies of Self-Reliant Societies." *Journal of Anthropological Research* 35, no. 1(1979): 18–29.

Commoner, Barry. *The Closing Circle.* New York: Knopf, 1971.

Conklin, Harold C. "An Ethnoecological Approach to Shifting Agriculture." *Transactions of the New York Academy of Sciences*, 2nd ser., vol 17, no. 2(December 1954): 133–42.

Conover, Patrick W. "The Potential for an Alternate Society." *The Futurist*, June 1973, 111–16.

Cook, Earl. "The Flow of Energy in an Industrial Society." *Scientific American* 224, no. 3(1971): 134–44.

Cooke, G. W. "The Carrying Capacity of the Land in the Year 2000." In *The Optimum Population for Britain*, edited by L. R. Taylor, 15–42. London: Academic, 1970.

Coon, Carleton S. *The Hunting Peoples.* Boston: Little, Brown, 1971.

Cotton, Steve, ed. *Earth Day: The Beginning.* New York: Arno, Bantam, 1970.

Cowgill, George L. "Population Pressure as a Non-Explanation." In *American Antiquity* 40, no. 2, Part 2, Memoir 30 (1975): 127–31.

Cowlishaw, Gillian. "Infanticide in Aboriginal Australia." *Oceania* 48, no. 4(1978): 262–83.

Culbert, T. Patrick. *The Lost Civilization: The Story of the Classic Maya.* New York: Harper & Row, 1974.

Dakeyne, R. B. "Conflicting Interests on Bougainville." *Pacific Viewpoint* 8, no. 2(1967): 186–87.

Dalton, George. "Economic Theory and Primitive Society." *American Anthropologist* 63, no. 1(1961): 1–25.

———. Primitive Money." *American Anthropologist* 67, no. 1(1965): 44–65.

———. *Economic Development and Social Change: The Modernization of Village Communities.* Garden City, N.Y.: Natural History, 1971.

DASA. Defense Atomic Support Agency. *Proceedings of the Third Interdisciplinary Con-*

ference on Selected Effects of a General War. DASIAC Special Report 120, vol. 3 (DASA 2019–3). 1971.

Dasmann, Raymond. "Future Primitive: Ecosystem People Versus Biosphere People." *CoEvolution Quarterly*, no. 11(Fall 1976): 26–31.

Deevy, Edward S. "The Human Population." *Scientific American* 203, no. 3(1960): 195–204.

Dentan, Robert K. *The Semai: A Nonviolent People of Malaya.* New York: Holt, Rinehart & Winston, 1968.

Dewhurst, J. Frederic, and Associates. *America's Needs and Resources: A Twentieth Century Fund Survey Which Includes Estimates for 1950 and 1960.* New York: Twentieth Century Fund, 1947.

———. *America's Needs and Resources: A New Survey.* New York: Twentieth Century Fund, 1955.

Diamond, Stanley. *In Search of the Primitive.* New Brunswick, N.J.: Transaction, 1974.

———. "The Search for the Primitive." In *The Concept of the Primitive*, edited by Ashley Montagu, 96–147. New York: Free Press, 1968.

Divale, W. J., and Marvin Harris. "Population, Warfare, and the Male Supremacist Complex." In *American Anthropologist* 78, no. 3(1976): 521–38.

Dole, Gertrude. "The Use of Manioc Among the Kuikuru: Some Implications." *Anthropological Papers* (University of Michigan Museum of Anthropology), no. 67(1978): 217–47.

Dowling, John H. "The Goodfellows vs. the Dalton Gang: The Assumptions of Economic Anthropology." *Journal of Anthropological Research* 35, no. 3(1979): 292–308.

Dumond, Don E. "Population Growth and Political Centralization." In *Population Growth: Anthropological Implications*, edited by Brian Spooner, 286–310. Cambridge: MIT Press, 1972.

Eames, Edwin, and Judith G. Goode. *Urban Poverty in a Cross-Cultural Context.* New York: Free Press, 1973.

Ehrlich, Paul. "Eco-Catastrophe." *Ramparts*, September 1969, 24–28.

———. *The Population Bomb.* New York: Ballantine, 1968.

Ehrlich, Paul, and Anne Ehrlich. *Population, Resources, Environment.* San Francisco: W. H. Freeman, 1972.

———. *The End of Affluence.* New York: Ballantine, 1974.

Ehrlich, Paul, and Richard L. Harriman. *How to Be a Survivor: A Plan to Save Spaceship Earth.* New York: Ballantine, 1971.

Ehrlich, Paul, et al. "Long-Term Biological Consequences of Nuclear War." *Science* 222, no. 4630(1983): 1293–1300.

English, Richard D., and Dan I. Bolef. "Defense Against Bomber Attack." *Scientific American* 229, no. 2(1973): 11–19.

Fabun, Don. *Food: An Energy Exchange System.* Beverly Hills, Calif.: Glencoe, 1970.

Fairchild, Hoxie Neale. *The Noble Savage: A Study in Romantic Naturalism.* New York: Columbia University Press, 1928.

Fei, Hsiao-t'ung, and Chih-i Chang. *Earthbound China: A Study of Rural Economy in Yunnan.* Chicago: University of Chicago Press, 1945.

Finkel, A., ed. *Energy, the Environment, and Human Health.* Acton, Mass.: Publishing Sciences, 1974.

Firth, Raymond. *We the Tikopia.* New York: Barnes and Noble, 1957.

Flannery, Kent V. "Origins and Ecological Effects of Early Domestication in Iran and the Near East." In *The Domestication and Exploitation of Plants and Animals,* edited by Peter J. Ucko and G. W. Dimbleby, 73–100. London: Duckworth, 1969.

Foster, George. *Applied Anthropology.* Boston: Little, Brown, 1969.

Freeman, M. M. R. "A Social and Ecological Analysis of Systematic Female Infanticide." *American Anthropologist* 73, no. 5(1971): 1011–18.

Freydberg, Nicholas, and Willis A. Gortner. *The Food Additives Book.* Toronto: Bantam, 1982.

Fried, Morton. *The Evolution of Political Society.* New York: Random House, 1967.

Friedman, Jonathan. "Marxism, Structuralism and Vulgar Materialism." *Man* 9, no. 3(1974): 444–69.

———. "Hegelian Ecology: Between Rousseau and the World Spirit." In *Social and Ecological Systems,* edited by P. C. Burnham and R. F. Ellen, 253–70. ASA Monograph No. 18. London: Academic, 1979.

Garwin, Richard L. "Anti-Submarine Warfare and National Security." *Scientific American* 227, no. 1(1972): 14–25.

Garwin, Richard L. and Hans A. Bethe. "Anti-Ballistic Missile Systems." *Scientific American* 218, no. 3(1968): 21–31.

Geertz, Clifford. *Agricultural Involution: The Process of Ecological Change in Indonesia.* Berkeley: University of California Press, 1963.

George, Susan. *How the Other Half Dies: The Real Reasons for World Hunger.* Montclair, N.J.: Allanheld, Osmum, 1977.

Glasstone, Samuel, ed. *The Effects of Nuclear Weapons.* Atomic Energy Commission. Washington, D.C.: U.S. Government Printing Office, 1962.

Goldberg, Edward D. *The Health of the Oceans.* Paris: UNESCO, 1976.

Goldsmith, Edward, et al. *Blueprint for Survival.* Boston: Houghton Mifflin, 1972.

Goody, Jack. *The Domestication of the Savage Mind.* Cambridge: Cambridge University Press, 1976.

Gould, Richard A. "Uses and Effects of Fire Among the Western Desert Aborigines of Australia." *Mankind* 8, no. 1(1971): 14–24.

———. "Comparative Ecology of Food-Sharing in Australia and Northwest California." In *Omnivorous Primates: Gathering and Hunting in Human Evolution,* 422–54. New York: Columbia University Press, 1981.

Goulet, Denis. *The Cruel Choice: A New Concept in the Theory of Development.* New York: Atheneum, 1971.

Grainger, A. "The State of the World's Forests." *The Ecologist* 10, no. 1(1980): 6–54.

Great Britain. *Britain 1982: An Official Handbook.* London: Her Majesty's Stationery Office, 1982.

Greenwood, Ted. "Reconnaissance and Arms Control." *Scientific American* 228, no. 2(1973): 14–25.

Gross, Daniel R., and Barbara A. Underwood. "Technological Change and Caloric Costs: Sisal Agriculture." *American Anthropologist* 73, no. 2(1971): 725–40.

Gustafson, A. F., C. H. Guise, W. J. Hamilton, Jr., and H. Ries. *Conservation in the United States.* Ithaca, N.Y.: Comstock, 1939.

Gutkind, E. A. "Our World From the Air: Conflict and Adaptation." In *Man's Role in Changing the Face of the Earth,* edited by William L. Thomas, Jr., 1–44. Chicago: University of Chicago Press, 1956.

Haas, Jonathan. *The Evolution of the Prehistoric State.* New York: Columbia University Press, 1982.

Hagood, Mel A. "Which Irrigation System?" *Proceedings of the 11th Annual Washington Potato Conference and Trade Fair,* 83–86. Washington Potato Conference, Moses Lake, Washington: 1972.

Hallam, S. *Fire and Hearth.* Canberra: Australian Institute of Aboriginal Studies, 1975.

Hallpike, C. R. "Functionalist Interpretations of Primitive Warfare." *Man* 8, no. 3(1973): 451–70.

———. *The Foundations of Primitive Thought.* Oxford: Clarendon, 1979.

Hamblin, Robert L., and Brian L. Pitcher. "The Classic Maya Collapse: Testing Class Conflict Theories." *American Antiquity* 45, no. 2(1980): 246–71.

Hamilton, Annette. "A Comment on Arthur Hippler's Paper 'Culture and Personality Perspective of the Yolngu . . .' " *Mankind* 12, no. 2(1979): 164–69.

Hardin, Garrett. "The Tragedy of the Commons." *Science* 162, no. 3859 (1968): 1243–48.

Harris, David R. "The Origins of Agriculture in the Tropics." *American Scientist* 60, no. 2(1972): 180–93.

Harris, Marvin. *Culture, Man and Nature.* New York: Crowell, 1971.

———. *Culture, People and Nature.* New York: Crowell, 1975.

Hartmann, Betsy, and James Boyce. *Needless Hunger: Voices from a Bangladesh Village.* San Francisco: Institute for Food and Development Policy, 1982.

Hassan, Fekri A. *Demographic Archaeology.* New York: Academic, 1981.

Hayden, Brian. "The Carrying Capacity Dilemma: An Alternate Approach." *American Antiquity* 40, no. 2, Memoir 30 (1975): 11–19.

———. "Research and Development in the Stone Age: Technological Transitions Among Hunter-Gatherers." *Current Anthropology* 22, no. 5(1981a): 519–48.

————. "Subsistence and Ecological Adaptations of Modern Hunter/Gatherers." In *Omnivorous Primates: Gathering and Hunting in Human Evolution*, edited by Robert S. Harding and Geza Teleki, 344–421. New York: Columbia University Press, 1981b.

Hecker, Howard M. "Domestication Revisited: Its Implications for Faunal Analysis. *Journal of Field Archaeology* 9(1982): 217–36.

Heer, David M. *After Nuclear Attack: A Demographic Inquiry.* New York: Praeger, 1965.

Heilbroner, Robert L. *The Great Ascent: The Struggle for Economic Development in Our Time.* New York: Harper & Row Torchbooks, 1963.

————. *An Inquiry into the Human Prospect.* New York: Norton, 1974.

Hemming, John. *Red Gold: The Conquest of the Brazilian Indians.* Cambridge: Harvard University Press, 1978.

Henry, Jules. *Culture Against Man.* New York: Random House, 1963.

Herskovits, Melville J. *Economic Anthropology.* New York: Knopf, 1952.

Hickerson, Harold. "The Virginia Deer and Intertribal Buffer Zones in the Upper Mississippi Valley." In *Man, Culture and Animals: The Role of Animals in Human Ecological Adjustments*, edited by Anthony Leeds and Andrew P. Vayda, 43–65. Publication No. 78. Washington, D.C.: American Association for the Advancement of Science, 1965.

Hippler, Arthur E. "The North Alaska Eskimos: A Culture and Personality Perspective." *American Ethnologist* 1, no. 3(1974): 449–69.

————. "Cultural Evolution: Some Hypotheses Concerning the Significance of Cognitive and Affective Interpenetration During Latency." *Journal of Psychohistory* 4, no. 4(1977): 419–60.

————. "Comments on *Causality Among Cross-Cultural Correlations*, by Janet Reis, and *Ideological Bias*, by Walter Precourt." *Behavior Science Research* 14, no. 4(1979a): 293–96.

————. Review of *Aborigines and Change*, edited by R. M. Berndt. *Journal of Psychological Anthropology* 2, no. 4(1979b): 507–10.

————. Review of *The Mardudjara Aborigines*, by R. Tonkinson. *Journal of Psychological Anthropology* 2, no. 4(1979c): 493–94.

————. "The Yolngu and Cultural Relativism: A Response to Reser." *American Anthropologist* 83, no. 2(1981): 393–96.

Hobbes, Thomas. *Leviathan.* New York: Liberal Arts, 1958. (Originally published in 1651.)

Hubert, M. King. "Energy Resources." In *Resources and Man*, ed. National Academy of Sciences, 157–242. San Francisco: W. H. Freeman, 1969.

Hunter, Beatrice Trum. *Food Additives and Federal Policy: The Mirage of Safety.* Brattleboro, Vt.: Greene, 1982.

Jacobsen, Thorkild, and Robert M. Adams. "Salt and Silt in Ancient Mesopotamian Agriculture." *Science* 128, no. 3334(1958): 1251–58.

Jannuzi, F. Tomasson, and James T. Peach. *Report on the Hierarchy of Interests in Land in Bangladesh.* Washington, D.C.: Agency for International Development, September 1977.

Johnson, Allen. "Time Allocation in a Machiguenga Community." *Ethnology* 14, no. 3(1975): 301–10.

Johnson, Allen, and Clifford A. Behrens. "Nutritional Criteria in Machiguenga Food Production Decisions: A Linear-Programming Analysis." *Human Ecology* 10, no. 2(1982): 167–89.

Kaberry, Phyllis M. *Aboriginal Woman: Sacred and Profane.* London: Routledge, 1939.

Kahn, Herman. *On Thermonuclear War.* Princeton: Princeton University Press, 1961.

———. *Thinking About the Unthinkable.* New York: Horizon, 1962.

Kahn, Herman, and B. Bruce-Briggs. *Things to Come: Thinking about the 70's and 80's.* New York: Macmillan, 1972.

Kahn, Herman, and Anthony J. Wiener. *The Year 2000: A Framework for Speculation on the Next Thirty-three Years.* New York: Macmillan, 1967.

Keenleyside, H. L. "Critical Mineral Shortages." In *Proceedings of the United Nations Scientific Conference on the Conservation and Utilization of Resources, 17 August–6 September 1949,* 38–46. Lake Success, N.Y.: United Nations, 1950.

Kelly, Raymond C. "Demographic Pressure and Descent Group Structure in the New Guinea Highlands." *Oceania* 38, no. 1 (1968): 36–63.

Kermode, G. O. "Food Additives." *Scientific American* 226, no. 3(1972): 15–21.

Klein, Richard G. "Stone Age Exploitation of Animals in Southern Africa." *American Scientist* 67, no. 2(1979): 151–60.

———. "Stone Age Predation on Small African Bovids." *South African Archaeological Bulletin* 36(1981): 55–65.

Knudson, Bob. "Time Management—It Pays." *Proceedings of the 11th Annual Washington Potato Conference and Trade Fair,* 71–76. Washington Potato Conference, Moses Lake, Washington, 1972.

Knudson, Kenneth E. "Resource Fluctuation, Productivity, and Social Organization on Micronesian Coral Islands." Doctoral dissertation, University of Oregon, 1970.

Koch, Klaus-Friedrich. "Cannibalistic Revenge in Jalé Warfare." *Natural History* 79, no. 2(1970): 41–50.

Kohr, Leopold. *The Breakdown of Nations.* New York: Dutton, 1978. (Originally published in 1957.)

Kunstadter, Peter. "Natality, Mortality and Migration in Upland and Lowland Populations in Northwestern Thailand." In *Culture and Population,* edited by Steven Polgar, 46–60. Cambridge, Mass.: Schenkman, 1971.

Lancaster, P. A., et al. "Traditional Cassava-Based Foods: Survey of Processing Techniques." *Economic Botany* 36, no. 1(1982): 12–45.

Landsberg, Hans H. *Natural Resources in America's Future: A Look Ahead to the Year 2000.* Baltimore: Johns Hopkins University Press, 1964.

Landsberg, Hans H., Leonard L. Fischman, and Joseph L. Fisher. *Resources in America's Future: Patterns of Requirements and Availabilities 1960–2000.* Baltimore: Johns Hopkins University Press, 1963.

Lappé, Frances Moore, and Joseph Collins. *Food First: Beyond the Myth of Scarcity.* Boston: Houghton Mifflin, 1977.

Lathrap, Don W. *The Upper Amazon.* New York: Praeger, 1970.

———. "Our Father the Cayman, Our Mother the Gourd: Spinden Revisited, or a Unitary Theory for the Emergence of Agriculture in the New World." In *Origins of Agriculture*, edited by Charles A. Reed, 713–51. The Hague: Mouton, 1977.

Lee, Richard B. "What Hunters Do for a Living, or How to Make Out on Scarce Resources." In *Man the Hunter*, edited by Richard B. Lee and Irven De Vore, 30–48. Chicago: Aldine, 1968.

———. "!Kung Bushman Subsistence: An Input-Output Analysis." *Contributions to Anthropology: Ecological Essays.* National Museums of Canada Bulletin 230 (1969), 73–94.

MacNeish, Richard S. "Speculation About How and Why Food Production and Village Life Developed in the Tehuacan Valley, Mexico." *Archaeology* 24, no. 4(1971): 307–15.

Malinowski, Bronislaw. "An Anthropological Analysis of War." *American Journal of Sociology* 46, no. 4(1941): 521–50.

———. *Freedom and Civilization.* New York: Roy, 1944.

Malthus, Thomas R. *An Essay on the Principle of Population* (parallel chapters from the [1st] and [2nd] editions). New York: Macmillan, 1895. (1st edition originally published 1798, 2nd edition originally published 1807.)

Marple, Gary A., and Harry B. Wissmann, eds. *Grocery Manufacturing in the United States.* New York: Praeger, 1968.

Marsh, George P. *Man and Nature.* New York: Scribner's, 1864.

Martin, Paul S. "Prehistoric Overkill." In *Pleistocene Extinctions: The Search for a Cause*, edited by P. S. Martin and H. E. Wright, Jr., 75–120. Proceedings of the 7th Congress of the International Association for Quaternary Research. New Haven: Yale University Press, 1967.

Martin, Thomas L., Jr., and Donald C. Latham. *Strategy for Survival.* Tuscon: University of Arizona Press, 1963.

Mazur, Allan, and Eugene Rosa. "Energy and Life Style." *Science* 186, no. 4164(1974): 607–10.

Mead, Margaret. "Warfare Is Only an Invention—Not a Biological Necessity." *Asia* 40(1940): 402–5.

Meadows, Donella H., Dennis L. Meadows, Jorgen Randers, and William W. Behrens III. *The Limits to Growth.* New York: Universe, 1972.

Meggers, Betty J. *Amazonia: Man and Culture in a Counterfeit Paradise.* Chicago: Aldine, 1971.

Meggers, Betty J., and Clifford Evans. *Archeological Investigations at the Mouth of the Amazon.* Bulletin 167. Washington, D.C.: Bureau of American Ethnology, Smithsonian Institution, 1957.

Mellars, Paul. "Fire Ecology, Animal Populations and Man: A Study of Some Ecological Relationships in Prehistory." *Proceedings of the Prehistoric Society* 42(1976): 15–45.

Mining Magazine. "Bougainville Project Nearing Completion." *Mining Magazine* 124, no. 5(1971): 377–81.

Modjeska, Nicholas. "Production and Inequality: Perspectives from Central New Guinea." In *Inequality in New Guinea Highlands Societies,* edited by Andrew Strathern, 50–108. Cambridge: Cambridge University Press, 1982.

Montagu, Ashley. "Sociogenic Brain Damage." *American Anthropologist* 74, no. 5(1972): 1045–61.

Morgan, Lewis Henry. *Ancient Society.* New York: Holt, 1877.

Morris, David M. *Measuring the Condition of the World's Poor: The Physical Quality of Life Index.* New York: Pergamon, 1979.

Mosley, Michael Edward. *The Maritime Foundations of Andean Civilization.* Menlo Park, Calif.: Cummings, 1975.

Murdock, George P. "Human Influences on Ecosystems of High Islands." In *Man's Place in the Island Ecosystem,* edited by F. R. Fosberg, 145–52. Bishop Museum Press, 1963.

Myers, Fred R. "Always Ask: Resource Use and Land Ownership Among Pintupi Aborigines of the Australian Western Desert." In *Resource Managers: North American and Australian Hunter-Gatherers,* edited by Nancy M. Williams and Eugene S. Hunn, 173–95. AAAS Selected Symposium No. 67. Boulder, Colorado: Westview, 1982.

Naroll, R. "Does Military Deterrence Deter?" *Trans-Action* 3, no. 2(1966): 14–20.

Nash, Manning. *Primitive and Peasant Economic Systems.* San Francisco: Chandler, 1966.

National Academy of Sciences. *Resources and Man.* San Francisco: W. H. Freeman, 1969.

———. *Long-Term Worldwide Effects of Multiple Nuclear Weapons Detonations.* Washington, D.C., 1975.

National Research Council, Committee on Mineral Resources and the Environment. *Mineral Resources and the Environment.* Washington, D.C.: National Academy of Sciences, 1975.

Neel, James V. "Some Aspects of Differential Fertility in Two American Indian Tribes." *Proceedings of the Eighth International Congress of Anthropological and Ethnological Sciences* 1(1968): 356–61. Tokyo: ICAES, 1968.

———. "Lessons from a Primitive People." *Science* 170, no. 3960(1970): 815–21.

Nelson, Richard K. *Hunters of the Northern Ice.* Chicago: University of Chicago Press, 1969.

Newcomb, W. W., Jr. "Toward an Understanding of War." In *Essays in the Science of Culture,* edited by Gertrude Dole and Robert L. Carneiro, 317–36. New York: Crowell, 1960.

Nicklin, Flip. "Krill: Untapped Bounty From the Sea?" *National Geographic* 165, no. 5(1984): 626–43.

Nietschmann, Bernard. *Between Land and Water: The Subsistence Ecology of the Miskito Indians, Eastern Nicaragua.* New York: Seminar, 1973.

Nougier, Louis-René. Essai sur le peuplement prehistorique de la France. *Population* (Paris) 9(1954): 241–73.

Nulty, Leslie. *The Green Revolution in West Pakistan.* New York: Praeger, 1972.

Odum, Howard T. *Environment, Power, and Society.* New York: Wiley, Inter-Science, 1971.

Oliver, Douglas L. *Bougainville: A Personal History.* Honolulu: University of Hawaii Press, 1973.

Otterbein, Keith. *The Evolution of War: A Cross-Cultural Study.* New Haven: Human Relations Area Files, 1970.

Pacific Northwest River Basins Commission. *Columbia–North Pacific Region Comprehensive Framework Study.* (Main Report with 16 vols. appendices.) 1971–1973.

Paddock, William, and Paul Paddock. *Famine—1975!* Boston: Little, Brown, 1967.

Payne, Roger. "Among Wild Whales." *New York Zoological Society Newsletter,* November 1968, 1–6.

Peoples, James G. "Individual or Group Advantage? A Reinterpretation of the Maring Ritual Cycle." *Current Anthropology* 23, no. 3(1982): 291–310.

Peterson, J., ed. *The Aftermath: The Human and Ecological Consequences of Nuclear War.* New York: Pantheon, 1983.

Pimentel, David, et al. "Food Production and the Energy Crisis." *Science,* 182, no. 4110(1973): 443–49.

Platt, John. "What We Must Do." *Science* 166, no. 3909(1969): 1115–21.

Polgar, Steven. "Population History and Population Policies from an Anthropological Perspective." *Current Anthropology* 13, no. 2(1972): 203–11.

Porter, Bernard. *Critics of Empire.* London: Macmillan, 1968.

Radin, Paul. *The World of Primitive Man.* New York: Dutton, 1971.

Rapoport, Roger. *The Great American Bomb Machine.* New York: Dutton, 1971.

Rappaport, Roy A. "The Flow of Energy in an Agricultural Society." *Scientific American* 224, no. 3(1971): 117–32.

———. *Pigs for the Ancestors: Ritual in the Ecology of a New Guinea People.* New Haven: Yale University Press, 1968.

———. *Ecology, Meaning, and Religion*. Richmond, Calif.: North Atlantic, 1979.

Redfield, Robert. "The Folk Society." *American Journal of Sociology* 52, no. 4(1947): 293–308.

———. *The Primitive World and Its Transformations*. Ithaca, N.Y.: Cornell University Press, 1953.

Reichel-Dolmatoff, Gerardo. *Amazonian Cosmos: The Sexual and Religious Symbolism of the Tukano Indians*. Chicago: University of Chicago Press, 1971.

Reser, Joseph. "Australian Aboriginal Man's Inhumanity to Man: A Case of Cultural Distortion." *American Anthropologist* 83, no. 2(1981): 387–93.

Reynolds, Vernon. "Ethology of Urban Life." In *Man, Settlement, and Urbanism*, edited by Peter J. Ucko, R. A. Tringham, and G. W. Dimbleby, 401–8. London: Duckworth, 1972.

Ribeiro, Darcy. *The Civilizational Process*, translated by Betty J. Meggers. Washington, D.C.: Smithsonian Institution Press, 1968.

Richards, Paul W. "The Tropical Rain Forest." *Scientific American* 229, no. 6(1973): 58–67.

Riches, David. "The Netsilik Eskimo: A Special Case of Selective Female Infanticide." *Ethnology* 13, no. 4(1974): 351–61.

Ryan, Peter, ed. "Bougainville Copper Project." In *Encyclopedia of Papua New Guinea* 1: 92–102. Melbourne: Melbourne University Press, 1972.

Sahlins, Marshall. "Evolution: Specific and General." In *Evolution and Culture*, edited by Marshall Sahlins and Elman R. Service, 12–44. Ann Arbor: University of Michigan Press, 1960.

———. "The Segmentary Lineage: An Organization of Predatory Expansion." *American Anthropologist* 63, no. 2, pt. 1 (1961): 322–45.

———. "Notes on the Original Affluent Society." In *Man the Hunter*, edited by Richard B. Lee and Irven DeVore, 85–89. Chicago: Aldine, 1968.

———. *Stone Age Economics*. Chicago: Aldine, 1972.

Sahlins, Marshall, and Elman R. Service, eds. *Evolution and Culture*. Ann Arbor: University of Michigan Press, 1960.

Samuels, Michael. "Popreg I: A Simulation of Population Regulation Among the Maring of New Guinea." *Human Ecology* 10, no. 2(1982): 78–84.

Sapir, Edward. "Culture, Genuine and Spurious." In *Culture, Language and Personality*, edited by David G. Mandelbaum, 78–119. Berkeley and Los Angeles: University of California Press, 1964. (Originally published, 1924.)

Saucier, Jean-François. "Correlates of the Long Postpartum Taboo: A Cross-Cultural Study." *Current Anthropology* 13, no. 2(1972): 238–49.

Schneider, David. "Abortion and Depopulation on a Pacific Island: Yap." In *Health, Culture, and Community*, edited by B. D. Paul, 211–35. New York: Russell Sage Foundation, 1955.

Schrire, C., and W. L. Steiger. "A Matter of Life and Death: An Investigation into the Practice of Female Infanticide in the Arctic." *Man* 9, no. 2(1974): 161–84.

Schumacher, E. F. *Small Is Beautiful: Economics as if People Mattered.* New York: Harper & Row, 1973.

Scoville, Herbert, Jr. "Missile Submarines and National Security." *Scientific American* 226, no. 6(1972): 15–27.

Sengel, Randal A. "Comments." *Current Anthropology* 14, no. 5(1973): 540–42.

Service, Elman R. *Primitive Social Organization.* New York: Random House, 1962.

Shaler, Nathaniel S. *Man and the Earth.* New York: Duffield, 1905.

Shantzis, Steven B., and William W. Behrens III. "Population Control Mechanisms in a Primitive Agricultural Society." In *Toward Global Equilibrium*, edited by D. H. Meadows and D. L. Meadows, 257–88. Cambridge, Mass.: Wright-Allen, 1973.

Shweder, Richard A. "On Savages and Other Children." *American Anthropologist* 84, no. 2(1982): 354–66.

Smith, Philip E. *The Consequences of Food Production.* Module in Anthropology no. 21. Reading, Mass.: Addison-Wesley, 1972.

Sofer, Cyril. "Buying and Selling: A Study in the Sociology of Distribution." *Sociological Review*, July 1965, 183–209.

Solow, Robert M. "The Economics of Resources or the Resources of Economics." *American Economic Review* 64, no. 2(1974): 1–14.

Spaulding, Willard M., Jr., and Ronald D. Ogden. *Effects of Surface Mining on the Fish and Wildlife Resources of the United States.* Bureau of Sport Fisheries and Wildlife Resources Publication 68. Washington, D.C.: U.S. Government Printing Office, 1968.

Spoehr, Alexander. "Cultural Differences in the Interpretation of Natural Resources." In *Man's Role in Changing the Face of the Earth*, edited by William L. Thomas, Jr., 93–102. Chicago: University of Chicago Press, 1956.

Spooner, Brian. *The Cultural Ecology of Pastoral Nomads.* Module in Anthropology no. 45. Reading, Mass.: Addison-Wesley, 1973.

Steinhart, John S., and Carole E. Steinhart. "Energy Use in the U.S. Food System." *Science* 184, no. 4134(1974): 307–16.

Stonier, Tom. *Nuclear Disaster.* Cleveland and New York: World, Meridian, 1964.

Sussman, Robert W. "Child Transport, Family Size, and Increase in Human Population During the Neolithic." *Current Anthropology* 13, no. 2(1972): 258–59.

Suttles, Wayne. "Affinal Ties, Subsistence, and Prestige Among the Coast Salish." *American Anthropologist* 62(1960): 296–305.

Sweet, Louise. "Camel Pastoralism in North Arabia and the Minimal Camping Unit." In *Man, Culture and Animals: The Role of Animals in Human Ecological Adjustments*, edited by Anthony Leeds and Andrew Vayda, 129–52. Publication No. 78. Washington, D.C.: American Association for the Advancement of Science, 1965.

Talburt, William F., and Ora Smith. *Potato Processing.* Westport, Conn.: Avi, 1967.

Tax, Sol. "Anthropology for the World of the Future: Thirteen Professions and Three Proposals." *Current Anthropology* 36, no. 3(1977): 225–34.

Taylor, Gordon Rattray. *Rethink: A Paraprimitive Solution.* London: Secker & Warburg, 1972.

Toffler, Alvin. *Future Schock.* New York: Bantam, 1971.

Trowell, Hugh C. "Kwashiorkor." *Scientific American* 191, no. 6(1954): 46–50.

Turco, R. P., et al. "Nuclear Winter: Global Consequences of Multiple Nuclear Explosions." *Science* 222, no. 4630(1983): 1283–92.

Turnbull, Colin. "The Importance of Flux in Two Hunting Societies." In *Man the Hunter,* edited by Richard B. Lee and Irven DeVore, 132–37. Chicago: Aldine, 1968.

Underwood, Jane H. "The Demography of a Myth: Abortion in Yap." *Human Biology in Oceania* 2, no. 2(1973): 115–27.

UNESCO. *Tropical Forest Ecosystems: A State-of-Knowledge Report.* Natural Resources Research XIV. Paris, 1968.

United Nations, Department of Economic Affairs. *Proceedings of the United Nations Scientific Conference on the Conservation and Utilization of Resources, 17 August–6 September 1949.* Lake Success, N.Y., 1950.

United Nations, Food and Agriculture Organization. *Third World Food Survey.* Freedom from Hunger Basic Study No. 11. Rome, 1963.

United Nations, Trusteeship Council. "Report of the United Nations Visiting Mission to the Trust Territory of New Guinea, 1968." *Trusteeship Council Official Records: Thirty-fifth Session (27 May–19 June 1968).* Supplement No. 2. New York, 1968.

———. "Report of the United Nations Visiting Mission to the Trust Territory of New Guinea, 1971." *Trusteeship Council Official Records: Thirty-eighth Session (25 May–18 June 1971).* Supplement No. 2. New York, 1971.

U.S. Bureau of the Census. *Statistical Abstract of the U.S.: 1984,* 104th ed. Washington, D.C.: U.S. Government Printing Office, 1983.

U.S. Department of Commerce. *Census of Agriculture.* Vol. 1, *Area Reports,* pt. 46, "[state of] Washington." Washington, D.C.: U.S. Government Printing Office, 1969a.

———. *Census of Agriculture.* Vol. 5, pt. 4, "Sugar Crops, Potatoes, Other Specified Crops." Washington, D.C.: U.S. Government Printing Office, 1969b.

U.S. Department of the Interior, Bureau of Land Management. *Draft Environmental Impact Statement: Proposed Federal Coal Leasing Program.* 2 vols. Washington, D.C.: U.S. Government Printing Office, 1974.

U.S. Environmental Protection Agency. *Legal Compilation: Statutes and Legislative History, Executive Orders, Regulations, Guidelines, and Reports (General),* vol. 1. Washington, D.C.: U.S. Government Printing Office, 1973.

U.S. National Advisory Commission on Civil Disorders. [Kerner Report.] Washington, D.C.: U.S. Government Printing Office, 1968.

U.S. National Commission on the Causes and Prevention of Violence. *Justice: To Establish Justice, to Ensure Domestic Tranquility.* Final Report. Washington, D.C.: U.S. Government Printing Office, 1969.

U.S. President's Materials Policy Commission. *Resources for Freedom* [Paley Commission Report]. Washington, D.C.: U.S. Government Printing Office, 1952.

U.S. President's Science Advisory Committee. *The World Food Problem: A Report of the Panel on the World Food Supply.* 3 vols. Washington, D.C.: U.S. Government Printing Office, 1967.

Vanek, Joann. "Time Spent in Housework." *Scientific American* 231, no. 5(1974): 116–20.

Vayda, Andrew P. "Primitive Warfare." In *International Encyclopedia of the Social Sciences,* vol. 16, 473–98. New York: Macmillan, Free Press, 1968.

Wagley, Charles. "Cultural Influences on Population." *Revista do Museu Paulista* 5(1951): 95–104.

Walker, B. H., et al. "Stability of Semi-Arid Savanna Grazing Systems." *Journal of Ecology* 69(1981): 473–98.

Washington Potato Commission. *Proceedings of the Annual Washington Potato Conference and Trade Fair.* Moses Lake, Washington: Washington Potato Commission, 1962.

Webster, David. "Late Pleistocene Extinction and Human Predation: A Critical Overview." In *Omnivorous Primates: Gathering and Hunting in Human Evolution,* edited by Robert S. Harding and Geza Teleki, 556–95. New York: Columbia University Press, 1981.

Weiss, K. M. "Demographic Models for Anthropology." *American Antiquity* 38, no. 2, Part 2, Memoir 27 (1973).

White, Leslie A. *The Science of Culture.* New York: Grove, 1949.

———. *The Evolution of Culture.* New York: McGraw-Hill, 1959.

White, Lynn, Jr. "The Historical Roots of Our Ecological Crisis." *Science* 155, no. 3767(1967): 1203–7.

Wiesner, Jerome B., and Herbert F. York. "National Security and the Nuclear-Test Ban." *Scientific American* 211, no. 4(1964): 27–35.

Willey, Gordon R., and Demitric B. Shimkin. "The Collapse of Classic Maya Civilization in the Southern Lowlands: A Symposium Summary Statement." *Southwestern Journal of Anthropology* 27, no. 1(1971): 1–18.

Winterhalder, B., and F. A. Smith, eds. *Hunter-Gatherer Foraging Strategies: Ethnographic and Archaeological Analyses.* Chicago: University of Chicago Press, 1981.

Woodburn, James. "An Introduction to Hadza Ecology." In *Man the Hunter,* edited by Richard B. Lee and Irven DeVore, 49–55. Chicago: Aldine, 1968a.

———. Stability and Flexibility in Hadza Residential Groupings." In *Man the Hunter,* edited by Richard B. Lee and Irven DeVore, 103–10. Chicago: Aldine, 1968b.

World Bank. *World Development Report 1983.* New York: Oxford University Press, 1983.

Wright, Quincy. *A Study of War.* 2 vols. Chicago: University of Chicago Press, 1942.

Yde, Jens. *Material Culture of the Waiwai.* Nationalmuseets Skrifter. Etnografisk Roekke 10. Copenhagen: National Museum, 1965.

Yengoyan, Aram A. "Infanticide and Birth Order: An Empiricial Analysis of Preferential Female Infanticide Among Australian Aboriginal Populations." In *The Perception of Evolution: Essays Honoring Joseph B. Birdsell,* edited by Larry L. Mai, Eugenia Shanklin, and R. W. Sussman, *Anthropology UCLA* 7 (1981): 255–73.

York, Herbert F. "The Great Test-Ban Debate." *Scientific American* 227, no. 5(1972): 15–23.

Young, Vernon R., and Nevin S. Scrimshaw. "The Physiology of Starvation." *Scientific American* 225, no. 4(1971): 14–21.

Zubrow, Ezra B. *Prehistoric Carrying Capacity.* Menlo Park, Calif.: Cummings, 1975.

INDEX